Divorce
Sharia Style

Divorce Sharia Style

Tales of Rebellious Women of Anatolia

HASAN ALI ÇELIK

To the memory of my mother and father

This is a work of fiction, based in part upon actual events, stories, and persons; however, many of the names used herein are fictitious. Any similarity to actual persons, living or dead, or any actual event, is entirely coincidental and unintentional.

Copyright © 2023 by Hasan Çelik

All rights reserved, including the right to reproduce this book or portions thereof in any form whatsoever. No part of this publication may be reproduced or transmitted in any form or by any means, electronic or mechanical, including photocopying, recording, or any other information storage and retrieval, without the written permission of the author.

ISBN 979-8-218-10577-8 (eBook)
ISBN 978-1-0880-7066-6 (TP)

Library of Congress Control Number: 2022921552

All artwork and photography by Hasan Ali Çelik

PRINTED IN THE UNITED STATES OF AMERICA

CONTENTS

Introduction ix

PART ONE: DIVORCE SHARIA STYLE

1. Crazy Kirez 3
2. Given Away, Husband Number One 5
3. Migrant Laborers 7
4. A Useless Husband, Divorce by Sharia 10
5. Husband Number Two 11
6. The Great War 13
7. The Left Behind 14
8. Betrayal of Trust 16
9. Bad News 18
10. Are the Dead More Fortunate than the Living? 20
11. Weep, Eyes, Weep Salt Tears 22
12. Jackals Abound Where There Are No Dogs 24
13. In Father's House Once More 25
14. Fortunate Girls and Brides 26
15. Third Time Lucky 27
16. Mobilization—The War for Independence 29
17. Wars End, Work Never Does 31
18. Days End, Work Does Not 32
19. To Aydın—Once More, Far from Home 34
20. Şükrü—The Child Grows Up, the Youth Calms Down 35
21. Kirez's Daughter, Fatma 37
22. Old Ways Die Hard 38
23. One Mishap Worth a Thousand Warnings 38
24. Rahim 40

25	Rahim Looks for a Wife	43
26	The Abduction of Fatma	44
27	Fatma's Thoughts	47
28	Kirez—the Lioness's Love of Her Cub	49
29	Fatma's Destiny	51
30	Both Husband and Father	52
31	Abdullah	54
32	The Road	55
33	False Witness	58

PART TWO: LOVE AND STRUGGLE

Collarless Shirt and a Pair of Breeches	65
Moon Babies	75
The Popgun	86
The Little Peddler	100
A Glass, a Kid, and a Bunch of Grapes	115
The Mule Mailman	137
Guardians of the Black-Pea Field	139

1	I Start School	139
2	Hasan Çelik, Monitor	141
3	Will We Go to the Yayla?	144
4	The Sarot Yayla	145
5	Moving to the Yayla	147
6	The Goats of Manavgat	151
7	Rise in Anger, Lie Down in Grief	154
8	The Black-Pea Guardians	157
9	Lucky Man	160
10	Katıran Forest	161
11	Treasure on the Dry White Hills	164
12	My Legs! Oh, My Legs!	166
13	Yogurt on the Yayla	168
14	Why Some People Don't Eat Onions	170
15	A Dead Donkey Is a Clean Donkey	170
16	What Kind of Rope Is This?	171

17	My Tooth! Oh! My Tooth! ("Are you pulling a tack from a donkey's hoof, Uncle?")	172
18	Geriz: The Bridge Over Hell	174
19	Fed Up	176
20	The Black-Pea Harvest: Hard Work and Sorrow	177
21	Thirty-Seven Sacks of Peas	178
22	Back to the Village	179
23	Exactly Fifty Years Later	180
A Threat of Divorce by Sharia: If the Fish Doesn't Know it, the Creator Will		182

PART THREE: THE VILLAGE THAT THERE WAS

Basketmaker Ali's Fountains		191
Gypsies		201
1	Circumcision	201
2	How the Gypsy Women Outsmarted the Peddlers	208
Grass Thieves		216
Stampede		224
Herdsman Mustafa		230
1	The Yayla Tradition	230
2	Herdsman Mustafa	232
3	The Herdsman's Drenching	233
4	Death by Lightning	235
The Honor of the Village		237
1	Soğla Lake	237
2	Fertile Soil: If Blood Drops, Life Will Flourish	239
3	A Hail of Stones	241
4	The Governor and the Village Headman 1	243
5	An Inexperienced Peddler	244
6	The Honor of the Village	245
7	An Unforgettable Bayram	250
8	How to Go to a War	252
9	No Spunk Left in a Coward	253
10	The Second Day of Bayram Is the Best	255

11	Music Is Food for the Soul	256
12	The Governor and the Village Headman 2	257

Marriage by Abduction—Emile and Durdul 261
Şenay, a Girl on the Yayla 270

1	Şenay	270
2	The Abduction of Şenay	272
3	Şenay Runs Away to Mesut the Cutler	276

The Legend of Fiery Süheyla and Abdal Rüştü 280

1	The Cotton-Field Workers	280
2	Work Is Glory as Well as Gain	283
3	Dressing the Lamb	284
4	The Chatter of Guns	287
5	Fire and Gunpowder: Explosion of Marriages	288
6	Süheyla the Firebrand	290
7	Abdal Rüştü	293
8	Drums Sound Pleasant from a Distance	295
9	Who Won the Lottery?	297

Bozkır: Friday Farmers' Market 301
Decay and Dissolution 311

1	A Delayed Time Bomb	311
2	Firearms: Fortune's Foe	312
3	A Son Fires at His Father	315
4	Blood Feud	316
5	Decay and Dissolution	320
6	Tended, a Garden—Neglected, a Stony Wilderness	325

Elegy for a Lost Culture 329

Acknowledgments 333
About the Author 337

INTRODUCTION

I count myself doubly fortunate in that, as a child, I was able to observe with great curiosity the changes that began to appear in the village way of life, which had continued unbroken for hundreds of years. First, my family and I were able to continue the traditions and customs handed down to us from our forefathers, and, second, I belong to the generation that witnessed the innovations being implemented throughout the world and, little by little, tried to adapt to them.

I never saw the responsibilities placed on me at an early age by my family and those around me as a crushing burden. On the contrary, I saw the arduous duties that I was given, greater than my years allowed, as the steps I had to take towards maturity, and I made great efforts to carry them out. I considered that my father, mother, and relatives were devoting themselves to helping me grow and develop, protecting me while, at the same time, guiding me toward tasks I could only just manage. When I was six years old, my baby brother, Mehmet got sick with the *moon baby illness*: the spirit of another baby, born within the same forty days as Mehmet, caused the illness, as believed according to ancestral traditions. My mother gave me the responsibility to reverse the bad omen by secretly carrying a piece of my brother's clothes around the house of the one who had wished ill of him. When I was eight years old, when my mother seriously injured her knee, I undertook the task of providing food and warmth for her and my three younger siblings. At nine years old, I was entrusted with the duty of taking the donkey loaded with flour to Sarot Yayla, four hours each way, all by myself. The efforts I made to carry out these hard tasks were of great benefit in helping me grow up.

The day I finished primary school, my teacher said to my father, "Uncle, let Hasan be educated. If he passes the examination to go to the Village Institute, he can study there without being a burden to you." This was his advice, and it is impossible for me not to feel immense gratitude to him and to the many people I value for the help, both financial and moral, that they have given to me throughout my life.

As one who came from a village and had the opportunity to see many different ways of life, I cannot remain silent about the loss of the culture in which I was raised, which had been the way of life for hundreds of years, but which is now completely forgotten.

—Hasan Ali Çelik

Divorce
Sharia Style

PART ONE

Divorce Sharia Style

PART ONE

Divorce
Sharia Style

1
Crazy Kirez

As a village, Çat was quite big, consisting of three almost isolated neighborhoods—Ahmetli, Karagaç, and the biggest, Çat—each settled on a different steep side of the Taurus Mountains. Cascades of waterfalls resounded at the *çat*, or intersection, of three small rivers, each coming from a different valley, finally joining in the middle of the village.* The Çat houses had flat dirt roofs—the only flat places in the village, used for everything from drying fruits and vegetables to celebrating weddings and festivals. Wild olive, linden, and sweet hackberry trees, together with wild roses, covered the open spaces between the houses. Spring, summer, and fall, the aroma of these trees filled the valleys, inviting all kinds of migrating birds to feast on sweet berries.

In the Ahmetli neighborhood, a teenage girl lived with her family in a traditional hillside house. Kirez, like other girls in the village, wore her hair in a dozen or so narrow braids, somewhat covered by a small colorful scarf. Her eyes were dark and intense, and her gentle smile hinted at her confidence.

Her house, like most of the houses in the village, was a two-level building, built into the inclined hillside. The ground level, used as a barn for the animals and for storage, was at least twice as large as the second level, which sat on the back of the roof of the ground floor. The second level made up the living quarters for the family. The additional roof space of the ground level served as an extensive veranda.

Upon leaving Kirez's house, the first thing to strike the eye was a small, flat-roofed mosque where only older men visited during prayer times. The fountain, which supplied the water for all the people in this

---

* Çat, pronounced as "chut": the Turkish word for "to join" or "joint" is the name of the village because three rivers join in the middle of the village.

neighborhood, was about ten feet away from the base of this mosque. All day long, women and girls filled their vessels from the fountain and found brief precious moments to chat and gossip. During the early mornings and late evenings, young men and boys would also come to the fountain to water their animals at the trough.

When women came to fetch water from the fountain with their pitchers on their shoulders, they had to be alert not to cross in front of a male passerby. If a man was detected crossing in the direction of a woman's path, she had to stop and make sure her headscarf or shawl veiled her face, and then lower her gaze away from the approaching man, waiting for him to pass first. This was the old custom: no female, no matter what age, would cross the path of a man, either young or old. A sensitive man would immediately understand the situation and either hasten away or else politely say, "Pass, sister, auntie, daughter, don't wait for me," and show his pleasure at the respect for the tradition. Small girls who did not understand would not engage in this game of respect for the male sex. But the day always came when someone would warn, or even scold, a young girl, "My dear, you're a big girl now, you must obey the customs of your forefathers."

From an early age, Kirez disliked this custom. She did not like having to show respect to boys of almost the same age, together with whom she had played and grown up. For a time, in fact, she did not observe this rule, which had been imposed on her for no good reason; not indeed until one of her neighbors, whose words had power, complained to her father, Bayram. After that, however unwillingly, she had to obey the rule of not looking at or speaking to any man, with the exception of close relatives.

Kirez got on well with girls of her own age, married or single. She liked taking part in the entertainments the women and girls organized among themselves. She played the tambourine well and sang songs to accompany her playing. She had a talent for making all the young girls and brides in the village dance to the rhythm of her music at weddings and festival occasions. She loved to take up two wooden spoons and click them in time to the rhythm of the tambourine.

One particular skill Kirez had was to closely watch her father work, and learn how to do what he did, so that, if necessary, she could do the same job. With practice over the years, she developed a skill for the traditionally male job of pruning vines. When her father, Bayram, was away all winter working to earn money in faraway districts such as Aydın or Manisa, Kirez took on the job of pruning and cultivating the family gardens. Her mother, Hatice, trusted her daughter's skill, but Kirez became the butt of jokes and gossip by young women who jeered, "What do females know about pruning vines?" Perhaps because they were jealous or because they hesitated to be inventive and try anything new, some of these mean girls began to call her "Crazy Kirez." Kirez did not heed the gossip, merely saying, "I'm crazy because my brain is full."

Apart from vine-pruning, Kirez would take surplus products from their garden, such as dried raisins, onions, potatoes, white and purple turnips, and whatever else they had, load them onto the donkey in the stable, and go to the nearest town, Bozkır, to sell them at the Friday Market. With the coins she earned, she would buy salt, matches, kerosene, and other things the family needed.

2
Given Away, Husband Number One

There was an unchanging custom in the village: every young girl, upon reaching the age of seventeen or eighteen, would have a marriage arranged for her as soon as possible. When Kirez became eighteen, her father gave her to a family as a bride for their son, Cafer. Yes, the girl to be married would be given to a family. After that, she would become part of that family, and her own family would treat her like any other relative or visitor. It did not matter that Kirez did not know this young man, Cafer. It was the year 1910, the last days of the Ottoman Empire. Marriages were religious in nature, with the ceremony performed by the village cleric, while the young man and young woman sat in adjoining separate rooms.

Kirez was married to Cafer, with very little in the way of a dowry: simply a pallet, a bundle of clothes, a sack, and two pots. When young people from poor families married, the ceremony couldn't really be called a wedding. The day after the marriage ceremony, according to tradition, a celebration known as "the Bridal Ring" was held. It was attended by only the young girls and young women of the neighborhood. This entertainment was the most important and memorable event for a young girl going as a bride from one poor family to another. The girls and young women would dance while clicking wooden spoons to the rhythm of the tunes of an expert tambourine player until they were quite exhausted. As they danced, the young women would sing:

> *The stream flows, the stream*
> *flows, strewing sand.*
> *Come take me, stream,*
> *to a place of love,*
> *while mothers' hearts burn.*

Kirez began her new life in her new home together with Cafer's mother, father, and their two young children. Everyone in the new house addressed her as "Bride," and not by her given name. In return, Kirez had to address each household member with a special respectful title—father, mother, elder brother, elder sister. She was not allowed to call her husband by his name, Cafer, instead addressing him as "my husband." Everyone in the neighborhood addressed her as "Bride Kirez."

Bride Kirez, skilled in looking after the house, garden, and vineyard, was beloved by everyone in her new family. Her aim was to make herself and her husband become independent as soon as possible. In such a situation, it was up to Cafer to ask his father's permission to become independent from his family. In answer to such a request, the father would, in accordance with his means, give them some property and possessions, and a one-room section of the house for the couple to live in, with a portion of the stable if the young couple managed to own a cow or a donkey. Although her mother-in-law did not want to part with such a skillful bride, Cafer's father promised to think about it and agreed to his son's leaving home on certain conditions:

"Son, join those neighbors who will go to work in Aydın during this coming winter and work there for five or six months. You'll need a hoe and a spade when you arrive. It doesn't snow there in winter like it does here. There's plenty to do in the winter months, hoeing the vineyards, marking out fields, digging up roots, and cleaning the water channels. And by going to Aydın, you'll learn what it is to earn money and save it. When you come back at the beginning of next summer, we'll arrange a suitable section of the house for you and a stable for a donkey. Earn money and save up, and come home. Bride Kirez will stay with us until you come back and we'll do all we can to help."

3
Migrant Laborers

In the fall, a large number of the young and middle-aged men from the village Çat, having finished the necessary work in their own gardens and vineyards, harvesting and stripping the fields, and stocking up on flour, cracked wheat, and firewood, would become idle. In the winter months, they could keep themselves busy doing little chores around the house like clearing snow off the roofs, and feeding and watering the animals in the stable, but that would not bring any income. They usually spent time in the coffeehouse, playing games like backgammon and a card game called sixty-six, or gossiping and listening to others gossip. Those who were confident enough and wished to improve their family's situation would go to earn money by taking a job in the towns and villages of the southwestern province of Aydın. In those days of the Ottoman Empire, donkeys, horses, mules, and even camels were used for every kind of transport. A poor migrant worker heading to

Peasants traveling to find work

find work, however, would not take away his family's only donkey. He would travel on foot. A brave father setting off to walk to Aydın would be shod in moccasins he had made himself, and clothed in a collarless shirt, a woolen jacket, and baggy trousers made by his wife or mother, have his pallet tied in a bundle on his back, and his food tied up in a handkerchief attached to a stick carried over his shoulder.

The food from home would last for only two days. Then the traveler would make do with the food provided at a convenient village guesthouse, or else would look to fill his belly by buying cheap food paid for sparingly with a few kuruş from his pocket money. Cafer, Kirez's young new husband, taking his father's advice, set off for Aydın with some other villagers.

People suffering often remember traditional sayings such as "There's safety and strength in numbers," which might be translated to "Sweet or sour, if everyone is suffering with you, just enjoy and celebrate."

However, at times of severe hunger, thirst, or weariness, the inexperienced ones can't help but express their frustrations in very colorful swear words, directed toward their beliefs and religion, or their mothers and fathers who brought them into this life. At such times, the experienced workers just smiled at their anger, and perhaps told a joke or two to lessen the sufferings of younger Aydın-bound migrant workers, during these interminably long and weary journeys, stretching over weeks rather than days.

Not every young man could stand the job of being a casual laborer, far away from home in strange places, wielding mattock and spade each day with brute force but little experience. If a young man worked, it was because he wanted to earn two or three kuruş, but it took a real man to keep and save what he earned. If he went and spent the first money he earned on buying new shoes or boots, he couldn't save anything. A young man, intelligent but lacking in self-confidence, would ask an experienced, trustworthy relative or family friend he worked with to keep his earnings for him. A young man who wanted to show off would enjoy spending his earnings. Of course, every young man would want to show off upon returning to his village, and wished to be envied by all who saw him in his city-style jacket, trousers, and high boots. But buying these would mean he could not save anything from his daily wage, which, in any case, was a pitiable sum.

Swinging mattock and spade for days on end, a migrant laborer could not change his clothes every day, or even every week. These clothes, after being soaked many times with sweat and then drying in the heat of the sun, came to resemble the uncured hide of a sacrificial sheep—that is, they became as stiff as boards.

Either because he had no one among his coworkers to look after him, or because, like a child, he wanted everything that attracted his attention, Cafer saved no money in all the seven months he labored. He bought a pair of breeches cut in the English style, a shirt to go with them, and a pair of high boots, together with small presents for his mother, father, siblings, and wife, leaving him with only enough money for the return journey. When he came back home at the beginning of the summer, the money in his pockets was not enough to buy him tobacco.

It was the custom to greet whoever returned from migrant labor with a "Welcome home." The neighbors would say to the parents, "May your eyes be bright, your traveler has returned." The parents would reply, "To your good health and may your days be bright also." If only for a day, everyone would speak kind words, both inside the house and out. Those who received gifts would express their happiness.

On the second day the questions would begin:

"What did you do in Aydın?"

"How much did you earn?"

In the streets, coffeehouses, and gatherings, either directly or in a roundabout way, these questions would be asked. It did not take long to recognize which of the workers had saved money and which had returned penniless. It soon became clear which goat was white and which black!

Cafer's father said to his son, "My boy, it's been almost eight months since you left for Aydın. I hope you saved up a good sum of money. Give it to me and I'll keep it for you. Once in a while, a relative or neighbor may become needy and want to sell a small garden or a field with water. On such an occasion, if the price is reasonable, we'll buy it for you and you can start off with a small place of your own. It's not easy for a young couple to be independent houseowners. Bride Kirez is thrifty and skillful. If you have a place to plant and sow things, you'll settle down quickly."

Cafer hung his head and looked at the ground. He murmured hesitantly, "Father, the job in Aydın didn't go too well. All I earned was just enough to buy food and the clothes on my back."

His father's hopes were shattered. However, he didn't show his dismay. He said, "What can we do, son? Hopefully next winter, you'll save some," and the subject was closed.

Cafer considered he had gotten off lightly with so few questions. His good spirits returned.

4
A Useless Husband, Divorce by Sharia

At first, Kirez thought nothing of it when her husband told his father he had not saved any money. Probably, she thought, he didn't tell his father what he earned because he is expecting more contribution from his father, at the time of the separation from family. He must be hiding some of his earnings. In any case, he'll tell me all about it one day. She was not worried.

Cafer spent the first two days after his return visiting the people who had welcomed him home. On the third day, Cafer asked his wife, Kirez, for money to buy tobacco. At that time people made their own cigarettes by filling thin cigarette paper with finely shredded tobacco and rolling it into a tube. Kirez was shocked, but she couldn't say anything. She had ten mecids, very small silver coins, that she had saved up by working as a daily helper in other people's gardens and fields. Without letting Cafer see where she had hidden them in the stable, she took one and gave it to him. According to her calculations, as a packet of tobacco cost five kuruş, the money she gave Cafer would keep him in tobacco for four days, at least. But the very next day, Cafer again asked his wife for tobacco money. Kirez knew then there was no use asking him, "Did you smoke four packets of tobacco in one day?" At that moment, she realized something: I can't spend my whole life with such a useless and wasteful fellow.

She didn't give her husband any more money, but said to him, "Divorce me, man. I'm going back to my father's house."

Astonished, Cafer replied, "I will not divorce you."

In the Ottoman Empire, under Sharia law, women did not have the right to divorce their husbands. In any case, there was no precedent for it. If there were, it would have been impossible to find a case of it in a village community. Divorce was a one-sided affair. The man would say to his wife in the presence of two witnesses: "Let the law run from three to nine. Woman, you are divorced from me." He would repeat this statement three times and then his wife would be divorced. If there were small children, they would stay with the father. The woman had to return to her father's house, or, if she was an orphan, to the house of a close relative.

Cafer refused to divorce his wife. Kirez, realizing she would need a straitjacket for this madman, tried a different tactic. She asked her husband, "If I work as a day laborer for other people and earn twenty mecids to give you, will you divorce me?"

When it came to money, Cafer was all smiles. "No, I won't. But if you give me forty mecids, I will."

The whole of that summer, Kirez spent each day hoeing weeds from the vegetable patches, cutting grass, picking crops, digging potatoes, or carrying on her back the cracked wheat washed in the river. She earned one-quarter of a mecid a day by doing these and other such tasks. When she had saved up forty mecids, the village imam and a neighbor were called. In their presence, Cafer pronounced the required divorce statement three times and Kirez paid the money to Cafer, completing her divorce from him.

That was only her first divorce.

5
Husband Number Two

News of what Kirez had done spread throughout the whole village.

"What a crazy woman, not liking her husband and paying him to divorce her."

"Well, what do you know, she did herself good. Not every man is truly husband material! Maybe other bums will hear of this and get wiser."

In her father's house, Kirez began to work hard at doing what had to be done. Whenever she had a free day, she would work wherever she could find a job and save up money. She waited patiently for a new opportunity to present itself. She knew she wasn't going to stay in her father's house forever.

Mümine, a widowed neighbor of theirs, had been searching for months for a bride for her eldest son, Ömer. As they were poor, she was always rejected, but she went on searching, even if without much hope. She was happy to learn that Kirez had returned home. She told Ömer of her intentions. When he said, "I don't want a divorced woman," she said calmly, "Look here, I've been to at least six houses already to ask for a bride. They didn't even look at me. It's hard to be fatherless. We have no one to lean on. None of our relatives can be said to have any influence. I've known Kirez since her childhood. She's rather blunt and says what she thinks, but that's a fault that can be found even in the daughter of a district judge! She can do anything. Tomorrow or the next day, you'll be called to do your military service. I'll need a helper then. If you get married, your bride will help me. Your brother, Hese, is not an adult yet, and he doesn't know how to take care of a field or garden. I want to ask our neighbor Bayram for Kirez as your bride. If Kirez comes to you, pray and give thanks morning and night."

Ömer still refused, saying, "I can't do it, Mother. I won't take a widowed woman as a wife."

His mother persisted, fixing her son with a stern look. "Come to your senses. Being beautiful or a virgin isn't going to help fill a belly. Either you accept Kirez—that's if she'll have you—or I won't go begging to anyone else for a bride."

However reluctantly, Ömer was forced to accept. Mümine knew that it was difficult to live in a village as a single woman, a widow with a past. Trusting in Kirez's good sense, she made up her mind to ask for her as a bride for her son.

Mümine gathered a basketful of black mulberries from the garden at Akpınar as a present and paid a visit to her neighbors, Bayram and Hatice. She remarked that, for a sensible and skillful girl like Kirez, it was a blessing to have escaped from a no-good husband. She had decided to wait for a week or ten days before asking Kirez to become her son's bride, so she said no more.

Kirez understood why she had come. She saw no problem in the fact that she was a year or two older than Ömer. She already knew that he was a calm, good-tempered young man. She decided she would marry Ömer if, indeed, his mother came to ask for her.

At the end of harvest time, Kirez and Ömer were joined together by the imam in another religious ceremony. This was the second time Kirez was a bride. Her mother-in-law, Mümine, liked his bride very much, and Kirez soon became accustomed to her new family well.

Within a short time, Kirez and Ömer formed a good relationship. At the beginning, they behaved like two strangers, but soon a respect grew between them, which turned to love. In the end, helping each other and working together in the garden, vineyard, and fields built a feeling of trust between them.

6
The Great War

All this happened in 1913. Before a year had passed, the First World War began. Ömer, who would have been of military age within six months or a year, was immediately called up. Kirez was pregnant by then. Before he left to go into the army, Ömer advised her, "Do whatever my mother wants. Even though Hese, my brother, is five or six years younger than you, continue to call him 'Aga'—elder brother—listen to him and obey what he says."

Kirez replied, "Very well, I won't make you ashamed." Then she asked, "If our child is born while you are away, what name will I give?"

Ömer said, "Let Mother decide. I'll agree to any name she chooses."

Many young men from the village were conscripted into the army. It made no difference if they were married and had children to look after. The official who was rounding up soldiers called on every man, including the younger ones.

Those leaving said:

> *We leave now and go.*
> *We may not come back,*
> *we may come back,*
> *but may not see you.*
> *Give us your blessing!*

As they hugged their soldiers and bid them goodbye, those remaining said:

> *May this blessing*
> *be pure as mother's milk.*
> *May your path be open.*
> *Your ways are fortunate.*
> *Allah keeps you from all harm.*

As most of those who were departing had gone away to work each fall, they had no fears about walking to their recruiting office in Konya, the chief town of the province.

They all talked about which distant battlefront they would be sent to after they joined their units and had a little drill and training. Hoping to be sent to the same area as their fellow villagers, they walked for days to get to Konya.

They could not know they would be sent on foot or by train—where there was one—on journeys lasting for weeks, some going to the Caucasus, some to Iraq, others to front lines in Yemen, in Egypt, or on the Canal, strange borderlands of the Ottoman Empire they had never heard of. Fighting tirelessly, the poor young men who were conscripted to protect the sultan's empire would be wounded or die, yelling "Death or Glory!"

7
The Left Behind

At home, there were babies to be cared for, as well as elderly grandparents. Bread and food had to be provided. Gardens, vineyards, and fields had to be planted and sown. Firewood and kindling had to be gathered before winter came. If a cow or a donkey were owned, grass had to be cut and dried to be stored for winter fodder. Those who owned goats had to cut green leaves from boughs of oak in the village woodlands for their winter food. These chores had to be done whether there was a man in the house or not. At the very least, some wheat had to be obtained, washed, boiled, and made into cracked wheat. All of this work was to be done by the women on their own if there were no old folk at home to assist them. Boys and girls aged six or older had to take part and work to help the family stay alive. They learned to become adults while still children.

In the fall of 1914, no one from the village left for Aydın. News of the military roundup had swiftly reached every corner. This was bad news for everyone who heard it, and especially for those working in Aydın. War meant separation for an unknown length of time. The migrant workers, wishing to receive the blessings of their parents, took the road back to their villages as soon as possible. No one knows when a war will be over.

Kirez and many other brides, as well as young mothers, took it upon themselves to earn a living for the family. Young boys not yet of an age to join the army felt like grown-ups and took on adult responsibilities, thinking of themselves as "the man of the house." One of these young men was Hese, Kirez's brother-in-law. Even though he was only fourteen years old, he was tall and well built. His behavior as "the man of the house" started to frighten not only Kirez, but his mother as well. Taking no notice that she was pregnant, Kirez continued to do every kind of work that came to hand. In order not to give her brother-in-law any excuse to bare his teeth at her, she obeyed without questioning his orders such as "Bride, wash the clothes," "Bride, cook this," "Bride darn my socks."

Kirez did everything that was necessary, saying only, "Very well." Obedience cannot be found a fault.

In the spring, Kirez gave birth to a son. Her mother-in-law named him Şükrü. A young mother though she was, Kirez continued to do what was required. Carrying the baby in a cloth slung on her back, she went with her brother-in-law to work in the field, garden, or vineyard. The two would work together the whole day long. Kirez would breastfeed the child when he cried. As evening drew near, she would sling the child on her back and return home with Hese.

The family owned part of a field and a garden in the Akpınar area, named for its white water. It took an hour to get there over a difficult, narrow, rocky path. This land was the mainstay of the family and consisted of about two hectares of dry ground where barley and wheat could be grown, and half a hectare of well-watered land where vegetables could be grown. The vegetables were watered from a spring issuing from white rocks at the foot of the mountain. The field was split in two by a small gully along which grew four or five willow trees, and the edges of the planted area were bordered by fruit trees such as apple, plum, cherry, and a splendid black mulberry tree from which everyone passing by might pick the fruit. There hadn't been enough seed available the past fall to plant just wheat, so the field had been planted with a mixture of wheat and barley.

At the end of July, the harvest was ready. By going early every morning and returning home in the evening, in a week, Kirez and Hese finished cutting the harvest with their sickles. The harvested sheaves were placed in a level, grassy corner of the field and left for another week to dry.

8
Betrayal of Trust

A family that was able to produce a harvest was the envy of those who had no such opportunity, however small the harvest might be. In particular, the villages belonging to the four townships of Bozkır, Hadim, Ermenek, and Akseki—all parts of the province of Konya—were in mountainous regions, so a hectare or even a half or a quarter that could be planted and bounded by stones taken from clearing the inner part of the field was a very precious possession. It would be plowed with a plowshare drawn by an ox or a donkey. Where the ground was too steep for these animals to plow, the land was tilled with a mattock and planted by hand.

Early one morning the following week, the harvest was spread in a suitable place to be threshed. They bargained with a neighbor who owned a pair of oxen to drive the flint-bottomed sledge over the well-dried stalks. This work would be paid for in kind. While the neighbor was threshing, Hese and Kirez mixed the stalks so the threshing would be even. By late afternoon, the threshing floor had become like a soft bed. The neighbor finished the job and left for his home in the village.

The mixture of cut and crushed dry barley and wheat stalks needed to be separated as seeds and mesh of stalks. In order to winnow the husks from the grain, the mixture had to be thrown up into the air with a wooden spade when a suitable wind blew to scatter them. This job was to be done the next morning. Just like every evening, Kirez prepared to sling Baby Şükrü on her back and was getting ready to return to the village. Hese said, "Bride Kirez, we're not going back to the village this evening. We can't go and leave the harvest unattended. Thieves may come in the night to fill their sacks and steal our produce. We both have to sleep here tonight by the grain to be winnowed."

Lightning flashed through Kirez's head. She felt as though boiling water had been poured over her. She thought of what terrible things could happen to a woman who spent the night in the mountains with a young man who was not her husband. This means that all the time we've been working together far from the village at Akpınar, Hese's smiles and winning behavior have all been for this—to spend the night with his soldier brother's wife, thinking no one will see or hear of it, she thought to herself. With a frightened expression, she said, "Please, Aga, I can't stay. The child will get ill if he spends the night here. Excuse me, elder brother, but I can't stay. You stay here and watch the grain. I'll go home and prepare our food for the day and come back tomorrow morning early. Then we'll winnow the grain together."

Hese repeated his order. "You will stay here. You will obey me. We'll sleep tonight by the grain. You promised my older brother. You have to listen to me."

Kirez quickly swung the baby onto her back and began to walk as fast she could toward the village. Hese ran in front of her. "If you don't listen to me, you'll be sorry!" he threatened.

Without taking any notice, Kirez walked even faster and arrived at her home in the village. She did not tell her mother-in-law anything, but only said, "Today we finished threshing. We'll winnow the threshed grain tomorrow if there's a breeze."

From that day on, Kirez did all she could to help the household budget, winnowing the grain and working together with her brother-in-law at every kind of job. She took no notice of Hese, who took every opportunity to whisper in her ear, "See what trouble you'll get into for not doing what I asked." Even when visiting her parents, she said nothing of the indecent advances that had been made to her.

It seemed as though while the war went on, time stopped. For those who waited expectantly, every day seemed like a month. The children's cries of "Mum, I'm hungry! Grandma, I'm hungry" marked the day's passing, while the coming and going of the storks and the swallows showed the passing of the seasons. Everyone—brides, children, mothers, fathers, all—was waiting for news. For days, weeks, and months, even, they looked toward the roads coming into the village for a message or a letter from their loved ones at the front. At times they tried to make out whether the croak of the magpie perched on the eaves was to be considered good or bad news. Whenever they saw the village watchman, they asked him when he was going to the town to fetch the letters waiting there.

9
Bad News

About six months after the distressing event at harvest time in Akpınar, the village watchman saw Kirez at the fountain. He gave her a letter from her husband. Like all the other village women, Kirez did not know how to read or write. She was very curious to know what Ömer had written, so she immediately took the letter to show to her father. Her father, Bayram, read the letter silently to himself first. His face darkened. Kirez realized it was bad news. Then her father read the letter aloud. The news was not the worst, but it was very bad:

"As my wife, Kirez, cannot get on with my mother and my brother Hese, and is disobedient and disrespectful toward them, as well as not contributing anything toward the household, I am divorcing her in accordance with the Sharia rules of marriage."

Let the law run
from three to nine.

My woman, Kirez,
I'm divorcing you.
You are divorced.

Let the law run
From three to nine.
My woman, Kirez,
I'm divorcing you.
You are divorced.

Let the law run
From three to nine.
My woman, Kirez,
I'm divorcing you.
You are divorced.

As witnesses, Ömer had written down the names of two of his army friends.

Kirez swallowed, her throat dry. So her brother-in-law, Hese, had sent a letter to his elder brother telling him a number of lies, saying, "Kirez does this, Kirez does that."

Kirez began to cry silently as she breastfed the infant on her lap and, moaning, cursed Hese:

Evil brother-in-law,
may your neck be broken,
may you be washed
on the slab for the dead,
your eyes be blinded,
and force you to lead
the life of a dog.

She dried her tears on the edge of her headscarf. Sitting by her father's knee, she waited, hoping he would find a way out of this situation. Her father, Bayram, began to speak words of advice:

"See here, daughter, let this letter stay here. I'll hide it. Your mother-in-law and that rogue who calls himself a brother-in-law won't hear about it.

Go on living with them in the same house as if nothing is wrong. If others hear you're divorced, you'll have to come back and live with us. There may be people who want to insult a widow, and I don't have the strength to protect you. Let people continue to think you are the wife of a soldier. Not even a stranger would harass a soldier's wife. Since your mother-in-law is very fond of you, continue raising your child with her help. If you do come back to us as a divorced wife, you will have to leave your poor child in his father's house. A child belongs to its father. Your infant, Şükrü, is still very young. He needs to be breastfed for at least another year."

Kirez replied, "Yes, Father, but the fellow divorced me. What will happen in the end?"

Her father continued, "Yes, Ömer divorced you. If he dies in the war, the state will protect you as the widow of a war victim. If he returns home safe, even if he is sorry and wants to marry you again, he can't. To do that, he would have to follow the Sharia law that says, 'In order for a man to marry his divorced wife again, the woman must first be married to another man and sleep with him for at least one night and then be divorced.'"

Kirez said, "What's done is done. I can't remarry a man who divorced me without asking, even if he wants to take me back. Tell me, Father, what will happen to me at the end?"

Thinking hard, her father said slowly, "At the end of the war, when the soldiers start to come home, if you hear that Ömer is returning, pack up your things and come directly to our house. Now go and continue living with your mother-in-law as if nothing has happened."

Her mother-in-law loved her Bride Kirez and her grandson, Baby Şükrü, very much. They shared all their troubles. Even if Hese didn't like the way the two got on so well, he couldn't complain and break up the household.

10
Are the Dead More Fortunate than the Living?

The war went on and on. No regular mail came to the village, just notice of those who had become victims of war. From the house to which such a notice came, the sound of grieving was heard for forty days and forty nights. Many of the Çat villagers lost their husband, son, or father. Life changed completely for young widows with one, two, or even three children.

War widows who had no relatives to help them looked for different ways to raise their children. Some of them would hand over their son to a well-to-do farmer. In exchange for eighty to one hundred kilos of mixed grains for one year, the boy would undertake the work to be done in the field, garden, or vineyard of the house he had been given to, as well as look after the animals. Some of these boys would be made to sleep in the stable with the animals. They would not be fed well. Our ancestors used to tell this strange but well-known story of one of them:

One long hot summer day, one of these bond-children, sweating with the effort of cutting the harvest, was continuously scolded by his owned-woman: "You! Lazy child, you're not cutting the stalks cleanly." Finally, the youth couldn't stand it any longer and burst out:

Elder sister, elder sister,
those who drink ayran
harvest this way.
Feed me with butter,
I will lick the ground clean.

In a house where there was no son, a poor boy who was good looking and skillful might be lucky enough to prove himself worthy of a well-off family, entering into a promised marriage to their daughter, thus gaining a family to look after him.

A widow without relatives might give her daughter to be adopted by someone in the city when she was old enough to do housework. Such a girl had no right to any inheritance and was bound to work as a lifelong servant of the family that had adopted her. Rarely, after they had made use of her services until she was middle-aged, a good-hearted family would help her get married.

While the war waged on, no soldier returned home unless he had been wounded. Those who did return were seriously wounded, having lost at least one of their limbs. Those with an incurable disease were discharged before returning. Even if they were greeted with joy, this didn't last long. An unhealthy man cannot live without grief.

11
Weep, Eyes, Weep Salt Tears

World War I lasted four whole years. Then came the news: the war was over. The soldiers would return.

A telegram came to Bozkır saying that soldiers were beginning to arrive at Konya. The wounded would stay in the hospital there, while those who were healthy would begin to come back to their villages.

Some of the villagers were full of hope, while others waited full of fear. Parents who had been told earlier, "Your son became a victim of war, killed at such and such a place," or had gotten news of his death, began to weep all over again. It was not possible to forget those who would never come back.

Kirez had not received news that her husband was dead. She was not full of joy, but wept inwardly. According to Sharia law, she was a divorced woman. She couldn't stay any longer in her husband's house. She would be forced to stay far away from her son, Şükrü. Her beloved son, whom she had carried in her womb for nine months and had looked after and raised for four years, now belonged entirely to her husband's family. That was the Sharia law. Even if it weren't, that was what was recognized in this village.

"A child who has no mother may also be called a child without a father." Isn't this what our ancestors used to say? Without a mother, a child is a stranger in his father's house. He is treated the same as a bonded slave. His father, his stepmother—that is, his father's new wife—and even the neighbors would prevent a childlike Şükrü from having a pleasant childhood. Şükrü was only four years old. His mind was set on playing in the street with others his own age.

Two days before the soldiers were expected to return from the war, Bride Kirez bundled up her clothes and what belonged to her in an old piece of cloth during the night. The next morning, she got up early and made the soup for that day. When she was alone with her mother-in-law, she told her what had happened at threshing time three years earlier, and of the letter of divorce her husband Ömer had sent her. Then, after kissing her son, Şükrü, who was playing in front of the house, she picked up her bundle and returned to her father's house.

Şükrü was a child that had grown without knowing tears. At almost four years old, he had become accustomed to going places by himself when his mother went out to work as a day laborer. Wasn't he a child full of play wanting to go on enjoying life with his friends?

Kirez's mother-in-law, who loved her daughter-in-law, and got on well with her, moaned all day about her younger son, Hese. Whatever curses came to mind, she spat out freely:

> *May you never find happiness,*
> *be the butt of your enemies,*
> *always unlucky,*
> *your eyes be blind.*
> *May your head hang*
> *below your shoulders.*
> *Go to the hands of strangers,*
> *enter a dark place.*
> *Let's hear news of your death.*
> *May my eyes be blind to you,*
> *and never see you again*
> *either dead or alive.*

Two days after the news that the soldiers were returning, those the villagers were waiting for began to return in twos and threes. After coming by train as far as Konya, they managed to reach home after walking for two days and a night, their kit bags on their backs.

Kirez's husband, Ömer, was one of those who returned home from war safe and sound. He went straight home. He didn't expect to see Kirez there, and he didn't. He saw his son, Şükrü, for the first time. He was happy that he had a son. "Come, son, give your father a hug and see what I've brought you," he said, moving toward Şükrü. But his son, who had never seen this bearded man before, was afraid and shrank away from him, hiding himself behind his grandmother.

According to the whispers that went from ear to ear around the village, Ömer's mother never said to him, "Welcome home, son." She stayed sitting in a corner, clutching her grandson to her, weeping and saying, "My orphaned little one."

"What's the matter, Mother, why are you crying?" Ömer asked. "Has something happened to Hese?"

"I threw him out. I don't know where he's gone. May he go to hell," was her answer. She told him she had learned only the previous day of the letter about the divorce. She described how unhappy she felt, and went on, wailing, "My bride, my Kirez, my friend for life, always at hand, sharing my troubles! Just like this orphan child, I've no one left to support me."

12
Jackals Abound Where There Are No Dogs

It was not easy to keep the social life of the village going as usual during the First World War. Apart from the old men not drafted into the army, and the one village watchman, there was no one to check the lack of respect that disrupted the social order. All the nation's strength was put into fighting against the enemy surrounding them at seven points of the compass. The gap left by the young men gone to fight was used by some of the adolescent youths as an opportunity to behave badly. Kirez's brother-in-law, Hese, and four or five of those who, like him, had grown up without a father to teach them manners but were too young to go into the army, became drunk with a false feeling of freedom, and began to act arrogantly, carrying out secret misdemeanors. First, they carried out small thefts. Without being seen, they would go in the darkness of night to gardens and vineyards, particularly to those where there was no man of the house, and steal the fruit or vegetables. Their thefts were not confined to taking one or two apples, a bunch of grapes, or a few cucumbers to eat. They believed that what belonged to someone else was sweeter. Drawing courage from each other, these no-good youths would trample on all the vegetables planted in the garden, and spoil far more than they ate.

Knowing that they would not be punished for what they did, the members of this gang encouraged each other to do worse when the opportunity arose. They began to steal chickens and even goats from the stables they could get into. The group took what they stole and cooked it far off where no one knew them or would catch them, beyond the range of high mountains, in precipitous gorges, caves, and extensive valleys. They began to fear no one. As well as thieving, they intimidated and sometimes harassed defenseless women, and began to expose themselves in an unseemly manner, even if only in secret. Sooner or later, it would come to light which of these behaved as though he was a wolf in a village without a dog. The old people in the village waited with their eyes peeled for their heroes to come home from the war.

Some of the heroic soldiers who came home safe and sound began to seek and wipe out one by one those who had ruined their property, and, in particular, those who had blackened the honor of their family. Three of the men were shot in far corners of the mountains. Each of these rogues was thought unfit for a grave, and, after being shot, was left to rot and become, as the villagers said, "meat for the crows." Kirez's brother-in-law, Hese, was one of these, and his body no longer looked human when it was found.

No one ever found out what happened to the bodies of the other two. They were never seen again, either dead or alive, but according to rumor, they had escaped to a far-distant region of the country where they must have carried on with their lives in secret.

13
In Father's House Once More

After returning to her father's house after her second divorce, Kirez led a rather humdrum life. She tried to save money by working whenever she could. She did what work was necessary in her parents' house, garden, and vineyard. Her great sorrow was that she could not see her son, Şükrü, every day. Whenever she saw him playing with his friends, she would press the two or three of the candies she carried in her pocket into her son's hand, trying to keep their relationship alive and not lose him completely. But soon, Şükrü began to run away every time she saw him, and he was not as cheerful as he used to be. Not only did he not run to kiss her when he saw his mother, he did not even turn to look at her. Kirez continued to watch her son from a distance whenever she had the chance, but she realized that he was under pressure at home. There was nothing she could do. Without making it plain to her mother and father, she wept silently, saying to herself:

> Oh, my sweet son,
> my Şükrü, my lifeblood.
> Am I now a stranger,
> my orphan child?
> It was your fate
> to become helpless;
> my future's dark, too,
> not knowing where to go.
> Weeping sad tears,
> sorrow is my fate.

14
Fortunate Girls and Brides

The village put its best foot forward to marry off those bachelors who had returned safely from the war. Those young girls who, four years earlier, had been counted as children, and widowed brides with or without children, were married off to the young men their families thought suitable. Simple wedding celebrations were held, even though most of the people were poor. Wedding celebrations that were held on the roofs and accompanied by music were entertainment for men only. This was an opportunity for the young men who joined in the dances to show off to the women and girls watching from the nearby higher-level roofs. At one of these feasts, a lively young man dancing the folk dance called zeybek was attracted to Kirez, who was watching the dancing from a distance. Kirez, who herself enjoyed dancing at the women's entertainments, liked the looks of the young man. Abdullah, whose nickname in the Karagaç neighborhood was Gunner, was from a poor family, the only son who had returned from the war without harm. By custom, men were prevented from watching the women's entertainment, even from a distance. Young men generally allowed their own families and neighbors to choose a girl to their liking. There was almost no way for a young man to see the face of any young woman except those in his family.

This part of our story is complicated. Was it Kirez who sent word of her interest to Abdullah secretly with the help of a friend, or was it a neighboring woman, knowing that Kirez was a suitable young widow for him to marry, who played the go-between? The readers must decide for themselves.

Abdullah, this World War I hero, was a shy young man. Four years earlier, when only eighteen years old, he had been drafted as a soldier. At the same time, his three elder brothers became soldiers as well, and each brother was sent to a different front. One of his brothers, Kerim, had become deaf, and came home during the war; his two other brothers had been killed, one on the Caucasus front, the other in Libya.

Upon returning home safe and sound after the war, Abdullah learned that his parents had both died. The only relative he had to take an interest in him was one aunt named Rukiye. She told him she would do what she could to find him a suitable young widow to marry. She asked Abdullah, "Nephew, my dear child, is there anyone who takes your eye?"

Abdullah replied, "Aunt, whoever you like, I will like. If you find anyone suitable, ask her for me. I have no mother or father, and I am a poor man. Who would give their daughter to me? I'll even marry a woman whose husband is dead."

15
Third Time Lucky

A man of small stature, Abdullah had fought for four years on battle-fronts in Iraq, Arabia, and Yemen, and had spent more than six months in a British prisoner-of-war camp in Egypt. Kirez had not previously met this young man who sent his aunt to ask for her hand. In order to learn more about him, she went to visit a friend in Karagaç. She saw Abdullah walking along the road, smoking a cigarette. He was the young man she had seen dancing the zeybek at a wedding two weeks before. When she came home, she said to her father and mother, "Maybe my third marriage will be blessed. Send word that I am willing to marry Abdullah."

Kirez married Abdullah and moved into her new husband's small house in the Karagaç neighborhood. As she grew to know her husband better, she liked the way he behaved. Apart from his addiction to cigarettes, she found no fault in him. She cleaned the small one-room house and the attached stable, which Abdullah's father had left him. When Kirez did the housework, Abdullah helped her. And what a helper he was! Whatever Kirez asked him to do, he never said, "That's a woman's job." His behavior was unusual and very different from that of the other men of the village.

Very happy with her situation, Kirez immediately began planning for a settled home. Their house was in the lower part of Karagaç, on a steep hill underneath which flowed the Ulu River. In front of the house, about a hundred meters above the river, was a piece of worthless, rocky ground. Abdullah said to Kirez, "I'll break up the rocks on that steep piece of ground and make terraces, which I'll fill with as much soil and manure as I can find." He began work on this immediately.

Days and weeks passed as Abdullah toiled away without a break. Kirez carried the broken rocks on her back and piled them up in the places where they would be laid. She was happy to see her husband working so hard. The neighbors admired the way Abdullah worked so perseveringly with a spade, mattock, and crowbar. "Abdullah is like a mole, burrowing through the mountain," some declared. For the past four years, Abdullah had been engaged in digging innumerable trenches and foxholes along the front lines. Now he was digging away at his own mountain in order to make terraces on which to plant vines, and black mulberry, apple, plum, cherry, and sour cherry trees. What was weariness to him? He had cold water to drink when thirsty, soup to eat in the evening, and a woman to warm his bed at night. What in the world could be better than that?

For four or five months, Abdullah and Kirez worked without stopping and created three terraces flat enough to plant potatoes, onions, and beans. Where no terraces could be made, they dug small holes and planted vines of different varieties of grape. The simple dry food they made do with during this time was paid for with the money Kirez had saved up over three years of working as a day laborer, brought with her from her father's house.

16
Mobilization—The War for Independence

Meanwhile, Kirez became pregnant. Just when Abdullah was rejoicing at having a child, a general mobilization of troops was announced. As an ally of Germany, the Ottoman Empire had emerged defeated from the First World War, and its enemies began to occupy the whole of the mother country. Many veterans and patriots, unwilling to see their country vanish from the map and the whole population live as prisoners under the bayonets of the enemy, were roused to action. Together with his friends, General Mustafa Kemal, the hero of Gallipoli and other battlefronts, formed a new army to drive out the invaders, and the War for Independence began.

Soldiers, weary of fighting battles on many fronts, were once again called to serve their country. It wasn't only men who, like Abdullah, had come home from war who were called up, but every whole-bodied man, young or old. Moreover, each family was asked to provide as much as possible in the way of clothing or food for the newly formed army. The families took part in the War of Liberation by providing the soldiers with woolen socks, leggings, undershirts, shirts, and underpants they made themselves, as well as halters and tethering ropes for the animals.

Once again, while expecting a child, Kirez said goodbye to a soldier-husband going off to war. This time, she had a house, a home of her own, and a garden big enough to plant and sow. She set to work to get on with her life. Occasionally, when she went to visit her parents, she would see her first child, Şükrü, in the distance. She tried to please him by giving him one or two of the colorful candies she bought at the market and kept for him.

Many things were lacking when the War of Liberation started. One major, a war hero who came to Bozkır, asked every village to collect up all the hunting rifles to be found there. He also searched for and found houses that had strong donkeys and strong boys, not yet old enough to join the army, that could drive pack donkeys over long distances. Under the protection of a few gendarmes, the boys would drive these donkeys, loaded with weapons and gunpowder made secretly in the neighborhood of Çat, from Bozkır to Eğridir to deliver their loads to the army units there. Then, again under the protection of the same few gendarmes, the boys took the donkeys back to Bozkır and their own villages. This was one of the ways Bozkır and its villages contributed to the national war effort. Thirteen-year-old Rahim from the Çat neighborhood was one of those boys. Sixteen years later, this same Rahim would become a son-in-law of Kirez.

The War for Independence went on for a long time. Lacking or deficient in every necessity, the army struggled through bloody battles. This was a war of life or death. Although the enemy never occupied or even came near the region of Bozkır, from time to time, the people left in the villages heard from the war-wounded heroes who came home about the misery and deprivations the people suffered under the occupation.

Kirez saved up the money she earned whenever she could find work. When there was no work to be had, she worked in her own garden. She made preparations for the birth of her baby. She sewed clothes by hand from the striped sky-blue cloth she had bought at the market and made a cover for the cradle. In due time, she gave birth to a baby girl. Kirez called her Fatma after Abdullah's mother. With the money she had saved from her day jobs, she bought a donkey to carry the sacks and bags when she was coming from or going to the small garden at Mantaki, or to the Friday market.

Carrying little Fatma in a shawl on her back, Kirez worked and toiled in her house, in the garden, or as a day laborer. Sometimes, when an elderly neighbor could not get to the market to sell raisins or dry beans, Kirez would buy these and sell them for a small profit at nearby villages such as Dere, Sorkun, or Akçapınar, that she could go to and come back from in a day.

Kirez's desire to make a home was so strong that she found new ways to save money. The shoes she had worn as a bride had worn out. She debated whether to buy a new pair of boots or shoes made by hand by master cobblers in Pabuççu village and sold at the Friday market, but decided not to. She accustomed herself to walking barefoot to places such as vineyards or gardens. Even when going to sell goods at the Friday market or other villages, she would walk barefoot.

Kirez's aim in saving money was to get enough to buy a neglected but well-watered plot on the lower edge of her small Mantaki garden. This was a secret she kept to herself. She worked with great effort in the hope that her husband, Abdullah, would return home safe from the war.

Like an ant scurrying here and there, little by little, she saved up money. Before the news that the war was over and the soldiers were returning, she had managed to save up enough to buy from its owner, who lived in Bozkır, the one and a half hectares she wanted so much. She was quite confident that the produce from this field would be enough for them to live on. She calculated that they would be able to live without her having to go out as a day laborer, carrying her child on her back.

17
Wars End, Work Never Does

For the villagers waiting for the return of a husband, son, or relative, it seemed the War for Independence would never end. It was the fate of many of them to endure pitiless hardship and want. Three whole years had passed since the call for general mobilization when the news came that the last enemy had been driven out of their land.

Bride Kirez's luck had turned at last. Her husband, Abdullah, returned home without a scratch. When he came home, his two-and-a-half-year-old daughter hid herself in fear behind her mother's skirts, perhaps because the young soldier had had no chance to shave his beard or cut his hair. As soon as Abdullah saw his daughter, all the weariness of war left him. Later, Fatma would warm to her father and learn to call him "Baba."

Kirez questioned her husband about the war. By a twist of fate, in the great offensive, Abdullah had been one of the soldiers in the forefront going from battlefront to battlefront barefoot. He had fought fearlessly and without pity, dreaming nostalgically of his wife and the daughter he had not seen, and thinking of all the things he would do in his garden.

After Abdullah had been discharged and returned to the village, he worked all winter long, tending the neglected field Kirez had just bought. He dug up wild bushes and trees. By springtime, the former overgrown field was at last ready to plant and sow.

Kirez was very impressed with the skill she saw her husband had in looking after gardens and vineyards. It was Abdullah's greatest pleasure to prune the trees, dig and hoe the field, garden, and vineyard, and sow and plant all kinds of vegetables. Kirez wanted her husband to take their produce to market and sell it. Abdullah said, "Look, my dear wife, listen carefully. I've been a shy person since childhood. I remained shy during all the years I spent as a soldier, and I am still a shy man. I can't bargain with anyone to sell goods. You are already used to doing that; go yourself to the market and sell or make use of whatever we produce more of than we need. You decide and buy whatever is needed for the house. One thing: don't forget to buy my tobacco. I got used to smoking as a soldier; I can't do without a cigarette. Whatever money is left over, keep as you know best, and when the time comes, we'll try to find a new garden or vineyard."

Kirez was very happy to hear this proof of her husband's trust. This situation was not often seen or heard of in village life. The young couple's unusual behavior became a source of gossip for jealous neighbors. Kirez took no notice. She was a woman who spoke openly to everyone without distinction, be it woman or man, villager or townsman. She was outgoing, hardworking, and helpful whenever help was needed, and these characteristics increased the number of her friends among the villagers, her neighbors at the garden, and her customers in the marketplace. She continued to take the produce of their garden, vineyard, or field to the Friday market or to neighboring villages, and was trusted to bargain fairly for what they were worth.

18
Days End, Work Does Not

As fall approached, everyone in the village was in a flurry of activity. First of all, the produce of the gardens and fields that could be watered had to be collected and taken home. Even the roots were not wasted. Green or dry, every kind of vegetable, plant, or yellowing creeper, and even the fat osiers growing along the riverbank, were dried and later beaten into straw. No one knew how long the coming winter would last. The donkey in the stable, which carried every kind of load, was indispensable to the life of the young family. Kirez knew the importance of feeding this precious animal well. Throughout the whole summer, how to provide enough fodder for the animal during the long winter months was one of her most pressing thoughts.

There was a lot of work to be done before the rains came in September. Grapes had to be harvested and boiled to make pekmez, a special grape syrup, and wheat boiled and dried to make bulgur and cracked wheat for making pilaf.

Cracked wheat was the villagers' staple food. To make it required care. The money saved during the summer was used to buy red wheat from the market or from the villagers who produced it. This wheat is bigger in grain than the wheat used to make flour and is best for making into cracked wheat. As the threshing floor was earth, the wheat had small stones or bits of clay in it. First it was spread on a fleece by the side of the river and expertly washed free of dirt in the running water. The wheat was then carried in sacks to nearby houses, where it was boiled outside, in large copper cauldrons or vessels also used for making grape syrup.

When the special wheat had been boiled, each of the neighbors was given a small plateful, giving them a taste of freshly boiled wheat and also an occasion to express their pleasure and hopes that the cracked wheat would last all year long. Both children and grownups loved the taste of this fresh boiled wheat. Everyone rejoiced at this annual custom, especially if there were a few walnuts to go with the food.

The boiled wheat would be spread out on goat-hair clothes to dry on the flat roof of the house, which would take from three to five days, depending on the sun. While it was drying, it could not be left unattended. At least one person had to stay there to scare away birds or the neighbors' hens. At night, the grownups would sleep there on a pallet and the children loved to sleep there, too, looking at the stars over the completely dark village.

Before the wheat was made into the kind of cracked wheat suitable for pilaf, there were two other processes to be done. The dried whole wheat grains were spread out thinly on copper trays and round wooden boards so the stones could be seen and taken out. Then, in accordance with the family's needs, the wheat was milled by hand and made into the kind used for making pilaf, soup, and other dishes.

19
To Aydın—Once More, Far from Home

The young male population of the village had certainly decreased during World War I and the War for Independence. From their behavior, it was obvious that those young men who returned safe and sound understood the value of life. The heroes who returned to the village of Çat, perched on the slope of a mountain, engaged in their work with great vigor, as if they were still soldiers on the front line. Young men of families that were ironsmiths, potters, or millers made great efforts to become masters of these trades. Young men that had little or nothing in the way of garden, vineyard, or field were unwilling to spend the winter months uselessly. Many young men wished to go to places where they could earn money.

In the month of October, before the rains came, the young men began to form into groups to go to the provinces of Aydın, Izmir, and Manisa. They wished to find work as laborers and earn money during the winter in places where the climate was mild and the land fertile. These were the regions where, six months or a year before, they had fought against the enemy tooth and nail during the Great Offensive and won their freedom. This time, they would go with pleasure to a new kind of struggle. These war veterans declared it would be a case of "a trip and a trade."

In the winter months, Abdullah had no work to do in his garden or vineyard, and he began to join the other village youths going to Aydın to earn money. There, in villages such as Hıdırbeyli, Bağarası, Germencik, or Koçarlı, they pruned the vines and trees, repaired water channels, and did other such jobs.

Abdullah's diligence won the hearts of the landowners, and one of his employers made him a generous offer, saying, "Mr. Abdullah, I'll give you enough land to make a living. Go home and bring your family here."

Abdullah replied, "Sir, I couldn't stand the summer heat and the mosquitoes here. We were born and raised among the mountains. We're not used to a lot of heat. Also, my wife loves her village, her house, and her garden, and she'd never leave them. Thanks a lot, sir, but let me go now and I'll come back next fall and work for you."

Many laborers, like Abdullah, worked until the beginning of summer to earn money. As soon as the extreme heat began on the Aegean plains, the men, whom the local folk called "rednecks," began to long for the cool, sweet air of their own villages. By then, the mosquitoes had become unbearable at night.

The migrant laborers were in a fever to get home. Forming groups of two or three, they bought special gifts from the area for those who were missing them in the village, things like licorice roots used as medicine, olives, or dried figs. Abdullah also took slips he had cut when working from vines rarely found in his area. After bringing them back to the village, he would graft them to vines in his vineyard.

The migrant laborers returned home. They paid their debts. They took up working in their own gardens and vineyards. This was Abdullah's favorite occupation. He gave Kirez the money he had earned, saying, "You'll use the money better than me. We've saved up money, spend it as you will; buy goods or property, whatever you want. You're better at thinking of these things than I am. Don't forget to buy me tobacco when you go to market. We soldiers endured a lot during the war years on the battlefront. Cigarettes were our faithful friends."

20
Şükrü—The Child Grows Up, the Youth Calms Down

When he was a twelve-year-old child, Şükrü, Kirez's son from her second marriage, had been left fatherless. A short time later, after his protective grandmother also died, he found himself poverty stricken and quite alone in the world, and so he began to visit his mother from time to time. As he was quiet and well behaved, Abdullah grew fond of him. After his father and mother, an uncle on his mother's side would be the closest older relative of a male child. Feeling close to him, Şükrü began to address his stepfather, Abdullah, as Uncle. On seeing how skillful Şükrü was at using mattock and spade, in the fall, Abdullah asked him to go to Aydın with him. The landowner who employed Abdullah agreed to allow Şükrü to work alongside him. Abdullah taught Şükrü all the skills he knew and took care to see he grew up properly.

While Şükrü was working all winter under Abdullah's guidance, his employer grew to like the young boy. When spring came, Şükrü did not want to go back to the village with Abdullah. He began working in and around Aydın, and ended up living there. It wasn't enough for him to work as a day laborer for a living. He used his quick brain to learn new skills. According to the season, he would graft young olive trees, or work at soldering and tinning at an ironsmith shop. As he grew, he learned how to make candy by working in a candy shop. He started making a special candy and sold slabs of it at the market. Next, he learned how to make fizzy lemonade. He began to invent new things. At first, he sold these at the market and in the coffeehouses, then he began to sell wholesale. He became known in the region as Master Şükrü from Konya.

Şükrü's childhood in the village must have been more distressing than anyone knew, as he never returned there. He would send his mother presents through Abdullah or the seasonal workers from his village. The coffeehouses in the villages and towns around Aydın became like home and family to him, and at an early age, he took up smoking tobacco. He loved relaxing and playing games in the coffeehouses. He became famous as an expert checker player. There was a story about a checker game played in Ankara, which entertained his admirers. He loved to tell the tale:

> Once upon a time, I took some goods to Ankara. I delivered the goods to the wholesaler and got a room at a hotel in the business district called Hay Market. Asking around, I found a soup kitchen nearby and had enough soup to satisfy my stomach. Then I went to a coffeehouse. There, a large crowd was watching a game of checkers with great excitement. It was obviously a close game. Without saying anything, I started to watch too.
> When one of the players sacrificed a good checker by advancing another to become a king, the crowd exclaimed "Wow!" One of them cried out, "Oh, the game's over, not even Master Şükrü from Konya could trap this king!"
> As I heard this, I couldn't stop myself from saying, "If you let him take the second checker on the left, that will end up trapping the king."
> The people watching and the two players all looked at me as if to say, "Who does he think he is?" Some of them looked me up and down with a jeering smile and then fixed their eyes on the board again. The second player followed my suggestion

and captured the king. The player who lost his king got to his feet and shouted indignantly at me, "Hey there, why are you interfering? It's none of your business, man."

"I'm really sorry, friend," I said, "but it is my business. Master Şükrü from Konya, that's me!"

When they heard me say my name, everyone burst out with laughter. That evening I had a good time playing checkers with many different people in Ankara.

Kirez did not see her firstborn, her beloved child, Şükrü, for many long years. Naturally, as time went on, she missed him more and more. Like all the mothers in the village, she waited with tears in her eyes, praying for the day her longing would be satisfied. At last that day came.

Şükrü came to Çat to pay her a visit, bringing with him his bride, a beautiful woman he had married. Kirez was overjoyed. For Şükrü, it was the first time he had had the opportunity to see his siblings in the village, and his close or distant relatives on his father's side, since leaving so many years ago.

21
Kirez's Daughter, Fatma

Life for Kirez and Abdullah ticked by like a well-regulated watch. Abdullah spent his days quietly and simply. He spent half the year working as a gardener in Aydın, and half in the village working on his own property. As the years passed slowly by, the life of this young married couple, as well as that of the country, rapidly changed.

Fatma had been born at the beginning of the War for Independence. After she was born, three further siblings, Mehmet, Hatice, and Rukiye, were born and raised. Fatma became old enough to look after her siblings. She also began to help Kirez in the house and garden. She had undertaken the job of watering and hoeing a small garden called Belen Head, which her grandfather had given Kirez at the time of her marriage to Abdullah. This tiny garden was only good for growing vegetables. When Abdullah was away in Aydın, Kirez was able to trust Fatma to look after the small children and take care of this small garden. This was a great help, as Kirez was able to load her donkey with the produce from her gardens—grapes, green beans, sweet corn, onions and potatoes—and go to sell them in neighboring villages.

22
Old Ways Die Hard

When the War of Independence was over, the state regime began to change. First of all, Turkey was declared a republic. Following this, marriage and divorce were to be regulated according to new civil laws, not those of Sharia. Plural marriages were no longer allowed. Elderly people who already had two or more wives were allowed to keep them, so as not to trouble them. New marriages made in the village of Bozkır would only be legal after being registered at the government office in Bozkır. The village people called this "getting permission." From then on, divorces would also be "by decision of the Bozkır court."

Living under the new Republican regime didn't mean that the old ways and customs were completely ended in the villages. The older people, who had grown up in accordance with the old customs and regulations, found it particularly difficult to adapt to the changes. There were still those who had marriages performed by the imam without getting official approval, and divorced according to Sharia law. It took a long time for the influence of the knowledge and information given by the teachers who came to schools newly opened in the villages to take effect; in particular, getting the information across to the headmen of the villages was not easy. But, little by little, the laws and regulations concerning human rights became the norm.

23
One Mishap Worth a Thousand Warnings

Our forefathers used to say, "One mishap is worth a thousand warnings," or in other words, "It's the burned child that fears the fire."

I can't continue without recalling an experience that taught the people of Çat village the need to comply with the new order of things.

Sülüman, a poor man living in the Upper Village area, was the father of a thirteen-year-old daughter, Duriye, whom he had married off to Başar, the twenty-year-old son of Dodulu, a well-to-do farmer from the neighborhood of Çayiçi. No one, neither her father nor her mother, had asked Duriye, "Do you want to be married to this young man?" Duriye was a pretty child. She never spoke up against her father. In the words of the old order, she was a tractable child, nodding her head to answer "Yes" to her parents. Such children were said to have a mouth, but no tongue.

On the day after her wedding night, Duriye ran back to her father's house. She cried and sobbed, pleading, "Please don't send me back there again! Please, Father! Please, Mother!"

Sülüman beat his daughter soundly, then he took her back and left her at Dodulu's house. There, her father-in-law, Dodulu, and her young husband, Başar, both beat her, too, saying, "You won't escape from this house again."

That night, she again suffered unimaginable pain. Duriye thought of going to Kemer Bridge and throwing herself into the foaming waters of the Ulu River. She had in mind a sad song she had heard of during women-only entertainment at weddings. This song was the sorrowful legend of a young girl who, long ago, like her, had been forced into marriage. She had found a way out by throwing herself into the turbulent waters of the Ulu River.

The next day, taking up a water pitcher, Duriye asked her mother-in-law's permission to go out, saying, "Mother, let me go to the spring and bring back a pitcher full of cold water for you."

Pleased, her mother-in-law said, "Well done, Bride. Always behave this way."

Duriye went to the bridge, but when she saw the torrential river flowing joyously below her, she was frightened. She gave up the idea of throwing herself into it. She went on walking toward the spring on the other side of the bridge, but passed it, only stopping briefly to leave the pitcher in the overgrown thorn-berry bushes a little way from the spring. Covering her face with her scarf which she twisted tightly around her head, she walked quickly toward Bozkır, the town to which the village was connected. She had often heard the older people say, "It's only an hour's walk to Bozkır." With the air of one who knew where she was going, she continued walking. Taking care not to be seen by anyone, she sometimes hid in the bushes. It wasn't Friday, the day for the Bozkır market, and there were few people on the road. She had never been to Bozkır before, but she had heard that the government was there.

When Duriye reached Bozkır, she asked someone, "Where's the government, uncle?" and arrived in front of a tall building. She sat down at the foot of a wall near the entrance and began to sob.

The time came for the government offices to close, and the officials came out in ones and twos. One of them saw Duriye and came up to her. He asked why she was crying. Duriye went on sobbing as she explained her troubles. The official himself had a young daughter and immediately informed the governor of the situation. The governor ordered the gendarmes into action: "Go and arrest these five people: Duriye's father, Sülüman, and her mother; Başar, her husband by the imam; his father, Dodulu, and his mother."

At the trial in Bozkır, the girl's mother said, "Sir, I was against this marriage. But my husband said, 'What I have said, I have said,' and allowed this marriage to happen." The verdict was swiftly given. The girl's father, Sülüman, was sentenced to seven years in prison with hard labor. Dodulu and Başar, father and son, were each sentenced to six years' imprisonment. The judge said, "Let this sentence be a lesson to everyone. I will set the mothers free. I am releasing them as protectors of their young children."

The people of Bozkır and its seventy-five villages were very impressed by the court's verdict, accepting that "The government protects underage girls."

24
Rahim

Rahim was the youngest son of a well-to-do man who went by the name of "Big Ali," or "Ali Hoca." He had two siblings older than himself, Salah and Haşşa, and one younger called Anakiz. All of them were married and had a house of their own. Meanwhile, Rahim's mother found a young girl, Nazife, for Rahim to marry. However, Rahim did not leave his father's house as his siblings had done, but decided to live with his parents. He and his wife, Nazife, undertook full responsibility for looking after his parents. But Rahim's father frequently warned him: "Look, son, go on taking care of us, but get a house of your own. In the same way that a needle is attached to a cloth, keep your earnings separate. Otherwise, when I die, your siblings will become joint heirs of everything, from the knife in your pocket to your handkerchief and even the socks your wife knits for you. They'll divide up everything in the house, the stable, the garden, the land on the mountain, everything! It's a bad custom left us by our ancestors who said the son who lives with his father owns nothing. Your siblings will take everything you have."

But Rahim didn't listen. "Father, I won't have people gossip about me: 'The youngest son of the house left his poor father and mother helpless and went off to a house of his own,'" he declared. He remained with his old parents and continued to take care of them.

As Rahim and Nazife were living with the two old people, it was the young couple's duty to make good use of the family garden, vineyard, and fields. Rahim was the one who took what they produced to sell in distant villages. The couple first had a son they named Hilmi, and then, two years later, another they called Kiriş. The parents were happy to have lived to see their grandsons, the children of their youngest child.

When the younger grandson, Kiriş, was one year old, Rahim's mother died. Rahim was away peddling at the time. He only learned of his mother's death when he returned to the village four days later. A year later, his wife, Nazife, became ill and died within a short time. Four-year-old Hilmi and two-year-old Kiriş were left motherless.

Rahim's mother-in-law, Saliha, was one of those whose husband had been killed in the Great War at Gallipoli. She lived alone. Rahim had no way of looking after his children and was forced to leave them in his mother-in-law's care. He was struggling alone to take care of his father, and at the same time was obligated to help out his mother-in-law with his profits on peddling trips and from the produce of the garden, vineyard, and fields. A little while later, Rahim's father also died. This is how Rahim told the story:

There was no flour left in the house. I decided to go peddling to provide for us and my mother-in-law, who was looking after the children. I needed to get some grains to make flour. After borrowing a donkey-load of pots from Master Potter Kerim from Ömerli, I went to peddle my goods around Karaviran and nearby villages. When I got to Bağra village, I bartered these for barley, wheat, and other grains. Spending one day on the road, one in bartering, and one on the return journey made it three days in all. I arrived back in the village early in the evening of the third day. Without going home first, I went straight to the mill and left the grain there to be ground by morning. I came home, tied up the donkey in the stable, and, with the saddlebag over my shoulder, came to the door of the house. It wouldn't open. On looking closely, I saw that the door was not only locked, but sealed: a print of the seal of the village headman was tied to the door. Seeing me, the neighbor, Havva, gave me the bitter news: my father had died the previous day, and, of course, had been buried on the same day by the Islamic tradition. Then my siblings had called the village headman and had the house sealed.

"Come and sleep with us," the neighbors offered. But, keeping my feelings to myself, I went to the stable and slept in the hay. My false-hearted siblings never came to give me condolences, nor asked me to their houses. I was particularly upset by the behavior of my elder sister, Haşşa, who, ever since childhood, had asked me to do jobs she found for me to do. I needed to call the village headman and divide everything in the house among the siblings.

It was three days before I could get them all to come together. I had borrowed a pan from my neighbor, basketmaker Halil, and brought a measure of cracked wheat from my mother-in-law. During those three days, I lived on the cracked wheat I cooked on a fire of sticks on the front roof of the house.

Rahim and his siblings divided up everything in the house among the four of them: pans, plates, glasses, bowls, spoons, ladles. The fields, vineyards, and gardens, even the poplars and fruit trees growing there, were all parceled out in the same way. For example, the garden known as Giysilik, forty feet across and fifty feet long, situated by the stream that fed the mill, was lined into four strips and shared. It was divided up in such a way that half the forked apple tree growing along one dividing line belonged to Rahim and the other half to his sister, Haşşa. All the other lands and vineyards were shared out in the same way, divided up into narrow strips that made farming and market-gardening very difficult. Even though, during the process, the village headman, who acted as judge in this matter, reminded the siblings that dividing land, garden, and vineyards into small parcels made them almost worthless for production, Rahim's siblings, in particular his sisters, insisted on dividing every piece of land into four, saying, "While visiting each plot, we'll remember our father."

25
Rahim Looks for a Wife

After all his father's possessions had been split up and shared out, and while his children were being looked after by his mother-in-law, Rahim began to live in the room and stable that had fallen to his lot. But it could hardly be called a life. In a village, a thirty-year-old man without a wife wasn't considered to be living a life of any kind. Rahim was very willing and did whatever he could to find a girl or a woman to marry. A well-known village saying is "The wife is the mirror in the house." If there is no mirror in the house, you will not see a reflection of yourself, wherever you may look. He asked his elderly neighbors for help. Taking their advice, he sent his mother-in-law several times to widows who had two or three children themselves, to propose him as a prospective husband. Each of them rejected the proposal. A widow with children did not want to marry and have them mistreated by a stepfather. A woman with children to protect considered this more important to her than marrying a man who had land of some kind, a garden, or a vineyard. Rahim was in despair. Finally, he asked his distant relatives living in the opposite neighborhood to find a bride for him. They found out that in the Karagaç neighborhood, a woman called Crazy Kirez had a newly adult young daughter called Fatma. They also told him that Abdullah, Kirez's husband, a very quiet man, spent a large part of the year working in the Aydın region. Rahim sent a few of his respectable neighbors and friends with a proposal, saying, "Rahim would like to marry Fatma."

When Kirez learned from the delegation why they had come, she had a fit. "My daughter is only just fifteen. I don't have a daughter to give to a thirty-year-old man, especially one who's a widower. Go away. I don't want to see your faces here again."

Rahim was shocked when he heard Kirez's answer, and, naturally, he wondered what to do next. He turned over all the possibilities in his mind, hoping to come up with a solution. He wanted to talk to Kirez himself, but he lacked the courage. How could he explain anything to a madwoman whose husband wasn't there? He very much wished he could say, "Look, Auntie, I've got a house. I have this much in the way of land and goods. I am from a well-known, respectable family. I have lost my wife and I am desperate. If you will 'give' me your daughter, I will look after her well in this way and that." But he knew he would be thrown out before he could open his mouth.

Kirez's father, Bayram Torun, lived in the Ahmetli neighborhood. He was a kind, elderly man. Kirez's husband, Abdullah, was away, so Rahim decided to talk with Bayram, the senior man of Kirez's family in the village at that time. Bayram, Fatma's grandfather, listened to Rahim. He gave Rahim courage, saying, "Mr. Rahim, brace yourself to abduct Fatma. What can Kirez do? Can she give my granddaughter Fatma to a better man? As it is, in Karagaç where they live, there is a whole slew of good-for-nothing, idle young men. If you don't run off with her, one of them will. Fatma's father is away in Aydın, not at home, which means she has no one to protect her. My son-in-law, Abdullah, is a good, well-mannered man, but no one would be afraid of him. We have a place at Belen Head where we grow green beans and potatoes. Fatma keeps it hoed and well-watered. You can arrange things so that you find Fatma alone there. Go and think about it. If you have a mind to do it, abduct Fatma. This is still possible in the villages. Later it will be just the same as a marriage."

26
The Abduction of Fatma

Rahim explained the story himself:

When my elder sister and her husband, my brother-in-law, the imam of the mosque, locked and sealed the door of the house after my father's death, I was very angry. However, he who falls into the sea clutches at snakes. One evening, I went to their house and told them: "I want to consult you about something. There's a girl in Karagaç I'm thinking of abducting. Four days ago, I went to the Ahmetli neighborhood and spoke with her grandfather, Bayram. He gave me some encouragement.

But I'm not sure whether to trust in the newly declared laws or not. If I carry her off, will they put me into prison because she is underage, I wonder? She is very young. But I have no alternative. My children, Hilmi and Kiriş, are with their grandmother, but not well looked after. I came to ask for your advice. Hoca, in the times of the old regime, you were a teacher at the madrasa in Konya. I am hopeful that you are knowledgeable about the new laws."

This is what Sarı Hoca replied: "Now, listen well, Rahim. You say the girl is very young. If the government gets to hear of it, you'll go to prison. If her mother, Kirez, doesn't complain, the government won't interfere. Abduct the girl, but don't frighten her. Try to persuade her nicely. No cursing or beating. Here, take my new jacket. Best of luck."

I made up my mind to carry off a girl I'd never seen before because the girl's grandfather told me to abduct her in a gentle manner, and I was advised to do so by my brother-in-law, a teacher.

I found out where the small vegetable garden at Belen Head was. I went there every day and kept an eye on it from a distance. The first two days, nobody came. On the third day around noon, a short, thin girl with a hoe in her hand came to that garden. She opened the water channel going in the direction of the garden to water it. The water began to flow toward a line of potatoes. I watched her from my hiding place behind a hedge of roses in the garden next door. When I realized that she was the girl I wanted, I jumped over the hedge in front of her and caught her up in my arms. I carried the girl, who was no heavier than a small sack of wheat, to a corner of the field and threw her like a ball over the boundary into the neighboring field, jumping myself immediately after her. I picked the girl up again and carried her through the rows of gardens to get to a secluded spot above the Ulu River. I didn't pay much heed to her sobs, but just said, "Quiet, girl. I'm abducting you. Don't be afraid. My intentions are good."

With the girl in my arms, I crossed the river where it was shallow. Taking care no one saw us, I quickly crossed the gardens on the other side of the river and began to climb to the top of the opposite hill.

The girl cried out, "Put me down. I can walk by myself."

I put her down on the ground, but I still held her tightly by the hand. In a little while, we came to the thickest part of the woods and sat down. No one could catch sight of us there, among the trees and bushes. I decided to wait there until darkness fell. I talked without stopping, telling her, "I have this much property, a garden, a field to plant with wheat, a house to live in, with a stable." I described the best side of everything, telling her whatever came into my mind. It was lunchtime and there was a long time to go till it got dark. Thinking that, like me, she would be hungry, I had come prepared.

Once when I was in Bozkır, I had been in the same shop as two women from the city. The women asked for something called pastırma. When they left, I asked the shopkeeper what pastırma was. The shopkeeper replied, "Nephew, pastırma is very good meat. City women, in particular, like it very much. Here, take this small piece and taste it."

I tossed it into my mouth. It was salty with a funny smell. I didn't like it. When I was deciding to abduct the girl, I remembered what the grocer had said. I went to Bozkır and came home with a hundred grams of pastırma. I wrapped the smelly meat inside a soft piece of flatbread. And when I went to run off with the girl that day, it was in my pocket. We weren't going to wait in the woods till it was dark before eating anything.

I turned to the girl and said, "Since you have beautiful eyebrows, I would like to call you Karakaşli. Come now, stop crying and eat a few bites. Take this little wrap and taste it. City ladies are very fond of the meat in it."

Reluctantly the girl, still hiccuping, took a small piece and put it in her mouth. She chewed it and then swallowed it. I was pleased, but I didn't show it. I began to eat the wrap I had made for myself with plain, dry white cheese and the last of the grape syrup.

The girl ate all of the wrap in her hand, but she still went on sobbing from time to time.

I said to myself, Let her cry. Hopefully she'll feel comfortable later on and open up.

The girl had not spoken a word. She just went on sobbing and crying almost silently. From time to time, she heaved a deep sigh.

27
Fatma's Thoughts

They weep and weep,
those born and raised
in Karagaç.
At four years of age,
I saw my father
for the very first time.
He came to the house,
I remember, one evening,
with his hair and his beard
all tangled and rough,
a veteran of World War I
and the War for Independence.
He said, "Fatma, my daughter,
I am your father,"
and tried to embrace me.
Frightened, his daughter
cried and sought shelter
behind her mother's skirt.

Growing and blossoming
with beauty and talent,
the young girl Fatma
was watering the garden,
that unfortunate garden
at Belen Head,
dried up and waterless
before summer came.
Abducted from there
with eyes full of tears,
carried into the shade
and cast down in the forest,
bare feet bleeding
from thorns that pricked her

and tore at her clothes,
her legs and her trousers,
Fatma wept and she wept,
not quite of an age
to become an adult,
still barely fifteen.

While her mother worked hard,
she looked after her siblings,
the three younger ones,
the light of her eyes.
On good days or bad days,
they never were scolded;
no curses they heard
from their dear Fatma's mouth.
Early one morning,
in the garden at Belen,
so they wouldn't get wet
Fatma rolled up her şalvar.
Before she had time
to give it a thought,
a man like a giant
caught her up in his arms,
imprisoned her hands,
and carried her close
over mud, thorns, and rocks,
and the fast-flowing river,
straight to the dark of the woods.
Fatma, weeping, wondered,
"What of the future?"
Would she not smile again?
Never play games,
in days full of troubles
and work without end?

She wept as she listened
to the words of this big man,

*confusing her mind
as she endlessly wept.
She cried with warm tears
till her eyes saw no more
as night fell. Then he rose,
his huge bony fists
tightly gripping her hand.
She walked with faint hope
in the heat of the dark,
till they came to the door
of the big man's house.*

28
Kirez—The Lioness's Love of Her Cub

*Someone had seen
the abduction of Fatma,
done in broad daylight,
and told all her neighbors,
who told all their neighbors.
News spread to Karagaç
to the ears of her mother.
Kirez frothed at the mouth,
and before it was evening,
arrived at the door
of Rahim's house.
She waited in anger,
determined to rescue
her young daughter, Fatma.
Snatched from her home,
her dear daughter, Fatma,
who'd not had the chance
to grow into womanhood,
Kirez determined
her invaluable helper
would not be left long*

in such shameless hands,
exposed to the gossip,
the poisonous tongues
of the Çat village wives.
She waited with curses
foretelling the end
of Rahim, this madman,
and all of his family,
seven generations to come.
Then Rahim came
with her dear one, her Fatma.
Taking her hand, she said,
"Come, girl, let's go,
Walk in front to our house.
Let's not wait till tomorrow
but go straight to the government.
Let's tell them our trouble
and see what they say
of this shameless abduction
of an innocent child.
You're still underage.
Let this man go to prison
and, judged by state law,
rot away in the darkness.
Should it be easy
to run off with a child,
barely fifteen years old?
We have the state, and the gendarmes,
and witnesses, too,
who saw you abducted by force.
Come, daughter, Fatma,
come on, let's go home,
where your young sisters
cry, 'Let our dear Fatma
come home to us here.'
You're still but a child
and not yet a wife, dear.

Come home, my sweet rose,
my helper in all things.
Come, let us go now,
where your home's waiting for you."

29
Fatma's Destiny

Heaving deep sighs
as she heeded her mother,
Fatma was thinking
of bad days ahead,
as if she could hear
the gossiping neighbors—
"She spent a whole day
with a man on the mountain!"
She thought of the future
with no one protecting her,
no father, nor brother
in the Karagaç neighborhood.
Where the Hamsoğlu youngsters,
as strong as wild beasts,
act like packs of wild dogs.
A future with them would mean
trouble and shame.
She made up her mind,
and, choking back tears,
said to Kirez, her mother:
"Oh Mother, my mother,
this is my destiny,
this place where I am now.
This door is my door,
this hearthstone is mine.
If God gives His blessing
I will here rock a cradle,
my cradle in my house.

*Since this is what's written
I can't go with you.
Oh Mother, my mother,
I have to stay here.
I've made up my mind,
so go away, do.
Go to my old home,
my siblings are there.
Leave me alone here
for good or for ill.
It's my fate to remain
and I'll spend my life here.
Oh mother, my mother,
I won't go with you.
God wrote this for me.
Don't go to the state
or call up the gendarmes.
Don't grieve over me,
I'm resigned to my fate,
which is never to go
to my old home again."*

30
Both Husband and Father

What had Rahim done? He had abducted a girl, still a child, and gotten himself a new wife. When this tiny girl stood up against her mother and decided to stay with him, his pleasure was obvious. But he knew it wasn't all going to be that easy. Fatma's father was in Aydın, and her mother had gone home to Karagaç, upset that she had not persuaded her daughter to come with her. It was early evening and he was alone in the house with Fatma. He could not stop black thoughts of what might happen from crossing his mind, but he did everything he could think of to make her comfortable. First of all, he sprinkled four or five pieces of flat, dry bread with water. Then he poured a little grape syrup from the jug standing in a corner into a dish. He called Fatma: "Girl from Karagaç, you've cried a lot today, you're tired and hungry. Come and eat a few mouthfuls with me and tomorrow we'll start to arrange things."

After they had both eaten a little food, Rahim took down the folded pallet he used in the house and spread it next to the wall. Fatma took off her şalvar, lay down silently, and drew the cover over herself. Rahim did not lie down immediately. Belatedly, he said his evening prayers. Telling his beads, he recited the prayers quietly. But before he had gotten halfway through each prayer, devils came into his mind and he forgot what came next: What would happen if complaints were made to the government? What could he do? What would happen if the girl didn't like being married and ran away?

If she didn't run home, he knew Kirez would not go to the government office and protest. It was clear that, until Fatma was at least seventeen, he could not get official permission to marry her. "Well, let's see what the morning brings," he said to himself, and decided to call the imam early the next day and at least have a traditional religious ceremony.

Tired after a long, struggling day, Rahim also took off his şalvar, and the jacket his brother-in-law had lent him, and lay down by Fatma, who was already fast asleep.

Rahim's eyes would not close. Thinking of all the possibilities, good and bad, he stayed awake until dawn. Getting up slowly, without waking Fatma, he went to borrow a bowl of ayran, buttermilk, from a neighbor. When he came back, he saw Fatma was up and making a fire of sticks and kindling on the hearth. When she said, "Should I put some cracked wheat pilaf on the fire?" he was very happy.

"That would be fine. I love cracked wheat pilaf," he said. It seemed that this young girl, soon to be his wife, had learned how to do things properly, and that made him feel a little less uneasy.

Together, they both filled their stomachs with some flatbread and a plate of cracked wheat pilaf, and drank the ayran. Rahim went to find the village imam and asked him to perform the religious marriage ceremony after he had said the noontime prayers in the mosque. Then he went to the Karagaç and Ahmetli neighborhoods to ask both Kirez and her old father, Bayram, to be present at the marriage ceremony.

After lunch, Rahim spread a sack on the front part of the roof. He laid two or three cushions on top of it. In front of a small group consisting of Kirez, Bayram, the village teacher, and the nearby neighbors, Rahim and Fatma were married by the imam. Those present wished them well and the first steps were taken in this marriage, performed according to the rites of their religion but without any legal validity.

Years later, Rahim described the evening of his wedding day to the first child born of this marriage:

I abducted your mother and brought her to my home. Although she wasn't happy about it, she agreed to stay with me. The next day, we had an imam marriage ceremony, but I was still afraid that I might get into trouble because she was a child bride. I considered that she needed time to get used to me, as well as the neighborhood. For fifteen days, we ate and drank and went to my share of the garden and vineyard left to us by my father and lay down at night on the same pallet, but all that time, I never laid a finger on your mother. Our married life began only after those two weeks. However, since her age wasn't right, we couldn't marry officially. That had to wait.

We worked hard as husband and wife to put our life in good order. When we were able to get official permission, your little sister, Ayşe, had just been born. We went to the government office and wanted to register both of you at the same time. We hadn't been able to register you as soon as you were born. Now, the official there told us it would cost us a twenty-five-kuruş fine to register you so late. He advised us to register the two of you as newly born twins. That's why you're really one and a half years older than the birth date registered on your official identity card."

31
Abdullah

When he returned from Aydın, Abdullah was not pleased to learn that his daughter, named after his mother, was married. However, since he couldn't change the situation, he didn't try to do so. What was done was done. As he missed her a lot, he often went to his darling daughter's house to see her. Because some people knew he didn't enjoy playing cards or drinking tea at the coffeehouse in Çat, when asked where he was going, he would say he was going to the tobacco seller, Lame Abdullah the Smith. After buying a packet of tobacco and some matches, he would always go see Fatma. Later, he started to trust his first grandson, Hasan, and would send him for tobacco when he visited his daughter.

Before they grew old, Kirez and Abdullah raised their other two daughters and a son. They saw their oldest grandson become the first person from the village to go to university. They lived to see the birth of grandchildren and great-grandchildren as the years passed by. Abdullah was getting on at seventy years of age when one day he said, "My energy's all gone. My hands and my legs haven't any strength left in them. I really can't work anymore." From then on, he didn't leave the house, but sat for the rest of his life on a cushion near the fire in the hearth.

As the family was used to people growing old and feeble, they did not think of taking this veteran of the World War and the War of Liberation to a doctor. Nobody thought that he was ill. Even if they had thought of it, there was no way of going to a doctor in Bozkır. No one in the family had the money to spend on taking someone who wasn't ill around the hospitals in Konya or Ankara.

Abdullah's life continued without much change. Kirez patiently looked for ways of lessening his discomfort. Instead of rolling tobacco in cigarette paper to make cigarettes, ready-made cigarettes in a packet had become the way to satisfy his addiction. Kirez bought these for him regularly, and saw that he had food and drink. His daughters, son, and his grandchildren, as they grew up, visited him once in a while, almost like paying a visit at Bayram festivals. They pleased their grandfather by bringing small gifts.

32
The Road

Toward the end of her life, Kirez found herself obliged once more to take part bravely in a struggle over something close to her heart.

It was sometime in 1963. The garden and vineyard at Mantaki were the most precious of the family possessions. They learned that a well-watered field on the edge of this land had been sold to someone they didn't know well, a certain Master Kamil from the Ömerli neighborhood. They hoped that they would get on well with their new neighbor.

It seemed that a section of the road used by the owners of the fields in that area went through the field that had just been sold. This so-called road was like a narrow strip of land, just wide enough, in fact, for men with loaded pack animals to come and go along. Kamil, a potter in the Ömerli neighborhood, was known to be tight-fisted. He regarded this path through the middle of the well-watered and fertile field he had just bought as an unnecessary nuisance. One day, when the spring planting and sowing began, he plowed up the whole of the field, including the path.

Bad news spreads fast, they say. Kirez and her neighbors, owners of the nearby fields, could not believe what they heard. There was another road it was possible to take when going to the fields and gardens if this one was closed, but it was a roundabout and much longer one. First, you went from Çat to Bozkır, then you had to go through the Bozkır marketplace, cross over the bridge, and take the road that the Bozkır landowners used on their journeys. This meant it would take at least two hours for Kirez and the owners of the neighboring fields to get there from the village. At present, the walk from the village to the fields took half an hour, so going the other way would mean they would have to walk one and a half hours longer. Closing the path seemed an unreasonable and uncaring way to behave.

The next morning, Kirez and her neighbors used the usual road to their gardens, their donkeys loaded with manure. They walked across the bridge over the Ulu River near the mill at Mantaki. They saw the plowed furrows along the path which went through Kamil's field. Kirez exclaimed, "Come, neighbors, let's trample on these furrows and stamp the earth down until it's like it was before."

They all began to flatten the earth, which had been plowed up three days before. Kirez and some of those who had come with her directed the donkeys to do as they did and tread down the furrows. Some of them stood at the side of the path, murmuring, "Let's not tangle with this stingy rich man."

A little while later, Kamil came with other members of his family. They shouted and started to walk toward the group of women. They wanted to stop them from walking up and down along the plowed-up path. Kirez was still tramping the earth to make the path plain to see. A huge argument followed. Those who were acquainted with Kirez knew that she could speak at the rate of a hundred words a minute, and had a talent for quick thinking and clear speaking.

Kamil was a man who stuck to what he said. He began to threaten Kirez, saying, "Crazy Kirez, you are chewing up my plowed field. I'm going to report you to the authorities. You'll rot in prison until you come to your senses."

Kirez replied, "Oh, Kamil, you, dwarfish trickster, how can you close the path we've used for forty years? Are you going to become so much richer by producing three kilos more beans from the path you took into your field? I've heard you take pride in being the son of a teacher. You shameful upstart. By paying cash for a field, did you set your eyes on getting the public footpath as well? After making everyone your enemy, aren't you ashamed to show your face at the mosque? Go to court, go to the government, go to hell, or wherever else you want to go, but you're not going to become the owner of the path I've come and gone along for forty years. You hunchback washboard of a man, did you never hear of such a thing as neighborliness? Are you such a trickster, you miserable dwarf? Are you a highway robber to block our path like this?

In less than a month later, Kirez received a summons from the court: "On this day at this time, you are ordered to come to the court at Bozkır with a witness to defend yourself in answer to the case brought by Kamil, owner of a field, who says you insulted him and deliberately trampled on and destroyed the crop of that field he had plowed."

Kirez persuaded a few of her neighbors who used the same path to come to the court with her. She thought she might need them as witnesses. She heard that Kamil had engaged a lawyer. Kirez said, "I will explain everything I know to the judge. I don't have the money for a lawyer."

Kirez's husband, the war veteran Abdullah, was old and feeble and no longer able to leave the house. Her grown-up son, Şükrü, was living in another place. Her other son, Mehmet, and her two sons-in-law were working away from home in some distant part of the country. She had three daughters and her first son-in-law, Rahim, with their numerous children living in the village. Rahim made up his mind to support his mother-in-law and take her to the court and bring her back. On the appointed day, she climbed onto his mule and he took her to Bozkır.

33
False Witness

At the court, the judge gave Kamil, the plaintiff, the chance to speak first.

Kamil stated his case and then turned the matter over to his lawyer to speak for him. The lawyer declared that Kamil's field had been unlawfully trampled on, that the leader in this action was Kirez, and, after summarizing what had happened, called a witness and introduced him to the court. Kamil's witness was a villager from Pabuççu. The lawyer asked him, "How is it that you as a witness know whether or not there is a path from the village to Mantaki which crosses a field there? Explain to us so that the judge and everyone here will know."

The witness stated that at one time, he had worked as a patrolman for many years around Mantaki, in charge of distribution of the water from the small canal there. He knew all the paths the landowners took very well. He declared that there was no path going through Kamil's field. He repeated very clearly, "I used to use all existing paths when I was working as the patrol of the water channel there. There was no path going through Kamil's field, judge."

The judge then called the defendant, Kirez, to state her case. Kirez asked, "Judge, may I ask this witness a question, sir?"

The judge smiled and said, "Ask away. You may ask him any question you like."

Kirez said, "Tell us, witness! The water channel that you were looking after, where does its water come from?"

The witness said, "From the Big River, that is, the Ulu River."

Turning to the judge, Kirez said: "Judge, sir, winter or summer, there is a lot of water in the Ulu River. The water channels coming from the Ulu River are always full. No one keeps a man to regulate the water where there is no shortage. There are fields and gardens above the level of the water channels coming from the Ulu River. The channels from the river don't go up to them. These gardens and fields are watered from above, from a small stream coming from Kozağaç village. This stream dries up in the middle of the summer. Because of the water shortage, the owners of the gardens and fields, which are irrigated by that particular canal, quarrel a lot, saying, 'You used so much water, there's none left for me.' In order to prevent these arguments, those owners hire a man to regulate the water evenly so everyone gets his fair share. Everyone around here knows that a water regulator is never hired for the Ulu River channels. It's quite clear, judge, sir, that this witness is a liar. I don't know him at all. I bought my field there forty-one years ago. There was a path then. I and my neighbors who own land there have used that path for forty-one years. And what's the sense in a man from Pabuççu village being a water patrol there? Pabuççu's a long way from there. Field owners hire water patrols, it's true, but they hire one who knows the owners of the fields. Sir, this witness is a liar, my neighbors and I have never seen him before, we don't recognize him."

After the judge had listened intently to this village woman who looked old but spoke such good sense in an energetic manner, he announced, "I reject this case."

Kirez looked at him and asked, "Sir, what does 'reject' mean?"

Without waiting for the judge's answer, the crowd listening all cried, "Woman, you've won!"

On hearing this, Kirez said, "You see, don't you, dwarfish Kamil, lying, penny-pinching Kamil, I beat you in the court."

She began to dance in the middle of the court, singing and shaking her shoulders, and clicking her fingers rhythmically. This was at a time when no one in Bozkır and the villages around had seen a woman dance in the middle of a crowd of men. Those who had never seen such a thing in their lives, let alone in a court of law, said, "I guess this woman's gone mad."

In answer Kirez started to sing and dance:

*"I'm not mad,
And I haven't gone crazy.
I've won a path,
And I'm dancing from joy."*

Then Rahim, feeling embarrassed at seeing his mother-in-law dancing in front of everyone, took her arm and said, "Come, let's go, Auntie, you've won the case but it isn't proper to behave like this in front of the judge. Come, we're going," and led her from the court.

> Deli de değilim,
> Delirmedim de.
> Yol kazandım,
> Mal kazandım,
> Onun için
> Ben oynarım,
> Sevincimden Oynarım.

Kirez lived for the rest of her life fighting against injustice and behaving in a brave and honorable way. Shortly after Abdullah's death, she withdrew from public life. While still alive, she divided up her properties among her children in the village. Her daughters, especially those who lived in the village, made it their business to look after her and help her when she needed it.

Toward the end of her life, she danced for joy once more in front of many women, men, and children up at the yayla. Her first grandson, after living away from the village for ten years, had come back to the village.

> Esen, my Esen, came
> from the heights of the sky.
> I've been given the chance
> to see you once more.

If I die now,
I won't feel regret.
My heart is filled with love.

She sang and danced, clicking her fingers in time with the tune.
　I am neither crazy, nor mad. I earned my path in court. I dance because I am happy.

PART TWO

Love and Struggle

Collarless Shirt and a Pair of Breeches

The first festival I remember was in the summer. It must have been the Festival of Sacrifice. I remember my father sacrificing a lamb on the roof of our house, and someone using a finger to smear a red mark right in the middle of my forehead with the fresh blood. It might have been either my mother or my father, or perhaps my elder brother, Hilmi.

The festival customs could have been invented for the village children. The waiting began months before the time. There was plenty of food, and a great variety of it. For once, at least, even the orphans could fill their bellies with meat. It was the children who first rejoiced when their relatives came to visit. It was to the children that the festival candy was given first. Happy laughter was heard, even if only once or twice a year.

What the children longed for most were the new clothes bought or made for them. For the rest of the year, it was the custom to wear old, patched clothes. But it was very sweet to live in expectation of new clothes to wear for the festival.

Two or three weeks before the festival was the time to shop for the children's presents at the Friday market. One or two meters of floral or striped cotton cloth and plain scarlet or sky-blue material would be bought. At that time, there were no ready-made clothes to be had at the market, or even in the shops. There were haberdashers in town who stocked every kind of material. The material to be bought and made into headscarves was specially woven in the form of squares. For young girls in particular, there were striped silk sashes to be had.

When the material had been bought, the mother or the grandmother measured by hand and eye the amount needed for each part of the garment, and then cut the cloth accordingly. The pieces were then tacked and laboriously sewn together to make the finished garment. Those who had two or three coins to rub together would have a tailor make their clothes for the celebrations. These would consist of breeches, a collarless shirt for the young men, and chemise and şalvar (pantaloons) for the young girls of marriageable age. The clothes made by the tailors on their pedal sewing machines would look neater and more elegant. They would be eyed with envy by those whose festival clothes had been made at home.

There were no tailors' shops in our village, but they could be found in the nearby township of Bozkır, as well as in the neighboring village of Dere. As it was nearby and the prices were cheaper than those in the town, our villagers used to take their material to Dere. The breeches worn by the young men were made to a pattern by the tailor. The thick handwoven cloth, or whipcord, was sewn with a double stitch, which could only be done on a sewing machine.

My father carried on his trade in the outlying villages on a system of barter. He would exchange his goods for cheese, butter, or wool at the Yörük (nomadic, animal-herding peoples) encampments or at those on the Çalmanda summer pastures. He would sell the foodstuffs at the Friday market, and store the wool for six months or a year.

In our village, the elderly womenfolk made a living by spinning wool on a handheld spindle, then winding it into balls before weaving it into cloth on their hand looms. Our elderly neighbors, Emiş, Dürdane, and Bekeleli, who all lived alone, earned their bread in this way. That handmade woolen cloth measured two to three handspan in width and about three meters in length. A piece of cloth like this was known as a roll.

This material provided jackets, breeches for the men, and pantaloons for the women that offered protection from the cold and frost in winter months. It was necessary to treat handwoven material before it was sewn. This treatment consisted of felting it by twisting and beating it. After beating, the roll would shrink. In order to bring it back to its original length, the cloth would be soaked, then weighted and hung up to dry slowly. Although the young villagers joined together to stamp on the cloth with bare feet, the best way to beat the cloth was known as the "Dere Village Drubbing." A man called Sipsip invented a device that utilized the force of the stream running alongside his house. Mr. Sipsip would earn money from the surrounding villages by treating their rolls of cloth in this way: several rolls of cloth were put in the container, which turned like an energetic wheel with the force of the running water. The cloth would be beaten in this way until it reached the required density.

A pair of breeches

A well-beaten roll of cloth would be thick, but smooth as silk. If an expert tailor made a pair of breeches from this cloth, they would stand up straight by themselves. Worn with a belt and double stitched at the pockets and cuff, the breeches narrowed from the knees down toward the ankles, and looked strong and immensely elegant. After the tailor had stitched the breeches, he would iron them for the first and last time.

The iron, made out of a hollow piece of iron, was heated by embers placed inside the cavity. The breeches looked like two fat ears stretching from waist to knee before they were ironed; after being pressed to a good fit and with their double stitching, they made a fine sight.

The girls, seemingly unaware of the young men in their breeches, would observe them with secret excitement. The exchange of baggy trousers for breeches made the young men very happy. They wore their new breeches when they went to the store or to the market or to the coffeehouse, as well as to any wedding or entertainment. They didn't wear them when engaged in hoeing the vines, working in the fields, bringing firewood home from the mountains, or any such labor. When doing any kind of physical work, they would wear either baggy trousers or breeches that had lost their shape.

Middle-aged men would once more take to their baggy trousers. In fact, baggy pants made it easier to sit with their legs crossed when eating at the low tables, when mounting and dismounting from their animals, or when crouching on their heels at prayer.

My father had the wool he had stored up during the year treated and woven. Two weeks before the festival, he took out a roll of felt. "This will make a pair of breeches for Hilmi with maybe some left over," he said.

My brother Hilmi, who was eight years older than me, was excited by the thought of becoming a young man. Like his friends, he longed to have a pair of breeches.

Childishly, I murmured, "I want a pair of breeches too."

I don't know whether my father heard me or my mother brought the subject up that night. The next morning, my father gave the roll to Hilmi to have it stitched: "Hilmi, my son, go to the village Dere and give my greetings to Ahmet, the tailor. Let him make you a good pair of breeches. Ask him to make another good pair of breeches to fit a child like your brother Hasan, with the cloth that's left. Here is the money for the payment," he said, holding out his hand.

Hilmi grabbed the money and the cloth and ran off down the road to Dere.

That day, the whole of that day, I was overjoyed. It was a fact that I would be the only one of the friends I played with who would be wearing a pair of breeches. On foot, Dere village was half an hour away. All day, I waited for my brother to come home. Until I fell asleep,

I wondered what my breeches would look like. My brother still hadn't come.

It was late when Hilmi came home after waiting for his breeches to be made. Ahmet the tailor was very busy with the festival so near. When I woke up, I immediately asked, "Where are my breeches?"

After making Hilmi's trousers and measuring with his eye a boy about my size whom Hilmi pointed out to him, the tailor had looked at what was left of the cloth and declared, "There isn't enough cloth here for a pair of child's breeches."

I couldn't believe my ears. The festival would come and I wouldn't be wearing a new pair of breeches. I wept silently to myself all day long. My mother comforted me, saying, "Look, my son, I'll talk to your father and get him to buy a new piece of cloth. There's enough time before the festival to make a collarless shirt for you."

A week before the festival, my father bought the materials my mother had asked for. There was enough cloth with blue stripes for a shirt for me, cotton cloth with red flowers for my sister Ayşe, and enough dark blue cotton cloth for a pair of baggy pants for my mother. My mother approved of them all. "I'll do my best to sew these by hand ready for the festival, but it would be a good thing to have at least Hasan's cotton shirt made by the tailor. As it is, he can't have the breeches he wanted. A machine-stitched shirt would look much smarter. And what's more, his friends Vehbi, Muzaffer, and Bahri are all getting their shirts tailor-made. The only sewing machine in this village is your sister's. There's enough time till the festival. Take Hasan with you, give her the material, and let her measure him. I've seen her using the machine. It won't take her half an hour to cut and sew a child's collarless shirt. She will surely find time to sew a shirt for her nephew. Haven't you helped her all year long getting hay and firewood, when going up to the summer pastures and at the market? Whenever she called, 'Rahim, load up the hay from Çötü and bring it here,' 'Rahim, chop me two loads of wood,' 'Rahim, take me up to the summer pastures,' 'Rahim, I've a basin of grape molasses, take it and sell it at the weekly market,' or 'Rahim, come and tread my grapes,' you ran to help her."

"Enough, Karakaşli. That's a good idea," said my father. "A machine-stitched shirt would look good on Hasan." He took my hand and we went to my aunt, whose nickname was "my lady."

A little put out, my aunt said, "Well, Rahim, I'll give it a try," as she measured the cloth against my back. Then she said, "Hmm, this cloth will make a shirt for the child, but did you bring any buttons?"

Father exclaimed, "Oh, I forgot the buttons, but let's make do with the ones you have and Hasan will be happy. I'll get you buttons at next week's market and he'll bring them to you."

"Very well," said my aunt. "That's what we'll do. Come the day before the festival and I'll give you the shirt."

As I followed my father home, I skipped and jumped for joy.

My mother made a dress for my sister, Ayşe, the next child after me. The material was a very colorful cotton print with tiny flowers. So it would look as though it were machine-made, she put two rows of shirring on the front. Ayşe liked it a lot. There were four broken wooden spoons in the house. She took them, fixed them in her hands, and, imitating the rhythm of the girls' spoon dance, hopped around, playing and trying to sing the traditional song:

The stream flows
bearing the sand;
take me away,
down the creek.
Rabbits by the stream

know evening's here;
come over the stream.
Take me away
where life is sweet.

My mother sewed herself a pair of blue-flowered cotton pantaloons. My baby brother Mehmet was small enough for her to make him a shirt from the leftover cloth. I waited impatiently, counting the days till my new collarless shirt for the festival would come. In our village, it was custom for the younger children to put on their festival clothes on the eve of the festival. All adults, young and old, waited until the day of the festival.

For us children, the eve of the festival was known as the day full of good smells. That day, dough was kneaded and festival bread was made. Eight or ten rounds of pastry, rolled out thicker than usual, were put on the griddle and baked till crisp. This bread, eaten hot and known as Fat Bread, was spread with salted butter or with sesame or sunflower seed oil, and broken into small pieces. The mother of the house would take a plate piled with this hot, buttery bread accompanied by some raisins and dried chickpeas and call out, "Come, children, there's *smells* and snacks for you." On hearing the word smells, the children would rush to take the food and eat it with gusto, licking their fingers. The wonderful smell of the hot, oily bread would fill the whole of the village; the day before the festival was the one we children would long for.

At last, the day I had been waiting for dawned. As soon as I woke up, I said, "Mum, tomorrow is Good Smells Day! Come, let's go. Let's go to my aunt. Maybe she's finished my shirt."

"Hold on, son. I've a lot to do now. We'll go this evening," she said.

All day long I went around grumbling, "Mum, it's almost evening. How about getting my shirt?"

She replied "Wait a bit, son, don't burst yourself. I'll just go rinse the baby's diapers and wash them in the stream and then we'll be off at once."

While I kept the baby amused, my mother quickly washed the clothes and came back. After she had spread them to dry on the poles jutting out from the roof of the haybarn, she put my baby brother Mehmet into a cloth slung over her back. Upon leaving the house, she said, "Son, I've something to say to the old woman, Menevşe, so let's take the lower road."

As we passed the house of Hönker of the Rogues, I trod with my bare feet on some chicken droppings.

"Look where you're going and don't step on that again," she scolded gently.

The stream turning the mill wheel flowed directly below the lower road. The stream ran slowly and smoothly at the place called the Wash Place, where the women were wringing their clothes. "Power to your elbow, easy does it," my mother called out to them. Some of the women were using a stone to pound the clothes on a flat boulder, and others were rinsing or washing clothes, or boiling water in a cauldron or a basin. At that time, there were bloodsucking insects such as bedbugs and fleas in the villages. Their eggs were hard to spot in the clothes and boiling water was used to flush them out.

Menevşe was the mother of Stinking Mustafa. The elderly woman lived with her son, her daughter-in-law, and her grandchildren. She was well known in the village for helping young women heavy with child give birth. Everyone called her Midwife Menevşe. The women she helped would pay her by giving her food and clothing for the household.

This was the woman my mother visited. I didn't go inside. Instead, I dove into a game with her grandson, Ahmet, the same age as me. We began talking about our festival clothes. "I'm going to wear a collarless shirt my aunt's sewing by machine for Festival Eve tomorrow," I boasted, while he replied, "My granny made a new pair of pantaloons for me to wear."

My mother left the house, pressing a small bundle into Midwife Menevşe's hand as a little gift. "Did you know Esen? She was your midwife? It was she who helped me give birth to you," she told me. Without exactly understanding what she meant, I listened in silence and then ran in front of my mother toward my aunt's house.

I reached the house first and tried to push the door open, but it didn't budge. "Ma, the door's locked," I shouted. "My aunt must be out."

"They always keep their doors fastened," said my mother, rapping her knuckles on the door several times.

In those days, the wooden latch behind the door was only used to bolt the door at night upon going to bed. In the daytime, neighbors or relatives would visit without warning, just opening the door and going in. They would call out greetings such as "Hey there, how are things with you?" "God bless you," "The top of the morning to you," "How are you getting along with your mother-in-law?" and "May God be with you," and spend a little time there.

We didn't wait long before my aunt opened the door. Without asking us to come in, she said, "Karakaşlı, it's a good thing you've come. I was going to send you a message. I didn't have time to sew Hasan's shirt. Here, take back your material." She thrust the material, folded just as we had brought it, into my mother's hands.

My mother was shocked. After taking the material held out to her, she took a firm hold of my hand. Taking two steps backward, she said, "So that's it, sister? There isn't another sewing machine in the village.

You sew shirts, dresses, and baggy pants for others who pay you. That means you weren't about to sew a shirt for your own nephew. All year long, his father did all kinds of work for you for free. Shame on you! I hope I'll never need your help again."

Without making any reply to my aunt's feebly stuttered excuses, she wrenched a hold of my arm and took the road home. I sniffed the whole way to our house, wailing, "I won't have a new collarless shirt for the festival."

"Don't cry, son, don't cry. I'll sew you a new shirt myself."

When we got home, my mother held the cloth against my back and measured it, my neck, and arms, using hand and eye. She cut a few buttons from my old shirts and laid them aside in a bit of the material.

When will she get time to sew it? I wondered doubtingly.

We ate our evening meal of cracked wheat cooked with zucchini, spooning it up with pieces of flatbread. Not much later, my sister and I fell fast asleep. After my father had gone to bed, my mother began

İşlik, a collarless shirt

to sew a collarless shirt for me by candlelight, finishing it just before dawn. When I woke up, she said, "Son, I've finished your shirt. Wear it in good health."

Oh! What joy, what joy! The whole world was mine. There were no limits to the happiness of that village child, even if he didn't know how to express his thanks in words such as "Thank you so much, Mum, may you have a happy life," or say, "Health to your hands!"

My mother and father were the first to say, "Hasan, your collarless shirt looks so good on you, wear it in good health," followed by all the women of the village, who gave us snacks and smells, and all the relatives we went to visit for the festival the next day.

Over the years, most of the clothes worn by her husband and the ten children she raised were handmade by my mother. She saved up to have a tailor make clothes for her sons when they came of adolescence or were married. However, for the rest of her life, she never asked a favor of her sister-in-law.

When I finished university and started earning my own money, I bought a sewing machine for my mother in Konya and took it to the village. I'll never forget the sight of my mother's face when the machine was set in place and she began to use it. It was the same joy seen on the face of a child on the morning of a Festival Eve.

Moon Babies

Baby Mehmet went on wailing without stopping. Karakaşli tried to soothe him by giving him the breast from time to time, or giving him some of the bread she had softened by chewing to pulp, but she couldn't persuade her child to give up crying. It was just about lunchtime, but with having to stop every minute or so, she hadn't been able to finish weaving even one handspan of cloth. Half-angry, half-tearful, she muttered to herself, "That good-for-nothing man set up this hand loom, saying, 'Weave your cloth here.'"

Her daughter, Ayşe, was four years old, while her son, her right-hand man, was not yet eight. "Hasan, my son, rock the cradle, will you? The baby might go to sleep. Let me weave a bobbin at least before dark," she said, sitting down at the loom.

As he rocked the cradle, Hasan watched his mother working at the loom. It was amazing to see how she coordinated the movements of her hands and feet. While her feet moved the treadle to raise the warp threads in a pattern two up, one down, her right hand controlled the shuttle containing the weft thread moving backward and forward between them, while her left hand used a reed attached to a pulley to tighten the weave.

Little Ayşe's stomach must have been empty, as she had opened the bread bag lying by the hearth and was munching away on scraps of flatbread. In the cradle, Mehmet continued wailing. The young mother began to think there must be a reason for him to have gone on wailing like that for days. Her sister-in-law, Nergis, had warned her only the day before, saying, "Karakaşli, my girl, this child has the moon baby illness.

You must find a remedy. Otherwise, he'll go on wailing day after day and waste away from lack of milk."

Karakaşli's mind was occupied with wondering who could have cursed her baby for him to be so ill. "If only I knew which bad-mouthing woman, what mischief-maker has done this! If only I could find out what to do." One of the babies born within forty days of Mehmet's birth, one of his moon siblings, must have placed a curse on him. The question was, which one?

It was a big village. She began to consider. Apart from the big neighborhood of Çat where she lived, on the other side of the river there were the neighborhoods of Ahmetli, Ömerli, and Cingiller, while on the other side of the mountain was the district of Karagaç, where she had been born and raised. Thinking over the people of the neighborhood in turn, the first name that came to mind was Gök Fadime. She was certainly a mischievous woman, but her child was a girl. "Girls born within the same forty days as the boys don't make them ill, or only rarely," she had heard. In Ahmetli, there was a baby boy named Ali, but his father was a close relative, it couldn't be him. Karagaç was too far away for anyone from there to come and walk around her house to lay the curse. If there were such an ill-wisher, that person must have walked in a circle around the village, carrying either the sick child or one of the child's belongings. She didn't think that was likely either. She knew how difficult it would be to walk around Çat village, surrounded on three sides by mountains and bounded by three separate free-flowing rivers. In any case, such a person, if there was one, would have been seen and everyone would have heard about it by now. However, she still thought, You can't trust there not to be someone mad here. Karakaşli didn't believe that the solution was to walk in a circle around the village herself. Even if her husband had been there, it wouldn't have been a sensible thing to walk around the whole village in the spring.

The source of the Ulu River was in the mountains near the villages of Karacahisar and Sorkun. From there, it flowed down the valleys in a series of waterfalls. In the spring, it flowed along vigorously. "The Ulu River can catch birds on the wing," it was said, as the river bustled along, overflowing with joy. Once out of the village, it was impossible to cross the river where there was no bridge. Even a grown man would easily be swept away by the current. It was difficult to cross even its tributaries, the Yayla or the Şeykem rivers. Maybe on a summer's day when there was less water and a slower current, you could roll up your trousers and wade across. Let's say you did manage with great difficulty to cross the river four times. It would be a strenuous task to trek with a child on your shoulders over the rocky slopes of Ada Hill, along the precipitous sides of Quail Fall, over the hills covered with prickly plants and myrtle bushes behind Ahmetli, and across the steep scrubland of Karagaç. Even with a strong man beside you to share the difficult climb, it would take a whole day.

The young mother talked to her crying baby, saying, "Oh, Mehmet, do go to sleep and let me weave at least another hand's breadth," as she threw the shuttle as fast as she could. Nothing could put the child to sleep, not even the rhythmic sound of her feet keeping time with the movements of the reed compressing the weave, and of the pulley that controlled the direction of the shuttle, as well as the noise of the shuttle itself as it flew backward and forward. What if I tried the root of a tree? she thought.

The barberry tree, which is considered sacred, grows in the driest places, and even sends down roots into the rocks. Its tiny fruits are smaller than those of the garden barberry. The fruit—if you could call it fruit—only ripens as fall turns to winter. The skin and flesh are sweet and delicate, while inside there is a kernel as hard as stone. After the trees have shed their leaves, the fruit turns bright red, a magnet in winter for both birds and the children who long for fruit. Forcing its roots deep into the earth, this tree grows freely on steep slopes where nothing can be planted. Everyone considered this tree to be sacred, and it was not the custom to chop it down for planks or firewood; in fact, to do so was even frowned on. People left it alone for fear that a disaster might somehow fall on them.

When a barberry tree grows in places where torrential rainfall has made convenient runnels, single or several roots often remain above ground in the form of one or more arches. According to a centuries-old belief, if a sick person passes under such an arching root once, or the person's clothes are passed under it several times, it helps the person to recover.

Karakaşli's mind was constantly occupied with thinking about her baby's illness, until she hit on a solution that meant she wouldn't have to walk a circle around the village or confront anyone. On a slope near the Low Bridge over the Yayla River on the way to the yayla, she had clearly seen that kind of barberry root several times. She decided one of the baby's garments should be passed under that tree root. Telling her son what must be done, she said, "Hasan, dear, take this shirt of your brother's and go and come back like lightning," then added, "But watch out when you cross the bridge and don't go near the edge of the river."

Hasan didn't say, "I won't go," or "I'm afraid," or "I don't know where that root is." As always, he simply replied with a nod of his head. "Uh-huh." Then he stuffed his brother's shirt inside his own and left. Although it seemed as though Hasan wasn't afraid of anything, he was afraid of dogs.

At the end of the village, on the way to the yayla, there were several houses with dogs. He went slowly and cautiously past these until he was clear of the village. When he came to Uluyol, the place where shepherds collected their flocks together, he started running. After sprinting up Quail Fall slope past Tall Vertical Rock, he ran through the vineyards of Hunchback Kamil and the ravine where Kerim the Wrestler's vineyard was until he reached Low Bridge. Keeping to the center as he crossed over the narrow bridge made of thin planks with no guardrail, Hasan found the barberry tree his mother had described. At the foot of it, a twisted root arched upward before planting itself in the earth again. He passed his brother's shirt under the arch of this root seven times before putting it inside his own shirt again. Then, half-walking half-running, he returned home.

"Hasan, my blessed son, did you blow in from the sky?" his mother praised. She put the garment that had been passed under the sacred tree root back on the baby, murmuring a prayer that God would have mercy on him. But no change was seen in the sick child.

"Joy comes in the morning," she said, and filled the children's stomachs with the cracked wheat pilaf, turnips she had cooked on the stove over a fire of twigs, and the flatbread she had soaked in water. After being suckled, the baby fell asleep in the cradle.

As dawn was breaking, his mother gently woke Hasan. Telling her son to take the only cow in the stable to join the herd, she placed the remains of last night's pilaf in front of Ayşe, who was getting under her feet, grumbling she was hungry. Then she sat down at her loom and started weaving.

That morning, Baby Mehmet seemed no better. "Some evil-minded person must have walked around the house with a baby the same age as mine. I wonder who it could be," she muttered, and began to rack her brain once more.

Before a weaver starts to weave, the right amount of thread needed for the warp and the number of hanks of thread for the weft has to be calculated. In this way, there will be no thread, or very little, left over when the weaving is finished. Karakaşli Fatma, twenty-five-years old and the mother of three children, a woman who did not know how to read or write but could keep these measurements in her head like a rhyming jingle, was expecting an unseen, untouchable force to make her child better. She trusted in the centuries-old beliefs that there was power in a charm made from the root of a sacred wild barberry tree, that to come across a person with sky-blue eyes or a cock crowing out of time was an evil omen, that the cry of a magpie perched on the roof brought news from far off, or even that the wuthering sound of wind blowing among the rocks on the high mountains at night was a force for creation or destruction.

Karakaşli, hoping for the best, thought of all that could be done. She had heard and believed that Hızır, the legendary helper of people in trouble, would come when an unseen force silently crept up on them, bringing accidents or illness to test them. She began calling in a loud voice, "Hızır, Hızır, come and help me." The young mother's head was full of dark thoughts. Who had done this to Little Mehmet? It was surely one of the same-age children. In that case, it was no use hunting through every nook and cranny, or tying a rag to a sacred tree and making a wish for the spell to be broken. That wasn't the cure for this kind of ill-wishing. It must certainly be a child who was trying to cause harm and take away her son's spirit. She must find that child and think of a remedy.

Feeling quite alone in the world, the young mother was overwhelmed with despair; if only her husband had been at home, he might have been able to think of another remedy, even though he was a man. But he wasn't there. He'd been away from home for five or six months. Together with his fifteen-year-old son from his first wife, he had gone to work in the province of Aydın. He had sent home neither word nor money. Who knew which landlord's garden or vineyard they were hoeing, or what a miserable life they might be leading. Karakaşli felt sorry for them. If only my husband came home safe and sound, isn't there any nearby job, good or bad, he could earn an income from? she wondered.

Karakaşli didn't want to behave as though this goodwife or that were guilty, just like that. Thinking things over again, her mind was still fixed on Gök Fadime. Even though Fadime's own house was quite a long way off, her mother, Shorty Havva, and her brother, Murtaza, lived just two doors away from her house. If Fadime had come to visit her mother by the upper road and returned by the lower one, no one would have realized that, without having to find an excuse, she had made a circle round Karakaşli's house.

Karakaşli knew that it would cause a quarrel if she got up and went to Fadime's house and said politely, "See here, my friend, it's like this: my child's sick. Your daughter is one of the children born at the same moon-time as mine. How would it be if we found a cure together?" Fadime was touchy, just like her brother, who beat his wife every day. Karakaşli couldn't say, "Well, I don't care, even if it comes to a quarrel." She was afraid this would break up the friendship between her husband, Rahim, and Fadime's husband, Mahmut, the master blacksmith. Nor did she dare put the baby on her back wrapped in a shawl and walk secretly around Fadime's house. Someone would surely see her, stop to talk, and tell on her to Fadime.

Karakaşli decided to set aside the idea of walking around the house or the village and try something else that wouldn't make anyone suspicious. Her son, Hasan, was small and skinny, but he understood things and tried to do what she told him as well as possible. While his mother was busy, he would look after his two small siblings or go and fill two small pitchers with cold water from the spring; even when his father was at home, he would take the donkey from the stable to water it at the stream. Karakaşli had faith in her son. If Hasan went to play with the street children in Fadime's neighborhood, who would think anything of it? What's more, Mahmut the blacksmith's house and his forge were very close to the house of her stepson Hilmi's grandmother, Granny Saliha. From time to time, Hasan would go with his brother Hilmi to visit Saliha and take her a small gift. Karakaşli told her young son what he must do, and gave him many warnings.

This is how Hasan told this part of the story:

My mum took off my brother Mehmet's undershirt and put it inside mine, next to my chest. She tightened the baggy pants I was wearing. She told me, "Go straight toward the Upper Fountain. Go past Auntie Anakiz's house. Hang around there a bit. If you find a friend, play with him a little. Then go to Granny Saliha's house. If she's home, ask her, 'How're you doing, Granny?' and visit with her a while and then leave. Look around carefully. Don't let Mahmut's wife see you. Walk slowly down alongside the house. When you get close to it, take a bit of earth from the wall with your hand. Hold it tightly and come back here as quick as you can."

I left our house and walked straight in the direction of Ada Hill, past Musa's house and coffee shop. I walked past Auntie's house and hung around for a bit by one of the forges. I love watching the red-hot iron being beaten and then made into knives. When I see how the goat's horn is heated over the embers and then flattened between two iron plates clamped together, I'm amazed. That day, I watched Lame Abdullah the master ironsmith making knives in his workshop. I played a bit with his son, Ali, who was the same age as me. Then I said, "I'm off to see Granny Saliha," and walked up the slope behind the fountainhead. There were several women waiting in line for water. I didn't pay them any attention, but looked ahead and went on walking. I passed below the thief Ahmet's house and got to Granny Saliha's house. She wasn't home, so I went straight on.

I got to the corner of Mahmut the blacksmith's house and was just pulling a bit of earth from the wall with my left hand when a lightning blow struck me on my head. "Mother! Mother!" I screamed, and began running home with tears running down my face.

That woman, Fadime, shouted after me, "You'll not live long, not after stealing earth from my wall and running away."

Her husband, Mahmut, hearing the commotion, rushed out of the forge, cursing wildly. "I don't know what you're making such a fuss about, woman. What would he be doing with earth from the wall?"

In spite of the hard blow I had received, when I reached home, running at full speed from pain and fear, I was still holding the earth tight in my hand. I opened the door, rushed inside, and slammed it shut. Straight away, my mum took the earth from my hand and sprinkled it over my brother Mehmet lying there in his cradle, then quickly put the shirt I had carried close to my chest back on him.

Before five minutes had passed, a stone came flying at our door and we thought it would break. Fadime had planted herself on a neighbor's roof across the street and was shouting over and over again at the top of her voice, "Karakaşli, you whore, come outside! I don't know what I won't spit in your mouth."

In spite of being small, my mother sprang forward like a tiger to open the door and began screaming at the top of her voice: "You're the whore, you bitch! I'm not about to be afraid of you. You're the one who walked around my house and made my baby ill. Are you strong enough to deny it? Those who aren't hurt, don't cry!"

The two mothers screamed at each other, hurling insults by the score. Each of them dragged up the other's past misdeeds, one by one. The screams and retorts of the two sounded like the tumult between the Ulu and the Yayla Rivers when they crashed into each other in the spring, frothing with melting snow and rain. It's difficult to decide which river is the highest in the foaming water.

The neighboring women, hearing the commotion, began to collect outside, asking, "What's the matter? What happened?" They tried to stop the war of words, all speaking at the same time, trying to become the referee. That was the first time I saw that, when two or more women gather together, it is possible for a woman to hear her own voice the voice of the one speaking to her, as well as the comments of those around, all at the same time.

Just at that very moment, Hızır, his messenger of goodwill, arrived. Eyüp's wife, Ayşe Nine, one of the old women of the neighborhood, whose spit was known to help cure a certain itching of the skin, raised her voice, shouting, "Stop it, you women, stop!" Then she said, "As tradition and custom tell us, go and get bread and exchange it with each other. Bring water and exchange that. Let each of your children eat and drink from what was exchanged, so peace may be made between them. Never again will your daughter, Fadime, or your son, Fatma, fall ill of this sickness. Come, find a roof that doesn't take sides, do as I say, and put an end to this bad day with its unseemly quarrel." The neighboring women approved of this solution, a custom they all knew about.

The two mothers, exhausted by their screaming and shouting, were in any case willing to go to the roof of the nearby house of Niyazi, the grape jam seller, and exchange bread and water. Each of them went home and brought a piece of flatbread; one of them brought water in a pitcher, the other in a jug. Each of the mothers chewed the bread came from the other to soften it, and then fed it to her child, and each gave her child some of the other's water to drink. Meanwhile, both women started to say a few words to each other in a more cordial manner. After that, trusting that neither of their children would harm each other's spirit ever again, they collected their bits and pieces and went home, more or less at peace.

That day, my brother's Mehmet's crying lessened. That night, he slept without crying at all. The next day, his illness was completely gone.

Peacemaking ceremony of Moon Babies

Baby in cradle, weaver-mom, hearth, and exposed root

Mahmut the Blacksmith's house and shop

The Popgun

"Hasan, Hasan! Open the door!" Hasan heard someone say. The voice of his mother came accompanied by tears and groans. It was the voice his mother used when she was upset.

Frightened, he rushed to open the door onto the street. His mother was sitting there with her back to the door and her legs stretched out in front of her. When she saw her son, she cried pitifully, saying, "What's going to become of me, son?" She took hold of her right knee, rubbing it gently with her hand.

"What happened, Mum, did you fall?"

"I fell, yes, I fell, my dear. I was coming from the fountain. The pitcher on my shoulder was full. As I was coming past the guesthouse, my foot slipped and I fell with a thump on my knees. I'd stepped on some ice. These good-for-nothing shoes made me slip. I broke my pitcher. I couldn't get up or walk. I've crawled here along the ground with great difficulty. How about you, have you managed to light the stove, my son?" she asked.

"Yes, Mum, I've lit it." Grasping his mother's arm, he tried to help her inside over the threshold.

Before going to fetch water, his mother had asked him to light the stove and warned him, saying, "Be careful to keep your sister away from it."

Hasan went out of the door, saying, "I'll go and fill this empty basin and these two jugs and come back quickly before it gets dark." Without hearing his mother call anxiously after him, "Don't run too fast or you'll fall, son," he took the road winding up to the fountain in the upper village.

Mother broke her knee

He and his sister Ayşe, who was three years younger than him, both had empty bellies. The plan had been for his mother to bring clean water from the fountain and make cracked wheat pilaf. As Hasan climbed up toward the fountain, it was as if he could taste the sweetness of the well-cooked pilaf in his mouth. The house was nearer to the mill stream than to the fountain, but food was never cooked with water from the stream. The water in this small stream coming from the bigger river and running through the village to turn the mill wheel was often cloudy, especially in winter. Moreover, it was said that the villagers in Dere had built latrines right at the river's edge. The good water needed by all the people in Çat came to the fountain from a source on Erenler Mountain. It was brought there by water pipes made by the villagers. In front of the constantly running fountain was a long trough suitable for animals to drink from.

Hasan was thinking this over as he came near the fountain when he caught sight of his playmates from the upper neighborhood—Ali, Lame Abdullah's son; Lefty Şükrü's Alibeğ; Reşit, son of Musa from the coffeehouse, and others. They were playing a special winter game known as popgun, shooting pellets at each other from homemade wooden popguns. On seeing Hasan going toward the fountain carrying the empty vessels in his hands, one of them fired his popgun directly at Hasan, saying, "Here, take this!" and the others all began to use him as a target for their pellets.

Although Hasan knew the missile was only made of tiny juniper seeds and wouldn't hurt him, he still flinched. He fled toward the fountain as if to escape, not because he was afraid, but because he didn't have a popgun of his own and couldn't shout in answer, "Hey, what's up, take this. This is how to shoot, you dwarfs." He had tried several times to make such a popgun himself, but no matter many times he plunged the packing needle heated at the stove into the walnut branch, he never ended up making a hole in it.

Upon reaching the fountain, he quickly filled the containers. In order to put distance between himself and the popgun shooters, he took a different path home.

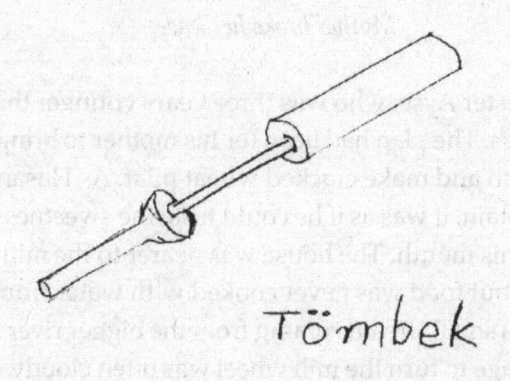

Tömbek

popgun

In wintertime, the sun went down early behind the mountains surrounding the village. The water from melting snow and ice in places where the sun shone would start to ice over as soon as it was left in the shadows. It was just like cream settling on the top of boiling milk. Hasan walked down the hill, taking great care not to step where it was icy. When he came home, the house was in darkness. Ayşe was whining away. His mother lay stretched out on the floor, breastfeeding Mehmet. Taking a match from a niche in the wall, Hasan lit the kerosene lamp. That year, he was six, going on seven years of age, his mother told him. She taught him how to light the lamp and how to kindle a fire in the stove with twigs. He took a shovelful of kindling from the tin stove and threw it onto the fire in the hearth that had burned slowly all day long, to make it blaze. He placed the trivet over it and put the pan his mother always used on top. Then he began to make the dish known as cracked wheat pilaf, or plain pilaf, with cracked wheat, water, and salt, following the instructions his mother gave him from where she lay. He fed the fire under the pot before the heat died down. When the flames burned higher, he drew the logs to the side so the fire didn't roar. If the fire looked like it was going to go out, he added new branches and blew them into flame. The smoke from the embers made his eyes smart and tears run, tickled his throat, and made him cough. Hasan took the pilaf off the fire early, unable to stand Ayşe's wails any longer. The pilaf was cooked, but still soggy. Suddenly, the thought that his father liked it this way came to his mind.

His father, and his eldest son, Hilmi, who was fourteen years old, were not at home. They, along with many other men from the village, had set off that fall to earn money by digging up licorice roots. In order to get the money needed for the journey and the pickaxes he would buy when they got there, his father had taken the pot of butter, mixed with rock salt that mother had collected during the summer, and sold it at the Friday Market. That was why the pilaf was cooked with water only, without adding any fat.

Even if the watery pilaf they ate in the half-light with flatbread dipped in water had no oil in it, it still tasted good. His mother had judged the amount of salt well. Anyway, he had always heard the elder folk say, food can be eaten without oil but not without salt.

His mother was in a bad condition. Her knee not only throbbed, but went on swelling. In order not to alarm Hasan, she didn't complain much. However, she couldn't stand up. That night, she told Hasan to take the pallet, quilt, and pillow from the closet and spread them out on the floor. Ayşe instantly fell asleep. When the baby was also sleeping in his cradle, mother and son blew out the lamp and drew the ragged coverlet over them.

For a long time, his mother uttered long, drawn-out groans of "My knee, oh, my knee" that made Hasan very worried. In the Ömerli district where the potters lived, there was a woman called Lame Eva who had had her leg cut off. She limped along on a wooden peg leg. Hasan had heard that when she was busy using her feet to tread the mud into clay suitable for making pots, she had dislocated her knee. Lack of attention to this had made it swell like a balloon, and later it became gangrenous so that her leg had been cut off at the knee. He snuggled up closer to his sleeping sister. Pulling the coverlet over his head, he filled his mind with worrying thoughts of Lame Eva. How do you cut off a leg? I wonder if my mother's leg will get gangrene and be cut off? He wept silently under the quilt for a long time, but at last, he fell asleep.

When morning came, Hasan started to do what was necessary in the house, following his mother's instructions to the best of his ability. He lit the fire in the hearth and, after chopping wood into a suitable size for filling the stove, made a meal of cracked wheat as well as he could. He hauled water from the fountain or the stream and, when snow fell, shoveled a space in front of the door. But when the flatbread on hand had been eaten up, it wasn't in little Hasan's power to knead the bread in the bread trough, roll it with the rolling pin, and cook it on the griddle.

The swelling on his mother's knee continued for several days. Morning and evening, she baked an onion in the ashes and made a poultice for her knee. Later, she wrapped it up in a paste of flax seeds. Patiently, this young mother continued using the different methods of treatment and the cures practiced in the village area for many years. The swelling on her knee remained much the same, but at least the pain became less.

None of her relatives, rich or poor, came to ask how she was. None of her sisters-in-law, aunts, or brother-in-law knocked on the door to ask, "How is this young wife with three children getting along in this wintry weather? Do they have enough food and drink?"

Hasan's mother, Karakaşli Fatma, had, for the time being, completely given up the weaving she used to do in daylight. When her neighbors didn't hear the sound of her daily weaving, some of them got anxious and came to inquire. "I hope you'll be better soon," they said. One of them, Ümmügüssün, although she wasn't a relative, offered to help as much as she could. Mother decided to borrow bread from her until she was well enough to knead it herself. Every time she got bread from her neighbor, Hasan would weigh the amount of bread they had taken. Everyone's flatbread was different in shape and thickness, so the weight was different too. Karakaşli followed the tradition of not overstepping another's rights and insisted on weighing the bread in order to return the exact amount she had borrowed. In those days, scales were made by boring holes in two pieces of wood and attaching strings and pans for weights known as okka and dirhem: Four hundred dirhem made one okka. The modern unit of a kilogram was equal to three hundred and twelve dirhem. Even though these old scales and weight units were no longer used at the Bozkır Friday market, they were still kept as heirlooms and used by the villagers.

Hasan vaguely remembered that two years earlier, his father, Rahim, and his mother, Karakaşli, had taken shares in a weaving cooperative established in the village. The loom was to be paid for with the calico and striped cloth they would weave.

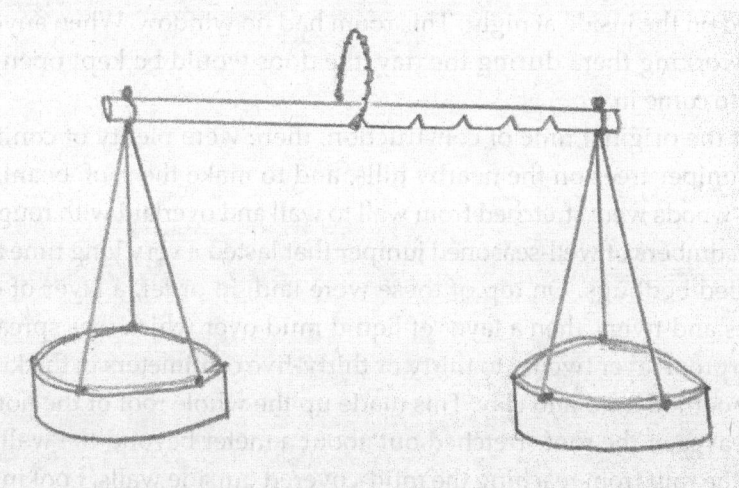

Wood scale

Their home, which had been left to them by Hasan's grandfather, Ali Hoca, consisted of a space about the size of a medium-size room. The adobe for the walls was made with straw mixed with mud. The windows were two small openings, each placed between two of the wooden supports for the outside walls, which were about one meter thick. Barred or wired on the outside, the windows allowed light to enter, and the windowsills provided a place to put all kinds of lamps, lanterns, pine-chip torches, or other paraphernalia. The floor of the room was made of beaten earth. Once a year, clean, liquid red clay was spread over it and beaten with a flat stone until it became shiny. Even if the floor was as hard as concrete when it dried, a sack could be thrown on this earthen floor and sat on. Before a wedding or betrothal feast, the walls would be whitewashed with liquid white clay. Bands of blue clay would be drawn around the windows and the hearth. Flowers made from the same color clay adorned the house. Both young and old enjoyed the pleasingly earthy odor of the fresh plaster.

This room, also called the home, had a smaller room opening off it, which was known as the summer quarters. In there was a hearth, a piece of wood over it to hold the water vessels and one or two sacks, a small alcove big enough to hold jugs and pitchers, and wood and kindling to light the stove in the evening. The outside door of the house opened to the summer quarters. The door could be locked from the outside or barred on the inside at night. This room had no window. When anyone was working there during the day, the door would be kept open for light to come in.

At the original time of construction, there were plenty of conifers and juniper trees on the nearby hills, and to make the roof, beams of these woods were stretched from wall to wall and overlaid with roughly hewn timbers of well-seasoned juniper that lasted a very long time and repelled bedbugs. On top of these were laid, in order, a layer of oak leaves and twigs, then a layer of liquid mud over which was spread a waterproof layer twenty to thirty or thirty-five centimeters in thickness of smoothed mud and clay. This made up the whole roof of the house. The eaves of the roof stretched out about a meter beyond the walls to stop the rain from reaching the mud-covered outside walls. Looking at it from the outside, the roof looked quite level, but in fact, all the roofs sloped very slightly toward the streets. This was to channel the rainwater toward the gutter, where, at a certain point, a pipe discharged it into the street about two meters from the eaves of the house. On the roof was a cylindrical roller made of marble. At each end of it were holes for handles made of wood. This was used to roll the roof when the rain started or after snow had been cleared off it so that water didn't drip into the house. That is, the earth on top of the roof was compressed by means of this cylindrical roller.

The houses of siblings, uncles, and cousins, either on the mother's or the father's side, were arranged side by side. It was custom to keep the roofs at the same level. As the village was built on the slopes of the mountains, the roofs were the only places that were flat. Social occasions, such as wedding and engagement feasts, as well as festival celebrations, all took place on the large roofs stretching out in this way. On any normal day, people stepped out onto their roofs to take an airing or look at the view. This made it easy for the village folk to have a chat or exchange gossip without having to go into each other's houses.

The roofs were used for many other activities in the summer. At haying times, the grass would be spread on the roof to dry and later, the dry grass is threshed into soft straw, with a flail drawn by a pair of oxen. Green beans, tomatoes, and other vegetables and fruits, as well as the year's supply of cracked wheat to be boiled, would all be spread out on the roof to dry after having been washed clean of stones and earth in the stream. The roof also provided a convenient level area for the children's games such as spinning tops or popgun shooting.

Let's continue by looking a little further at the room Hasan called his home. The hearth was on the east wall. This consisted of an alcove in the wall from which a narrow opening like a pipe stretched up inside the wall to a chimney on the roof. This space, which helped the smoke to escape, was called a smokestack or muharı. Before it emerged from the roof, there was a small round hole from which the smoke from the iron stove set up in winter could escape. The fuel for the hearth used to bake bread or cook food, even to boil water, was always wood, usually brushwood.

On the south wall, there was a small wash place, an area hollowed out in the wall and screened by a curtain, which little Ayşe called "Mom and Dad's place for a dump." The water used here would empty through a small hole into the stable below. To the right of this wash place, there was a small, narrow-mouthed jar which had been buried in the wall when the house was first built. Also known as "the hole in the wall," it was high enough to be out of the children's reach and used to keep matches, spices, and medicines, as well as keeping seeds for spring planting safe from rats. Against the back wall of the house was the niche in which the pallets, duvets, and pillows spread on the floor at night would be piled up in the morning and screened from sight by a curtain. A loom was set up near the window. Just next to it was a spinning wheel for rewinding the bobbins used in weaving. The baby's cradle stood against the opposite wall.

Hasan's "home" (the medium-sized room and adjoining small room called the summer quarters) were on the second floor of the building, situated on top of several storage rooms that made up the ground-floor. The roof of the ground floor expanded beyond the walls of these two upstairs rooms, creating an open flat space to walk onto. The first step outside the summer quarters was this strip of roof, not the street. One could climb to this strip of roof by first ascending a short flight of steps from the narrow street. The family could take in the fresh air on the flat strip and the rest of the big flat roof over the ground floor. The ground floor rooms below were a straw barn and five tiny rooms where wood, grains, pickles, and grape molasses were stored. These lower rooms had no windows, but a little bit of daylight came in from a small round opening overhead, defined by a small pottery cylinder, in a way a primitive skylight, called the hole at the top.

The house had been built at least two hundred years ago. As the family grew, new rooms and stables had been added on. The stables and straw barns were conveniently situated below the living spaces. The windowless lower rooms made up a quarter of the grandfather's property. When he died, two of Hasan's aunts had insisted that the property be shared in their father's memory, and so lots were drawn and it was divided up, room by room. The aunts, each of whom lived in the house of the man they had married, neglected to look after their shares of the stable, the grape press, and the woodshed for many years. They had not done the necessary jobs of clearing and rolling the roof in the winter months. Hasan's father had long wanted to buy his sisters' shares, but they could not be persuaded. One of them had, for a long time, insisted that she wanted to exchange her share for a field or a vineyard. Since there was little land to cultivate in the way of fields, vineyards, or gardens, neither of Hasan's parents had been in favor of this. The other sister, saying, "If my husband should ever turn me out of the house, I'll have a place to go," had not wanted to sell her share either. Hasan only knew these properties, the home of his grandfather, as an empty ruin in which the neighborhood children played house.

For fifteen years, the house of four rooms, two summer quarters, and three stables stood neglected, then one spring day, without any warning, it collapsed. Stones, earth, and bits of broken wood crashed down on the street beside it. It was only by chance that there was no one passing by at the time.

One of the aunts finally agreed to sell her share for cash. The other aunt still insisted on exchanging the ruin for some real property. Finally, his father unwillingly agreed to buy both parts of the ruin, one on the lower level and the other on the upper, in exchange for cash and a piece of land on the steep hillside in the region called Çötü. As the woodwork of the dilapidated rooms was mostly in pieces, Hasan's father was very annoyed and mourned, saying of one of the aunts, "My backbiting elder sister didn't sell the place until it was in ruins, and much of the timberwork belonging to your grandfathers was wasted."

Hasan's father, having bought the ruin in memory of his mother and father for a heavy price in money and land, had a great desire to pull it down and replace it with a larger one. He started making all kinds of preparations. In the winter months, no one in the village could earn money doing any kind of work. For this reason, he had gone, with many of the other men from the village, to Aydın, taking his fourteen-year-old son, Hilmi, with him.

In the winter, men streamed from the villages in Anatolia to the plains to earn money by tearing up licorice by the roots, earning themselves the nickname of grubbers. The big landowners, known as Beğs, had no difficulty in finding cheap labor to dig up the roots of licorice bushes and clear the fields in order to plant cotton in the fertile soil. All the people from our village, apart from the old, the craftsmen, and the women and children, went that winter to labor there. When these seasonal workers were told that the roots they grubbed up were theirs for the taking, they were very happy. They set to work in accordance with the precept "He who works hard earns a lot." That winter, like Rahim and his young son Hilmi, the villagers coming from the villages around Bozkır worked with greater enthusiasm in tearing up the licorice roots. Their day's spoils were sold through a middleman for six kuruş a kilo.

The Beğs of Söke, owners of the scrubland stretching as far as the eye could see, were overjoyed when it became possible to plant and sow this cleared ground.

Hasan's mother, Karakaşli, was still only twenty-five. This young woman, whose head only reached her husband's shoulder, spent that winter alone with her three children in that shoebox of a house. Their store of food consisted of a large earthenware jar of cracked wheat and a hillock of flour.

Her husband had recommended his wife spend all day at the loom, as long as there was enough daylight. The kilos of thread bought on credit from the cooperative in Konya were to be woven into broadcloth or calico to earn some money, if not much. That's what her husband was counting on when he set off for Aydın. However, Karakaşli frequently complained to those who came by: "He went off Aydın, leaving me with just a jar of cracked wheat!" The whole winter long, her complaints and recriminations continued. Still, it didn't escape her son's notice that, from time to time, his young mother would sniff the towel her husband had used.

As long as the swelling on her knee continued, his mother couldn't sit at the loom, and Hasan had to chop the firewood for the hearth and the stove. He struggled to lift the ax, too heavy for his spindly arms, and split the logs for the day. In the smokehouse, one of the dark rooms on the lower floor, thin stumps of oak were stored, and Hasan used the doorstep as a support when he chopped them into kindling. The wood was hard to split and he got very tired of having to wield the ax at least fifteen times to chop it into sticks only two or three fingers wide. "Oh, I wish I had the time to make myself a popgun," he would sigh.

As the doorway in which Hasan chopped wood was hidden away, no one saw the child's struggles. Only a neighbor's young son, Hüseyin, who lived in the neighboring village Dere and came by occasionally to visit his mother, would wander by and call out, "Hi there, woodcutter," then put his head around the door and watch with interest while Hasan chopped away.

One day while Hasan was struggling to chop the wood small enough to fit the stove, Hüseyin noticed some long poplar wood lying next to the woodpile. Pointing to the timbers, he said, "Hasan, you must be tired. I can chop that kindling for you in a minute. But there's something I want in return. I need two of those long poplar branches."

Hasan stopped and saw in his mind the popgun he had been dreaming about for weeks. "All right, you can have them, but will you make me a popgun?" he asked.

Hüseyin replied, "Of course I will. I'll make you two, one long and one short. The end of these straight poplar branches will be perfect for making popguns."

Hasan was not of an age to understand the value of the poplar branches as thick as an arm, which his father had prepared and left to dry, intending to use them for building. In exchange for two poplar branches, I'll get the popgun I've been longing for, he thought.

Dürdane's son Hüseyin, after he had chopped the oak wood into sticks of suitable size for the stove, repeated his promise to make the popgun. Then he tucked the two poplar branches under his arm and, hoping no one would see him in the evening twilight, quickly made his way home.

Hasan didn't mention Hüseyin's offer to his mother. When his mother saw that he had split the thicker logs as well as the thinner ones he chopped every day, she was very pleased. She said happily to herself, "My little Esen is becoming practiced at this," and stroked his head, saying, "You have become an extension of my hands, my son. She called him "Esen," which meant "like wind," when she was happy about something he did.

Chopping wood at the threshold

For three or four weeks, Hasan continued to be the man of the house. During that time, his mother's swollen knee got better. Karakaşli started to weave cloth, bake bread, and do the housework like other adult folk. Meanwhile, whenever Hasan found an opportunity, he would take the popgun his friend from Dere had made so expertly for him and go and play in the streets or on the roofs with his friends. The boy never brought his popgun home after play, but hid it in the woodshed. A feeling of guilt he didn't understand made him keep the toy out of his mother's sight.

The winter days grew shorter and shorter. The frosty weather increased. At home, the kerosene needed for the lamp and the salt for cooking had gone down a lot. Karakaşli and her children were tired of eating the same tasteless food made of cracked wheat or the boram made with the winter squash and beetroot her mother sometimes sent. They were pleased when their young mother made hash potatoes on the stove with the ones stored in the stable for seed.

The weaving was done, and quite a lot of broadcloth and calico had been stored away. But nobody on God's earth came to the village to buy even a meter of cloth. She had sent five or six rolls of cloth with the village representative to the cooperative in Konya. No money had been given in exchange because, in fact, her husband, Rahim, had gotten all the threads with money loaned by the merchant. Karakaşli hadn't known about that. After taking what was owed for the thread, the merchant hadn't even been able to give the person from the cooperative a lira to take back to Karakaşli.

This news made Karakaşli sad and angry. If she could have asked someone to bring her a kilo of sesame oil and a goat's head, she and her children could have put a little fat and meat in their bellies. When things got very tight as she toiled from morning till night, she would mutter, "That good-for-nothing man sold my oil and went off to Aydın without leaving me even forty pennies." The matches were also finished. One morning, the fire in the hearth and the stove burned out completely. Karakaşli gave Hasan a shovel and sent him to the neighbors to beg for a burning kindling. She warned her son to put an extra log on the fire at night so it wouldn't go out again.

One morning when Hasan woke up to go to the outside toilet, he heard the sounds of sobbing from a house in the upper village. A little later, some people came to their house and, in a low voice, asked

Karakaşli for six meters of broadcloth. She measured the cloth and gave it to them, taking in exchange the money they gave her.

"Mother, did they buy some of our cloth?" Hasan asked.

"Yes, my son," she replied. "It's for Leftie's shroud. He had pneumonia. He was very ill. Last night, he died. The cloth they bought was for his winding sheet. The poor man was so young and a father. Such a pity. May God give them patience."

Hasan couldn't remember hearing of anyone he knew dying. His idea of death was only a vague memory. Ages ago, he had heard of the deaths of his grandfather, his father's first wife, and the younger brother of his elder sibling, Hilmi. To hear of the death of someone from the village was a strange and terrifying thing.

With the money from the cloth she'd sold, Karakaşli was able to buy some kerosene for the lamp, salt, and matches they needed, as well as a few items of food from the Friday market that week. The children were delighted, especially with the bread from the market and half a kilo of halva. It seemed strange to Hasan to feel relief and happiness from having money in their hands when someone had died, and he felt his stomach churn. It was difficult to understand how the sorrows of another family could bring relief to his own.

The Little Peddler

The houses in the village Çat had been built on the sharp slopes of the Taurus Mountains. Two rivers, the Ulu and Yayla, came from the deep mountain valleys and divided the village into three main sections. The two rivers joined together in the middle of the village, and flowed freely toward the plain of Konya.

The people of this village were very hardworking and full of energy. As there was not enough land to be cultivated, the villagers were not farmers, but had created other jobs for themselves. Many families worked at different jobs according to the season. Individuals of this village were known by the work they did and by the names of these jobs: peddler Mustafa, ironsmith Hese, basketmaker Bekir, miller Arda, builder Tevek, potter Osman, weaver Ayşe, and so on. In order of importance, the jobs that brought the most income to the village were peddling or being a packman, pottery making, doing seasonal farmwork in Aydın, milling, basketmaking, being a blacksmith, herding, and even gambling.

The packmen or peddlers took the goods produced in their village, loaded them onto a mule or donkey, and took them to distant villages or towns. When they got to their destination, they exchanged what they were carrying for the main products of that village. In grain-growing areas, these were usually wheat, barley, garbanzo peas, lentils, and oats. In areas where these did not grow well, they bartered their goods for crumbly cheese, clarified butter, animal hair and wool products, raisins, or grape syrup.

These packmen made the most profit by selling pottery goods. Pots were made of suitable-quality clay, which existed in the village mountains, and were fired by the master potters and families of the Ömerli district. Many varieties of pots, large and small, were made this way, as well as every type of water pitchers, jugs, and ewers, some with one handle, others with two, and different types of vessels and containers such as washbasins, crocks, bowls, beakers, and jars. In addition, the potters took orders and made covered cooking vessels, chimney pots, and roofing tiles.

When Rahim was a young man, he took care of the family lands with a well-fed pair of oxen. He enjoyed the work and regarded himself as a successful farmer. However, after the passing of his father, he became one of the village men who took up peddling. In fact, Rahim could not have supported a family with five children by working as a farmer on his inheritance of one-quarter of a field and a vineyard. He earned a living by being a peddler, using a mule and a donkey as the beasts of burden. He got the pottery for his sales trips in two ways: either becoming a partner of a pottery master—providing the clay and the wood for a potter for the full share of the product that came out of the kiln—or by taking the pottery on loan, with the promise to pay it back after the completion of his peddling trips.

Rahim was diligent in performing the ritual prayers; he never missed a service at the mosque when he was in his village. He liked to say his prayers at the proper time. Even when he was walking on the long roads, he would hand over his mule to a trustworthy person near him for a minute or two, perform his religious duty at the proper time of day for namaz, and then run to catch up with the rest of the caravan. When he got to a village, he loved going to pray at the mosque with the rest of the congregation, after leaving his goods in safe hands. Rahim did not like to go on his peddling trips by himself. He liked to journey to distant villages with one of the other packmen like himself, such as Hasanoca, Sergeant Mehmet, Jughandles Bekir, or Ali, Hacı's son, all neighbors or distant relatives. When he went to smaller villages, though, thinking there wouldn't be enough customers for more than one packman, he loved to take one of his family members with him. When his own children were too small, he would take close relatives, like one of his elder brother's young sons, or the son of a close relative, like his cousins. In this way, not only did he not journey alone, but he also helped his relatives earn money.

Sometimes Rahim would take his oldest son, Hilmi, with him. But when he did so, they always quarreled a lot. Hilmi didn't like going peddling at all. At an early age, he had become used to joining his neighbors or a relative and going to work as a casual laborer, which he enjoyed. So Rahim waited with great impatience for his son Hasan to grow up.

A packman would prepare his goods the day before his trip; on the day of the trip, very early in the morning, he loaded the donkey or mule by tying the containers on with the ropes hanging from the saddle. His wife or a grown-up child, if there was one, would help. The loaded animal would walk for five or six hours without stopping, so the goods to be sold had to be well balanced and securely roped. Food for the journey and fodder for the animals, half a sack of hay for each, were the last to be tied on. Before dawn broke, they would leave the village, departing with farewells such as "God be with you," "Have a safe journey," or "God give you good luck."

After they had been on the road for an hour, dawn would break. By that time, the packmen would have passed through village Dere and be on their way up a long hill, nearing the red plains of Ahırlı just as the multitude of stars gave way to the brightness of the reddening sky. The packmen would hardly notice the slowly increasing twitters of birds and the hum of insects around them on the narrow trails. In order to prevent the loaded animals from bumping into each other left and right and breaking the pots, the packmen had to take care and always be on the lookout. Every so often, the silence of the dusty road was broken up by the sound of "Hey up, hey up," addressed especially to the donkeys, or the click of hooves on stony ground.

When Hasan first started going with his father, he was only eleven years old. "Aren't you ashamed to take this knucklebone of a child peddling with you when your donkey-headed son Hilmi sits in the coffeehouse all day, doing nothing?" his wife grumbled.

Rahim paid little heed to what his wife said. While they were loading up that evening, Hasan held the halter of the restless mule, his eyes closed, half-sleeping, half-awake, almost asleep on his feet.

"Don't overwork Hasan. He's still only little," his mother admonished, saying farewell as they set out on the road.

In charge of the loaded mule walking in front of him, Hasan listened to his father's warnings: "There's a narrow place ahead, son. Take care not to bump the load." Or, "Son, someone's coming. Hold the mule's head and take the side of the road." At places where he felt the road was wide enough and safe enough, he couldn't prevent himself from taking forty winks as he walked along, holding on to the back of the mule.

Even though it was tiring, Hasan found this first journey into the places he did not know very interesting. The roads he'd not traveled before, the fountains where he and the animals drank water, the wells, the wooden-wheeled oxcarts, the plants growing by the wayside or in the fields, the flowers, the insects, and many other things attracted him as he silently plodded along. They passed through villages he had only known as names. Who knew how many times he had heard of Ahırlı, İldoğan, Sandı, Yalıhüyük, Karaviran, or Bağra in the stories of trading told by his father and their packman neighbors. He tried to find a connection between the names and the villages he saw.

Hasan's interest in his surroundings lessened as the sun rose higher and the day grew warmer. As he was also a little hungry and thirsty, he began to feel tired. Toward noon, his father took a break among the willow trees at the side of the canal, his father's name for the wide, slow-running river. After unloading the pack animals, they attached the hay bags to their heads. Hasan and his father took their bundles of food from the pocket of the saddlebag and ate their meal of green onion and boiled potato in flatbread. It was early summer. The fruit to complement their meal had not yet appeared. Rahim was never without raisins in his pocket, however. Both of them sweetened their mouths with a few of these.

After they finished eating, Hasan was happy to have an opportunity to rest while his father said his prayers. After this short rest, Rahim and Hasan loaded up the mule and the two donkeys and started off along the road, made of pebbles and packed sandy soil, along the side of the canal toward the village. Rahim told Hasan the name of this village was Gökhüyük. He said that, so far, they had come six hours along the road, and it would be another five hours before they reached it, mentioning that they would see the villages of Lower Karaviran and Bağra on the way. Hasan had hardly spoken a word as he walked along. He continued walking in silence by the side of his charge, the mule, uttering only an "Uh-huh," meaning "I heard," and an "Eh," meaning "all right."

On the left side of the road were dark fields that had only just been sown. The bare fields stretched away as if to touch the far-distant mountains across the large, shining expanse seen in front of them. This was the reflection from Soğla Lake, the waters of which were drying up as the heat increased. Seeing a mirror image of the distant snowy mountains and hills reflected in the lake delighted Hasan.

The people of the neighboring villages were hard at work plowing the moist earth at the side of the receding lake. They were planting the things they needed, what they called garden produce, mainly garbanzo beans, melons and watermelons, and sunflowers to brighten the edges of the fields. Remembering his mother's saying, "Soğla garbanzo beans are easy to cook," Hasan was pleased to see this place.

Gökhüyük was a small village situated on an artificial mound called a höyük on the Seydişehir side of the lake. It was so far off the beaten track that Rahim had chosen it for this journey, hoping that no other packman would go there. When Gökhüyük appeared in the distance and his father said they had only another hour on the road, Hasan said with a smile, "Oh, that's good, Father, very good." By this time, he was very tired, and dragged his feet as he walked. Father and son both endeavored to walk through the knee-high dust made by the coming and going of people, animals, and the wooden oxcarts of the neighboring villages. When Hasan saw the village in the distance along an absolutely straight road, he imagined they would soon arrive there. But a little while later, his legs became heavy and he felt himself becoming weak. He began to falter and finally completely stopped, unable to even lift one foot.

Without panicking, Rahim said, "Son, you're not fit, that's why you're like a wet rag." Picking him up, he set him in back of the saddle on the laden mule. The term "wet rag" was used for a person or a pack animal who was so exhausted, he couldn't go another step.

Half an hour later, they arrived in Gökhüyük and stopped at the village guesthouse. It was time for afternoon prayer. The elderly people chatting outside the mosque near the guesthouse were happy to see the packman arrive. "Welcome," they called. "What's the matter with the child?"

Hasan was not much help to Rahim in unloading the animals. He could hardly stand upright to hold the halter of the mule being unloaded. He still didn't have the strength to walk. He could only try to hold the mule's halter sitting down. One of the villagers, after saying a few words to his father, laid Hasan on his back at the foot of the guesthouse wall. Lifting his legs, he helped him lean them against the wall.

The elderly villagers sitting in front of the mosque and others who came there began to bargain with Rahim over the pots he was selling. He wanted to exchange them for wheat, barley, or garbanzo beans. Local terms were used for the price and weight of the kind of pots to be exchanged. A different price was given for every pot according to what it was to be used for. The exchange rate was set according to the amount of wheat and the size of the pot. The bargaining went on in this way.

Meanwhile, Hasan was still lying down, leaning his legs against the wall, listening to the friendly talk of the villagers after afternoon prayers:

The ones who built this village came from Konya about two hundred and twenty years ago. Those who came first only knew how to farm small holdings, but they soon learned how to fish in the lake. There were four families then, and now there are seventy. Whenever the lake water gets low, the more fertile land there is, even if it's only a little. Wheat ripens late here, but the land's grand for barley, garbanzo beans, and garden greens. They worked hard to clear the reed beds so their children can now sow and plant in comfort. There are a lot of snakes, but there's no need to be scared. The snakes eat rats and field mice and other such harmful critters. Thank the storks who find and eat the snakes and frogs. God gave each living thing its means of life.

While this talk was going on, one of the elderly men called to Hasan, saying, "Come on, get up, son. You're all right now."

Hasan first lowered his legs and then, rather fearfully, got to his feet from the dusty ground where he had been lying for half an hour. The numbness had gone from his legs. Happily, he stood up straight, and, as if to make his father happy, he hopped and jumped around a few times.

Rahim went on selling off his pots until dusk had fallen, and then put what he had gotten in exchange into the sack he had brought with him. When the call for evening prayer was heard, he made his ablutions with water from a little pitcher, then told Hasan, "Son, keep a sharp eye on the goods until I get back from namaz." He hurried off to the mosque.

Sitting by the pots while his father was in the mosque, Hasan felt somewhat nervous and afraid. A village woman came up and asked him, "Little son, how many are there in the guesthouse?"

"Just me and my father," Hasan replied.

Shortly afterward, the congregation left the mosque. A young man with a tray of food in his hand came and said in a thick accent, "Excuse us, Uncle. Fill your bellies with this gruel and dry food. It's our turn to take care of the guesthouse. The stable's open. Come a bit later and feed your animals some of the hay from the haystack."

"Thanks a lot. God bless you," said Rahim.

The food the guesthouse keeper had brought was very welcome: hot cracked wheat pilaf, a bowl of ayran, and a few pieces of flat wheat bread.

"Their pilaf is very good, Father," said Hasan. "They've put garbanzo beans in it."

"My son," his father said, "the village is small, but its people are good folk and they look after the guesthouse well."

After eating their meal with great appetite in the half dark, Hasan's eyelids began to droop.

After collecting up the pots spread for sale in an orderly fashion, the packman whispered to his son, "Son, we'll sleep out here in the open next to our pots. The weather's not too cold. And I don't like sleeping inside if it isn't winter. There are always fleas or bedbugs. There's an empty sack in the room; let's give it a shake and put it down underneath our own empty bags and make pillows for our saddlebags."

Hasan listened to his father without saying anything. He helped him spread the sack on the ground. It made no difference to him whether they had pillows or not, whether it was dry ground or a sack. He laid his head on the saddlebag folded to make a pillow. He didn't even hear his father say, "Son, are you asleep already?" or feel the empty sack he covered him with.

Rahim did not go to bed, however. He went to the well nearby and drew water so the animals could drink from the trough. He took hay from the guesthouse keeper's haystack, filled the animals' hay bags, and hung them around their necks. He knotted the halters tight and shut the stable door so they wouldn't roam about during the night. Rahim preferred sleeping on a high pillow, so he shaped a grain sack accordingly. As soon as the bedtime summons to prayer were heard, he said his prayers as quickly as possible before lying down on the floor.

By now, the village was in total silence. The kerosene candles and lamplight that had been flickering behind the small windows of the village houses went out. Darkness covered everything like a magical canopy. Not even the sound of frogs and insects coming from the cultivated ground around the village could pierce this canopy or disturb the ears of the tired packmen.

> *Of stars, there were many,*
> *that night in the sky,*
> *streaming in cohorts to battle,*
> *the sharp spear of a comet*
> *or fiery arrows of flame.*
> *Only a shepherd to see them,*
> *fixing his eyes on his sheep,*
> *murmuring under his breath,*
> *"Seven thousand enemies over me.*
> *seven thousand enemies above"*

Waking up in this village of farmers was like a ritual to the sun. When the first streaks of red in the east began to disperse the darkness, birds, animals, and humans came to life, stirring at its silent touch. Children unwilling to open their eyes heard this awakening little by little, even though deeply asleep. Herds of cows went to graze, mooing sadly with the pain of leaving their calves, sparrows and swallows twittered and flew around the eaves, storks clattered their beaks as they prepared to leave their nests and go hunting, and the imam called the people to morning prayers. Even those reluctant to rise heard and got up.

In spite of all this noise, Hasan went on dreaming of being on the summer pasture at Eski Yurt playing with his friends, Bahri and Vehbi. He did not stir until his father called, as was his custom, "Hasan, come on, get up. Come, my son, my little bull, get up. Our customers will soon be here." When Hasan got up, he looked around, not quite sure where he was. Quickly, he went to the stables and urinated on the manure.

The sun had not yet risen, but it was light enough to see around. The pottery seller and his son first gave the animals their food and drink, and then began the serious business of setting out their wares to be sold. The men who had heard of the packman's arrival late in the evening came to choose the pots they needed before going to the fields. As the price of every kind of pot had been fixed by haggling the day before, they were able to make their purchases without losing much time.

At this time of the summer, the people of Gökhüyük were accustomed to making haste. There were garbanzo peas to sow before the plowed ground lost its moisture; barley to inspect, cut, and harvest before the ears dried out; and a plentiful supply of milk to take advantage of by making soft cheese and drying curds to use in the winter. That meant that in the early hours, when morning sunlight gave a pleasant warmth, they must get to work at once. The packman's son, observing the decrease in the number of buyers as they hastened off, realized he was hungry. He began to wonder when and what they would eat.

Breakfast at the guesthouse consisted of wheat bread and other food that was left from the previous night. The guesthouse keeper only provided the evening meal. In the morning, they had enough work to keep them busily rushing around. That morning was the first time Hasan had seen his father's cunning ways. Finding one of the women customers had a friendly manner, he said in a polite and ingratiating voice, "Sister, I can manage, but my son's belly is rumbling. Take this little ewer, won't you, and in return, cook us a little pilaf so we have something hot to eat this morning."

The village woman replied, "Now, Uncle, you don't have to do that. I'll go at once and, whatever God provides, I'll cook and bring to you."

"That'll do, my dear, that'll do. But take this ewer. Whether you need it or not, you can use this red ewer for water when you have a guest. It's worthy of your forebears and mine."

Without more ado, the woman took the small, bright red ewer.

More than half the pots had been sold. Midday would be a slow time for trade and the packman said to his son, "After we've eaten our bread, I'll take a few pots in my hand and show them around on the outer sides of the village." This way, he could sell to those too old or too shy to come to the guesthouse area. "While I am away, son, you could look after the pots spread out for any customers to see and tell them, 'My father will be back soon,' and mind you don't go off and play!"

Hasan was very hungry and couldn't prevent himself from looking now and again in the direction the woman had gone to make the pilaf. "What a warm-hearted auntie," he murmured to himself. Even though he ate cracked wheat pilaf every day, he could practically taste the warm morning pilaf and breathe its smell, but he kept his eye on the pots to sell. In his mind, he was wandering barefoot along the river in his own village.

Suddenly, he heard the words "Come, Uncle, may this food do you good," and his eyes brightened. The village woman brought a dish of pilaf, a small bowl of yogurt, and a few pieces of wheat flatbread and placed them by the packman's saddlebags, saying, "Uncle, if you need hay, come and take it," before going back to her house.

Father and son quickly filled their bellies. Hasan loved using a piece of flatbread to shovel up the yogurt. His father said, "Son, ayran will go further," and stirred some water into the yogurt. Hasan made no objection. He remembered the saying he had heard in the village: "Let's shake the yogurt up with water and it will go further."

Rahim, knowing that between the next prayer time and the afternoon one, there would be no big sales, slung a saddlebag on his shoulder and took a few different kinds of pots in his hands, setting off to stroll around the neighborhoods. Most of the time, he saw only small children playing in the dusty trails between the houses. Raising his voice, he sang loudly but tunefully, "Fine pitchers, going cheap," trying to catch the eye of those women or older men not in the fields by displaying his pots. From time to time, he returned to the guesthouse to check on his son, who sat quietly, looking around him and keeping an eye on the goods spread out there. Once he said, "Son, this evening, we'll reduce the price of the remaining goods and, while we're near, let's go tomorrow to see Seydişehir. Tomorrow's Thursday, the market day in that town. If we find goods cheap there, we can get them and sell them in Bozkır."

Hasan had heard of Seydişehir and was pleased to be seeing it. The goods they had gotten in exchange would only need two animals to carry them. On their return, they could take turns riding the other. Rahim made sure to buy lighter goods and make a little more profit. Hasan simply listened in silence.

The evening sales went quite well. Only five or six vessels remained unsold. Saying they could get rid of these at the market in town the next day, together Rahim and his son got ready for the next day's journey. That evening, the guesthouse keepers were from a different family, but the food was much the same.

The concepts of a guesthouse and providing food were not strange to Hasan. In Çat, they were also keepers of a guesthouse started some time ago by a prosperous villager, Hasan's grandfather Ali Hoca. Even though his son Rahim, was not well-to-do, he had been determined to carry on the family tradition. Every day in the evening, Hasan's mother would say to him, "Run, son, to the guesthouse. See if there are any guests, and, if so, how many." He remembered taking food there for the guests. He didn't warm to the idea of being a packman who ate and slept using the hospitality of the guesthouse in a different village, even if his father was there too. He began to imagine his house, his mother, his siblings, the village and the river, the trees, and his friends. Well, let's just have a look at the town, Seydişehir, he said to himself. That night, their second in Gökhüyük, they slept in front of the guesthouse as before.

Earlier, Rahim had said to the keeper, "We don't want to load and tire the animals for nothing, brother. Please let us leave our grain sacks in your safekeeping and pick them up on our way back from Seydişehir tomorrow." Filling the grain he had gotten by barter into two sacks, he delivered them one by one to the guesthouse keeper's house, then, mounting their animals, father and son set off quickly toward the town of Seydişehir.

The market in Seydişehir was quite crowded. They went straight to the cattle market and tied up their animals in a corner. Then Rahim said to Hasan, "You stay here with the animals, son. I'll go and sell these last few pots. Who knows, perhaps the balance will be enough for a few cheap goods." And off he went.

The crowd in the market was similar to the one Hasan was familiar with at the Bozkır Friday market, although the different way they were dressed attracted his attention. The decorated head coverings of the women, their colored stockings, belts like none he had ever seen before, the saddle girths, and the embroidered linen halters all interested him. In answer to the question, "Child, are these animals for sale?" he answered, "No, Uncle," and went on sitting and observing what went on in the marketplace.

An hour or two later, toward noon, Rahim came back with the saddlebag on his shoulder. "Come, Hasan, let's go before it gets late," he said. Taking the animals, they went to the other side of the market. There, Rahim bargained with a villager for some saddle straw.

Saddle straw consisted of green reeds, one and a half meters long. The inside of saddle straw was composed of spongy material that when dry, weighed almost nothing, which made it very suitable for filling saddles for pack animals, riding saddles, and pillions for horses. Reed beds grew and flourished along the shores of some lakes. In order to carry the cut and dried reeds easily, they were made into long cylindrical bundles and sold like that.

Rahim gave the villager the money for the reeds he had bought. As soon as the money was in his hand, the villager threw it up in the air, then knelt and kissed the ground. "I earned this money honestly by the sweat of my brow. For days, I sweated in my canoe, choosing and cutting bundles of the largest reeds. May you also see the reward of your labors, my friend," he said. Hasan was delighted to see the happiness on this villager's face.

Although the saddle straw was light, it was too bulky for one animal to carry; they loaded it on top of two animals in such a way that they could ride, too, and off they went. "We've a twelve-hour journey ahead of us. We'll eat on the way. We'll stop at Gökhüyük to pick up the grain sacks, load them, and continue. Even if we go without stopping, we can't reach home before midnight. We'll give the animals an hour's rest on the way and let them graze. By God's grace, we'll get there early enough for the Friday market," Rahim told his son.

Hasan couldn't help asking, "Are we going to Bozkır without going home first?"

"Yes, that's right, son. If I can sell the saddle straw at the Friday market, I'll bargain with one of the potters for his pots. If we get to the market in good time, we'll finish the job and get home early," the packman added.

The animals' loads were light enough for them to ride a little, walk briskly a little, and get to Gökhüyük by evening. Picking up the sacks of grain they had left for safekeeping, they loaded the other donkey and continued on their way. The packman told his son, "We'll walk all night without stopping. When we get to Sandı Fountain, we'll water the animals without unloading them and let them graze by the roadside for ten or fifteen minutes. If we eat now, that will keep us going until we get to Bozkır."

Night was falling, and the packman picked up his son and put him on the mule. He opened the saddlebag and gave him a piece of bread filled with halva. "Eat this, son," he said, holding it out to him. The boy's stomach had been empty for some time, and he had been wondering when they were going to eat. He took what was put in his hand and ate with great appetite, happy his father had bought halva and bread at the market. Swaying from side to side on top of the saddle straw on the mule, Hasan was overcome by sleep and his eyes closed. As he dozed off in the silence of the plains, he heard his father chanting in his baritone voice one of the hymns he had heard him sing before:

> *With my friends the mountains,*
> *I will call to you, my God;*
> *with the birds of the desert,*
> *I will call to you, my God;*
> *with the fish of the sea,*
> *with those whose hearts are burning,*
> *and those awake at dawn,*
> *I will call you, my God.*
> *With Jesus in the sky above,*
> *with Moses on Tur Mountain,*
> *the Laws held in his hand,*
> *I will call you, my God.*
> *With those who speak with dolphins,*
> *with doves and nightingales,*
> *with the humble who love justice,*
> *I will call you, my God.*

His father's beautiful voice was like a lullaby to Hasan. He had been used to it since he was a baby. When Rahim was in the village, he used to take the place of his brother-in-law, the village cleric, and climb up on the roof of the mosque. Hasan had many times heard him chant the call to prayer, turning in every direction as he did so.

From time to time, the mule stumbled, and Hasan later remembered waking to the sound of his father performing the call to prayer:

> *God is great, God is great,*
> *God only is to be worshipped,*
> *this I know without a doubt,*

and I will proclaim it.
Muhammed is God's messenger
this I know without a doubt,
and I will proclaim it.
Muhammed is God's messenger,
come to prayer. Come to prayer.
Come, all you people, come, all you people.
God is great, God is great,
God only is to be worshipped.

A pottery-loaded mule

Suddenly he began to think of how, during the last year, both the village cleric and Hasan's father had begun to chant the call to prayer in a language he couldn't understand. Hasan didn't like this change. But neither Hasan nor his friends could say anything. When they asked their parents, they were told, "This is the old call to prayer. Before this, a new call to prayer was accepted. Now it's the old one again. What can we do? Those who changed it must have a reason, daughter, son."

By now, darkness had really fallen. The child packman went on sleeping on the swaying mule. The father packman continued driving the animals and murmuring to himself. In the darkness of night amid the calm silence respecting the living creatures now asleep, he was going over in his head what he had bought and sold and how much profit he had made. Calculating to himself in a low voice, he continued walking alongside the animals he was driving.

A Glass, a Kid, and a Bunch of Grapes

Nobody knows how old our province of Bozkır is, but in my childhood, it was known by its former name of Siristat. When Siristat was mentioned, the name of the first settlement of Bozkır village came to mind. When one said Bozkır, there was something official about it. Bozkır was where the government offices were, as well as the Ziraat Bank, where the yearly agricultural credit, or Panga, was handed out to the villagers; the gendarme post; the lockup, known as the hole; the weekly marketplace; the recruiting office; the registry office where official marriages took place, known by the villagers as the "permission office"; and, of course, the residential area where officials such as the district governor and the local judge lived.

Of the government offices, the one that affected the people most was the mail office. In most villages of Bozkır, the villagers without arable land would go as seasonal workers to places like Aydın, Adana, or Istanbul in order to earn money. They would send money to their wives, children, mothers, and fathers who remained behind. When a villager needed it most, the news that their loved ones had sent money would be greeted like a message from Hızır, the legendary helper of the poor, and make that person very happy. Hoping to be able to buy what the family needed, that person would choose the Friday market day to run to the mail office, with the notice in hand, and wait among the crowd in front of the director's office.

Whatever money the men, working half-starved and thirsty, were able to save was sent by mail order to their relatives. The villagers would regard the mail office director as their generous father. After getting their money, they would respectfully express their thanks in words such as "May you live long, may God bless you, Mr. Director" before rushing off to shop at the market.

İhsan Bey, the mail office director, was a kind, fatherly man, worthy of the respect shown to him. He was tall. Unlike most of the other officials, he was not a portly or formidable figure in his formal suit and tie. He was the kind of state official who, with a smiling face and calm, gentle voice, could put at ease the crowd waiting bashfully in front of the clerk's desk. Many of the officials posted to government offices, thinking of Bozkır as a hardship post, would quickly make strenuous efforts to find another post, but Director İhsan had, for years, served the people there, putting his heart and soul into his job. In fact, he was one of the rare officials who did not forget that it was these people who paid his salary.

The mail for Bozkır district came from the central mail office for the province in Konya. All kinds of letters, parcels, money orders, and even telegrams, sent or received, came through the Konya Mail Office. The job of sending or receiving mail from Bozkır to Konya was given out on tender to a local citizen of means. In my childhood, the person who undertook the carrying and delivering of mail on this basis was a man known in Bozkır by the name of Ali, the son of Grafter, or Truckman Ali. Since this man had a few trucks and an omnibus, he was able to carry the mail to and from Konya and was given the tender.

Mailbags containing letters, packets, official documents, and even cash from the bank had to be sealed with a heavy lead seal, loaded onto a vehicle to be taken from Bozkır, and delivered to the mail office in Konya. Mail from Konya was received there and delivered to the mail office in Bozkır. Both of these deliveries were carried out by young citizens trusted by both İhsan Bey, the mail office director, and the contractor, Truckman Ali. It was Truckman Ali's responsibility to find and choose these carriers and pay their monthly salary.

In spite of there being a lot of people looking for jobs, it wasn't as easy as you might think to find someone to trust with this duty. In fact, the dirt road from Bozkır connecting with the graveled highway to Konya was closed for four or five or even six months of the year in winter, and, even if it was passable, it wasn't a regular occurrence. In the winter months, the Republic of Turkey's mail deliveries and dispatches for Bozkır were carried by mule to or from Seydişehir.

Seydişehir was a district about fifty-five kilometers from Bozkır. The road from there to Konya could be kept open in the winter months. It was an imperative and necessary condition of the system that the mail office met the needs of the townships and villages, even in the worst of winter storms.

Truckman Ali and İhsan Bey were responsible for finding a strong young man with a healthy young mule to do this work. Farrier Mustafa Çavuş, the oldest of the farriers in Bozkır, was of the greatest help in this. Everyone trusted this fatherly man's expert knowledge of animal health. Mustafa Çavuş was counted as the veterinary surgeon of the Bozkır district, where there were no certified veterinary surgeons, and the villagers, who understood the important role of their pack animals in their lives, had implicit faith in him. They brought all their livestock to him to look at and had him shoe their mules and horses.

One September day in the year I started second grade at the primary school, my father came home from the market. Unloading his goods, he said to me in a jovial voice, "Come, son, tie the mule up in the stable and tip a basketful of straw from the stack into the manger. Don't mix the bedding straw with the fodder, remember. I'll measure out the barley myself." He had realized that I was grown up enough to be trusted to take the mule we called our breadbasket and tie it up in the stable. Hoping that Father had brought the customary gift from the Friday market, I could already feel the taste in my mouth of the pide bread made with special flour, as well as a sweet paste called Karagaç halva. Hastily finishing the job, I hurried into the house.

Gleefully my father said to my mother, "Karakaşli, it looks as though we'll have money for bread this winter." As her oldest child, I had always heard my father and the neighbors call her "Karakaşli," and it was years before I found out that her real name was Fatma. Father went on. "An opportunity has come up. Tomorrow, I'm going to Siristat again to see someone called Truckman Ali. Today, I had the mule shod. Farrier Mustafa Çavuş gave me some news. They're looking for a carrier for the mail. He's given them my name. If Truckman Ali likes me and my mule, next Monday, I'll talk with the mail office director," he said. "The salary will be one hundred and twenty-five liras a month," he added.

A little fearfully, Mother asked, "What does 'mail carrier' mean? Is it an official job? Will you go far?"

Father told her what he knew. "In any case, in winter, I can't continue traveling around selling pots and kettles, raisins, grape syrup, knives, and such. Even if I could, it wouldn't bring us much. If I get the job as postman, the monthly salary will be plenty for us. If I get it, I say, because Truckman Ali is going to see other people with horses or mules. We shouldn't tell anyone else about it yet," he added.

My father was then about forty years old, tall, with face and hands tanned by the sun from his travels as a salesman; his looks showed he had the strength to lift a fifty-kilo sack and balance it on the side of a large mule. He used to say he had been raised well, fed with plenty of food containing sugar or fat. If anyone asked, "What is your heart's desire?" he would jokingly reply, "Honey, cream, meat, bread, cheese, and halva." On the other hand, years later when he had his own family and children to raise, to ensure that the shortages of the household wouldn't make us downhearted, he would often say, "Bread is the sultan, pilaf the vizier, the rest are just the commoners."

After attending the required interview and being approved by both the contractor, Truckman Ali, and İhsan Bey, the mail office director, my father was given the duty of mail carrier on muleback to fetch and carry the mail between Bozkır and Seydişehir during the winter of 1949 to 1950.

When Rahim from Çat began his adventurous career as mail carrier, it created mixed feelings of hope and fear in the house. He explained to his wife that a mail carrier had to have self-confidence and be fearless. There was no need to be worried. He knew the roads to and from Seydişehir well from his travels as a peddler to the surrounding villages. Preparations for the winter months had to be made at once. "First of all, I have to inspect my kepenek"—this referred to a uniquely shaped heavy shepherd's coat made as one single piece of felt, formed from sheep wool; it was also used by travelers in extremely cold times—"and then make myself a new pair of stout leather moccasins. Karakaşli, get our neighbor Uzun Emiş to knit a pair of thick woolen gaiters and mittens. Last market day, I bought some wool cheaply from the Yörüks and now's the time to use it."

Two weeks later, one of the butchers in Bozkır slaughtered a hefty ox. My father bought the head of it for almost nothing. When he came home, he flayed the skin off it to make himself a pair of moccasins. Then he carefully parsed the flesh from the bone. My father loved to take pride in his skill, and weighed the meat he had obtained. Full of smiles, he said, "Exactly seven and a half kilos; let the children eat their fill of meat," he added.

The road linking Seydişehir with Bozkır was mostly graveled. This road was fifty-five kilometers long, and to travel that distance on foot took nine, ten, even eleven hours, according to the traveler's pace and the weather conditions.

Rahim, now the mailman with a mule, began his first journey in October. One Monday morning, he arrived at the mail office when the government offices opened at nine o'clock. He took charge of the sealed mailbags filled with mail packages. First, he stuffed the mailbags in an orderly way into his own bags, which were made of goat hair. To load the mail in such a way that it looked as though he was one of the usual peddlers was a cunning idea he had thought up himself.

The mailman, new to his job, tied the mouth of each sack tight with string, loaded the mule, and set off on the road. With the laden mule in front of him, he set off in dry, but chilly weather along the road he already knew well.

The road between Bozkır and Seydişehir was completely flat except for the bit between the villages of Akçapınar and Meyre. This section was a two-hour walk before coming to the village of İldoğan, where the road stretched across the endless plain. A large part of this flat area was covered by Lake Soğla. For the rest of the journey, the road wound along the lakeside, which was like a natural boundary on the eastern side.

In summer, this road was used by oxcarts and wagons laden with the harvest from the surrounding villages, but in the winter months, it was mostly used by itinerant peddlers going with their loaded pack animals to sell to the villagers roundabout. Our mule mail carrier was very familiar with these roads. He calculated how long it would take him to reach Seydişehir by nightfall. He thought about the snowy, stormy, bitingly cold days of winter.

There wasn't a single caravan stop, cave, or rock cleft along the road for the traveler with his loaded pack animals in which to take refuge from a sudden tempest, rainstorm, or other inclement weather. In such a case, one had to turn to one of the villages not too far from the road, such as Yalıhüyük, Akkise, Lower Karaviran, Bağra, or Gökhüyük, to find a convenient and safe shelter.

This wasn't an option for the mule mailman. As an official mailman of the Republic of Turkey, he had to continue on his way, whatever the cost, until he delivered the mail to the designated mail office. This mailman trusted himself and his mule. With stout moccasins on his feet; knitted woolen gaiters on his legs; his head, nose, and mouth covered with his scarf; a heavy coat stretching from neck to knee; and a forked stick held tightly in his gloved hands, he considered it his duty to continue along the road even in the worst winter storm.

The forked stick was almost always made from a young branch of wild olive. As its name suggests, it forked at the thinnest part. It was of convenient length to support and balance the first load after it had been roped to the saddle, while tying the second load on at the other side. It was also useful as a support when walking along a rough road, as well as to rest his arms by using it as a support for the load on his shoulders. It could also be used to keep the mule on the right track if necessary, or as a weapon to defend oneself from attacks by sheep dogs, or even wolves or wild boar. This forked stick was a peddler's most valuable tool.

The mailman was quite nervous on his first day in his new job. Thinking that the mail that day was not too heavy, he didn't unload the mule when he took a rest on a piece of flat ground by the road near the Akkise Bridge. In this half-hour stop, he gave the mule food and hay, and, after performing his noonday prayers, he ate his own meal.

Walking at a fast, even pace when he reached Seydişehir, it was dark. The government offices and, of course, the mail office had long since closed. He couldn't deliver the mailbags to the official in charge. He stopped off at a wayside inn, where he rented a place to sleep, then he tied the mule up in the stable and fed and watered it. While he was doing this, his eyes and ears were on his sacks, not knowing whether the innkeeper was to be trusted or not. He filled his belly with the food that was left. He covered himself with the coat he had spread by his sacks at the foot of the wall, and fell into an uneasy sleep, ready to wake at any minute.

The next morning, he woke early at the usual time. He watered the mule and filled its hay bag, said his prayers, and had his morning meal. At ten to nine, he was waiting with his laden mule in front of the Seydişehir Mail Office for the official to arrive.

After delivering the mailbags he had carried there, the mule mailman received the mailbags ready for Bozkır. He repeated the same procedure for hiding the mailbags that he had carried out at Bozkır. After loading the mail onto the mule, he passed by the bakery in order to buy a hot loaf for his lunch that day before starting to walk back along the road to Bozkır.

After walking for six hours, Mailman Rahim gave himself a half-hour stop to rest and eat. Wherever he found a convenient well or fountain along the road, he satisfied his own thirst and the mule's. Occasionally, he would meet an acquaintance, a peddler like himself, and exchange greetings.

Mailman Rahim, a postman of the Republic of Turkey

No accidents or incidents happened on the first journey there and back, and Mailman Rahim got to Bozkır at nine in the evening. On leaving the road, he did what he had been told to do by the director, and went straight to the house close by the post office and knocked on the door. İhsan Bey was very affable. After saying a few kind words to the mailman, he took delivery of the mailbags. "Rahim Efendi, Godspeed to your feet and those of your mule. You must both be tired. Off you go to your own house in the village and rest. Come back at nine tomorrow morning to pick up the mail."

"Sir," said the mule mailman, "it may be dangerous to get to Seydişehir after nightfall. Winter's not here yet, but when it rains a lot, the canal can overflow and damage the road. I want to get there before dark. Give me the mailbags now. I'll take them to the village and set out from home at dawn. And if I take a shortcut by going through Dere and Ahırlı, I can reach Seydişehir before it gets dark."

"Not this time," said Mail Office Director İhsan. "Come here at nine o'clock tomorrow morning. I spoke with the governor today. There are important documents that must get there quickly. They'll be ready by nine o'clock tomorrow morning. Come then, and we'll do what you suggest for the following journeys."

Mailman Rahim said, "Thank you, Mr. Director, but I've a favor to ask of you. If you'd write a letter to the director at Seydişehir to ask if I could collect the mail from there in the evening, too, it would be a good thing."

"I'll do that," the mail office director replied. "Good night to you, then."

Rahim thanked him and mounted his mule. He knew the dirt road to Çat village, five kilometers up the mountain, so well that he took no notice of the coal-black dark, but set off following the river, patting his mule and making encouraging sounds as they went along.

At that late hour, the road was peaceful. The sound of his mule's feet striking the stones mingled with the constant murmur of the flowing river below and the intermittent song of a night bird. As he passed close by the Mantaki Mill and, later, the North and South Mills, the noise of the water rushing through the millrace disturbed the silence of the night. He was glad to hear this, as it meant he was nearing home. The mule mailman, impatient to reach his house, clicked his tongue to encourage his mule to go faster. He thought about the director's considerate behavior, wondering what benefits he could gain from getting to Seydişehir in daylight.

"I went yesterday, Monday, and returned on Tuesday. I'll go again tomorrow, Wednesday, and I'll come back Thursday. Thursday's market day in Seydişehir. If the mail I bring isn't heavy, maybe I can find goods at a reasonable price at the market there; if I go early, then I can sell them for a profit at the Friday market in Bozkır. In any case, I don't have to travel on Friday, Saturday, or Sunday." Turning these ideas over in his mind, he reached his house.

All the children were asleep. Rahim's wife, Karakaşli, placed freshly cooked cracked wheat pilaf, a mug of ayran, a small dish of grape syrup, and flatbread softened in water on the sofra, a special cloth, in front of him. Rahim filled his stomach to bursting, recounting at the same time the doings of his two-day journey to his wife. He told her to go to the stable and give the mule some hay. After his long journey, he hadn't the energy to do it himself, and, as soon as his head hit the pillow on his pallet on the floor, he fell into a deep sleep.

Mailman Rahim knew that his journeys with the mail to Seydişehir would not always be as easy as pulling hair out of butter, and accidents might happen. As the days grew shorter and he had to travel by night, he started to carry a gun, even though it was illegal and unregistered. He told only the mail director, Mr. İhsan, and Truckman Ali of his need to carry the pistol, which he had kept ever since he was a young man. In fact, it wasn't long before he had to shoot one of three sheepdogs that attacked him near Yalıhüyük village.

The canal, built to take the overflow from the large reservoir at Beyşehir Lake to irrigate the Konya plains, ran parallel to the eastern bank of Soğla Lake. In years when rainfall was heavy, the canal overflowed; a sluice directed the extra water to Soğla Lake. It was still possible for the canal to overflow. Once, when there was continuous heavy rain, the canal overflowed and tore up the road. In order to cross the knee-high water, the mailman mounted his mule to cross from one side of the flood to the other. That day, he counted himself lucky that his mule was young and strong.

There were years when Soğla Lake froze over when it was bitterly cold in the depths of winter. One day, it snowed without stopping after the mule mailman left Bozkır. Four hours later, the road along the lake was covered with snow and impossible to distinguish. There was fog that day as well. Trusting that the mule knew exactly where the road went, poking the snow with his forked stick every three or four minutes to find the graveled surface, the mailman endeavored to continue along the road. Once, when he poked the snow and did not strike gravel, he stopped immediately. He used his stick a little further on, but he still didn't find gravel. With fear in his heart, and using his hand this time to dig the snow, he found a layer of ice. He realized he was on the lake. "God save me! Oh, Hızır, come!" he murmured in fearful prayer, but he calmly took hold of the mule's halter and retraced his footsteps. This time, he found the graveled road. He had really had a scare. He continued on his way, poking the snow more often in order not to miss the road. Late that night, he arrived at Seydişehir.

In spite of this and other similar difficulties, the mailman of the Republic of Turkey went on delivering the mail from Bozkır to Seydişehir, and bringing the mail for Bozkır back from there. For years, Mailman Rahim, who had neither health insurance nor pension, kept the frightening events of that day a secret from his wife and children.

One Friday afternoon in the spring of that year, Mailman Rahim set a city-dressed lady on the back of his mule and took her to his house in the village. He told his wife, "This lady, Emine Hanım, the wife of the mail office director, is curious to know what life in the village is like. She'll be our guest for two days."

Their house consisted of a single room, which the family—husband, wife, and children—slept in at night and used during the day. Without batting an eyelid, Karakaşli set to work on thinking of how to host a lady. First, she welcomed her guest with open arms and sat her down on the best cushion in the house, then she quickly kneaded some dough and filled the pastry with thinly sliced onions and keş, a nonfat crumbly white cheese. She lit the hearth and began to make keşli ekmek or gözleme, a kind of filled pancake, and baked it on the round tin sheet placed over the fire. We children sat looking at our visitor in silence, our eyes delighted but shy. The visitor's face and hands were very white, her hair was combed, and her dress very clean. Turning our eyes toward the floor, we tried to answer the questions she asked us.

The keşli ekmek my mother was spreading with salted butter was not the usual crescent shape, but cut into small, elegant triangles. It was obvious she was making great efforts in order not to embarrass herself in front of the lady from the city. It was obvious from her hospitable manner that she was proud to have a house guest from the city, thinking, The owner of a mule is respected and honored. An important person would not go to any ordinary home as a guest.

Our guest, Emine Hanım, was a talkative lady with a sweet voice. She asked questions about all the objects visible in the room, the jars buried in the wall, the floor, the ceiling, the curtained store cupboard hidden in the wall, and the wash place—in fact, everything that caught her interest. She seemed very content with the information.

That evening, Mother spread a double pallet on the floor for our guest. That night, we all slept together on pallets laid on the floor of the room.

The next day, the neighbors we regarded as our relatives, on seeing or hearing that we had a guest, came to welcome the lady from the city, and stayed for a short while. Some of those brought food to offer to the special guest.

Emine Hanım spent the whole day, partly inside the house, partly on the flat roof in front, talking to the neighbors who came and went. She asked for information about the things that interested her and answered the questions of those who were curious about her. The thing that our village women were most curious about was how city women did not become pregnant and have children so often as the women in the village. Many of them voiced their complaints, saying, "I'm tired of giving birth." The lady who came from the city seemed to them like a representative of the government. As though trying to find a remedy for their helplessness, each of them explained her own problems, woman to woman. They listened to the advice Emine Hanım gave. When they left, some of them were pleased, and some of them wrinkled up their noses, saying, "Our men?"

That evening, when our mothers and elder sisters courageously shared the information they had learned with their husbands, they heard a lot of colorful swear words directed at that lady from the city. Naturally, the wives were silenced and did not open their mouths again, but set themselves to work once more, resigned to their lot of bearing a child every other year, however fed up they might be.

Our guest, Emine Hanım, was pleased with her visit to the village. On the second day, she went with my mother to visit relatives in different neighborhoods of the village. This city lady spent another night with us, sleeping on the floor in our one room.

The next morning, my father set her on the mule and took Emine Hanım back to her house in Bozkır. When he came home, he made my mother happy, telling her he was pleased with the way she had shown respect and hospitality to their special guest. My mother also was happy, thinking she had entertained the guest well, and had pleased the mail office director. They hoped that in the coming fall, the job of mailman would be given to my father again.

At last, the weather began to warm up. The road from Bozkır to Konya was open once more. Buses and trucks came and went without interruption. As a result, the mail could come and go five days a week by a motorized vehicle. Mule Mailman Rahim, who had carried the mail all winter long with great effort and confidence without losing anything, was offered the job of carrying the mail by bus daily throughout the summer. This offer included a free bus ticket, as well as the same wages, so Rahim accepted it, hoping to be given the right to carry the mail the next winter too.

In fact, this offer fell in with Rahim's wishes. In summer, the mule did not work for at least two months. Every year in the middle of May, the mule was turned to graze—that is, taken to the highland pastures and set free. It was an old Turkish custom to set horses and mules free for at least two months of the summer to roam the mountain valleys and plains in order to recover their health. In these two months of complete freedom, grazing half wild, a stallion that accompanied the horses and mules performed its duty of herding them as one family, and they spent the summer filling their bellies and wandering over the upland pastures.

Mailman Rahim had no vineyard, garden, or field in the village worth speaking of, or bringing in any income, nor any herd of sheep or goats grazing on the upland pastures. While the mule was out to graze, he had work to do. He would go with a donkey to buy goods as cheaply as he could and exchange them for other things in other villages; in other words, he endeavored to earn a living by bartering. The job as a salaried mailman had come just when it was needed. Since he didn't deliver mail on Saturdays and Sundays, he was able to stay in the village and plant vegetables and tend vines on his small plot of land.

First, he took his wife and young children, the oldest being still only nine years old, to the yayla, the upland pastures, together with the cow and its calf and four Manavgat goats with kids. He said to his wife, "Hasan is in his tenth year. If need be, he can come and go from the village. But the other three, Ayşe, Mehmet, and Hayriye, must stay on the yayla, playing safely in the fresh air for two or three months. And if you let them look after the cow, that would be good too. Store up some of the butter for us to eat during the winter. That way, all summer long, we'll have ayran from the buttermilk."

Before letting the mule free to graze, Rahim brought two loads of firewood and kindling from the Aygır Wood and piled it in front of the one-room cabin house on the upland pasture. He didn't think it fit for his wife with a child in her lap to go into the forest, like most of the other women, and return carrying bundles of firewood on her back.

During the summer of 1950, he carried mail to and from Konya five days a week. The mail sacks contained letters, documents, packets, and even bags of money needed by the Ziraat Bank, the only bank in the district at the time. Whenever Rahim was required to carry a lot of cash, the mail office director insisted Rahim carry the bag stuffed with notes under his arm, even when getting on and off the bus, and he never let go of it until he had delivered it to the proper mail office.

One time, the bus broke down on the hill at Kışla. Everyone had to get off the bus and push. The postman joined in with the cash mailbag tucked tightly under his arm. In answer to the questions of other travelers, curious to know what he was carrying, after uttering a well-chosen oath, Rahim replied, "The letters of officials whose wives are . . . I don't know, constantly writing important documents and sending them to Ankara." In this way, he passed over questions that were outside his line of duty. He wasn't about to tell anyone that the packet he called "documents" contained a thick bundle of notes totaling exactly sixty thousand liras. After he had given up being a mailman, he told us this story, saying it was a day he'd never forget, adding the well-known saying, "It is better to be safe. Can the sea catch on fire? It is possible."

That summer, for the first time, Hasan was given an important responsibility. On Saturday or Sunday, according to what was needed, Rahim would load the donkey with flour, salt, matches, and fruit and vegetables, and send it up to his wife and children at the upland pastures. The road from Çat village to the yayla, also known as Yellow Grass Yayla, was mostly a hilly footpath going through narrow-necked passes. It took at least three hours on foot. One late-afternoon, trusting in the long hours of daylight, Rahim set Hasan behind the donkey loaded with two sacks. "Off you go, son. Make the donkey hurry and get the flour to the upland pastures before dark. Spend the night there. Tell your mother to get a goatskin of ayran or buttermilk and bring it back here tomorrow evening." Then he went off to the mosque for the late afternoon prayers.

Sacks of flour being taken to the upland pastures

As he was going to the mosque, Rahim didn't notice that clouds were gathering in the sky. When prayers were over, he realized that the sky was quite overcast. Since he had been out of the village during the week, he had missed gossiping with his friends after prayers, so he began chatting with some of them. He began by saying with some anxiety, "An hour ago, I sent Hasan up to the yayla with a donkey loaded with two sacks of flour."

Ali, the master potter, exclaimed, "What did you say, my friend? Look at the weather! It looks like it'll rain heavily. Even if you don't care about the flour, have a care for your son. I hope to God he won't get caught in a flood and run into difficulties."

Rahim, without any hesitation, took the road to the yayla at a trot.

This is how Hasan tells his side of the story:

After Father had loaded the flour, I set off with the donkey in front of me. I was very happy. You see, I was going to the yayla. I was thinking of how much I would enjoy the next day there. My closest friends in the village, Vehbi and Bahri, had stayed at Eski Yurt Yayla for a long time. Eski Yurt wasn't very far from Oba, the summer place of our particular village, and whenever I went up to the yayla, I would always visit them and enjoy playing with them. We loved to swim in the icy-cold waters of the lake, avoiding the dangerous sinkholes where the water seemed to spiral into the underground, and especially when the water level was high. Sometimes we enjoyed collecting mushrooms and sweet saffron on Esenek Mountain. With dreams of this in mind, I made the loaded donkey in front of me hurry, and took the winding road going to Uluyol,

Quail Falls, and the lower bridge to cross the Yayla River. At the foot of Yuvalca Hill, the loaded donkey slowed down. I noticed that the sky had suddenly become dark, but I continued going. When I got to the top of the hill and reached the narrow pass called the Big Rock, it began to drizzle. Suddenly, everywhere was lit by a flash of lightning. A terrific roll of thunder followed. It was as dark as night, and I got very frightened.

All at once, the dreams in my head turned upside down. If it rains very hard, the valleys of Çötü and Dördoluk will be flooded and I won't be able to cross, I worried, thinking that in the dark, a monster might come, and the two sacks of flour would be wasted if they got wet. I took the donkey's halter and turned back. Clicking my tongue and brandishing my stick, I began to hurry the donkey along. The road back to the village sloped downward, which helped the laden animal go faster. When I got to the top of Quail Falls, I saw my father coming toward me like the wind. The first words out of his mouth were, "Hey there, my clever boy, you're your father's son." Hurrying the donkey homeward, Father made me happy with his praise. His sweet words were like a warm embrace, and rang in my ears for years.

Before the rain turned to streaming torrents, we ran through the streets and reached our home. My father unloaded the somewhat-damp flour sacks and took them into the house. After putting the flour into dry sacks, he decided that I should go to the high pastures in daylight the next day. My father found me another job to do as well. When I got to the pastures the next day, he told me I was to put some salt on a plate, find where our mule had strayed to, and make the animal lick the salt off the plate. The flesh of a grazing animal gets flabby, but it gets fuller and firmer if you give it salt. Of course, that waylaid my plans of finding my friends and playing with them.

In the villages, the heat of summer only lasted two months. During this time, the grass on the high-plateau pastures, at first plentiful, loses its strength, partly from the many animals grazing there, and also from the lack of rain and the mountain springs becoming completely dry. The upland pastures become an arid mountaintop, and everyone gets ready to return as soon as possible to the village.

By the middle of August, most of the people had left the upland pastures for the village. A week later, Rahim went to bring the mule back from grazing and brought his family back home too. In two and a half months, the children had almost forgotten the village, and when they got to Quail Hill and saw it in the distance, they became very excited. Those who returned from doing military service, or from studying in a distant city, or people who come for a visit after a long trip had the same feeling when they saw their beloved village.

Rahim continued to carry the Bozkır-Konya mail safely by bus or, alarmingly, by open truck with only a guardrail. On returning home one Friday evening, he brought his wife and children some news, which at a first didn't seem of much interest to them.

"The mail office director's son, Yilmaz, finished university and is now a lawyer. He's going to open an office in Bozkır. Truckman Ali has a beautiful young daughter called Sevim. There was an understanding between the two families that the two young people would make a match of it, and for the last three years, they have been seeing each other semiofficially. This fall, they're going to get married, it seems."

Karakaşli said something like, "Good luck to them. But what is it to us?"

"You're invited to the wedding. This is your invitation. Take it."

"The director says we'll be invited to the wedding. It's not just words, he's going to send a man here to announce it according to the custom."

"That's all very well," said his wife, "but there's a big price to pay for being invited to the wedding for all to hear of our being favored and honored like that. We don't know much about city customs. I wonder what kind of gift would be acceptable," she said.

Rahim replied, "First let the crier come and announce it, and then we'll think about a suitable present."

The Saturday following, a stranger rode into the village on a horse that carried a decorated saddlebag. After asking, "Which is the Mailman Rahim's house?" he arrived at our door. Without dismounting, he said, "Uncle Rahim, on Sunday next week, you are invited to the wedding at the mail office director's house. This is your invitation." He took a nice water glass from the saddlebag and held it out to my father.

Just then, some nearby neighbors, looking with interest at the stranger, called from the roof, "What's happening?"

Mailman Rahim took the glass and handed it to his wife. "Thank you, nephew. Come, let's go inside. Let me offer you something to eat and we can have a drink of tea," he offered, but the young man said, "I've got Dere, Sorkun, and Ahırlı to go to yet, so I must be off now. Thanks all the same." And he went on his way.

After the young man had gone, the mailman and his wife, in answer to their curious neighbors' questions, told them in a pleased but somewhat embarrassed way that they were invited to the wedding in Bozkır. They knew it would be a cause for envy, but it was natural that both of them felt proud to have been invited.

That evening, husband and wife had a long talk about what present to give. "What would be suitable? What would be most needed at a wedding?" they wondered. The wedding was likely to be crowded, and a huge amount of meat and rice, as well as other food, would be needed. What could they offer that would be most useful? they wondered. Finally, they decided to give a well-fed kid. They didn't have one themselves, so they would buy one from Mehmet the Shepherd.

Three days before the wedding, Mehmet the Shepherd came in the evening with a year-old kid with a shining black coat, and horns not yet completely curled, walking by his side as he held it gently by the scruff of its neck. After bargaining, my father got the kid for twenty-seven liras. Before leaving, Mehmet the Shepherd gave strict instructions on how to treat the kid. "Goats don't like to be tied when they're walking. Let the kid walk in front of you when you take it to Bozkır. When going through a crowded place, take it gently by the scruff of its neck. Don't shut it up in the stable at night. Goats don't like to be closed in. Tie it up outside the barn with a loose rope around the bottom of its horns and throw down some fresh oak leaves for it to eat."

When morning came, we gave the kid some fresh grass. We had our breakfast of fresh cracked wheat pilaf, buttermilk, and green onions. Then Father said to me, "Hasan, my son, today it's your job to take the young goat to Bozkır and deliver it to the house of the mail office director. Don't hurry. Let the kid graze where there's good grass at the side of the road. Don't let it stray. When its belly is full, it will be easier to manage. You know the director's house. He may not be at home. Say to his wife, Emine Hanım, 'My father and mother send their greetings. This kid is our wedding gift.' Put this money in your pocket. When you've delivered the kid, buy two loaves from the market and half a kilo of Karagaç halva. Tie them up in your handkerchief. Come home without wasting time on the road."

I held the goat by the scruff until I got clear of the village. I let it go free when we reached the road to Bozkır, and as I shooed it along, it grazed here and there at the roadside until two hours later—an hour longer than usual—we arrived in Bozkır. When we got to the mail office director's house, I saw a lot of activity and other villagers with loaded animals. I guessed that these people were also invited to the wedding. A man from Asarlık village was unloading two big baskets of fresh grapes. Someone from Farit village was waiting to empty the two large baskets of tomatoes, cucumbers, and eggplant he had brought. Another from Karaca Ardıç had brought a donkey loaded with dry wood, and was busy chopping it into a suitable size to go on the fire under the cookpots. At the foot of the wall, a goat was eating grass by the side of the road. It was obvious that someone else besides us had brought the present of an animal as meat for the feast.

The wedding gift

The women preparing for the wedding feast were looking after those who came with presents. A woman who saw me come up to the door with the kid and said, "Come, my child, let's see, who have you come from?"

"I'm from Çat village," I replied. "My father's Rahim the Mailman. I've come to see Emine Hanım."

Overhearing our talk, Emine Hanım came over, gave me a pat on the head, and said, "Welcome, son."

"My father and mother send their greetings to you, my lady. I've brought our wedding gift," I told her.

"Well done, my dear," she said, and told one of the helpers to take the kid and tie it up with the other goat. Then she turned to me and said, "Wait a bit, don't go away. Just wait here for me," and she went into the house.

I was looking around, wondering whether, as in our village, the bride and her attendants would mount their horses and parade through the streets of Bozkır, when Emine Hanım reappeared. In one hand, she held a sandwich of soft flatbread as white as snow. You could see how round it was, suggesting there was a lot of filling inside it. In her other hand, she held a large bunch of plump, sweet-tasting red grapes, not suitable for making grape molasses, but best when eaten fresh. "Here, take these, my child, and eat them on your way home. Give my greetings to your parents and say thank you for me," she said.

Inside the bread was crumbly white cheese; I took a bite. The wonderful smell of the soft white bread and cheese, and the glorious taste of the two fresh grapes I was eating, was something not to be forgotten.

A bunch of grapes

    Two days later, my father, mother, and I went to Bozkır for the wedding. At that time, it was thought shameful for a woman to ride a horse or mule inside the village. My mother mounted the mule after we left the village and my father and I walked along together. When we got to Bozkır, Father tied the mule up in the stable of a man he knew and trusted. Together, we arrived at the house for the wedding. The crowd consisted mostly of families of the officials living in Bozkır, and we also noticed, on seeing their clothes, quite a number of invitees from other villages. Mother went to the place for women and we didn't see her again until after the wedding was over.

    Many people had gathered on the level space outside the house. There, the men watched the special dances of our area, performed by talented dancers and accompanied by the music celebrating the wedding. I noticed some women were watching from the balconies and windows above. While Turkish folk songs such as "Kozan Mountain," "Young Osman," "Saffet Efendi," "On the Karaman Hills," and "Mevlana" were being sung and local melodies played, the host invited the guests to sit down at the low tables of round copper trays on which the food was spread.

Father and I sat down at a table on the second floor of the house. We first ate a hearty portion of buttery cracked wheat pilaf with meat, and then stuffed peppers and tomatoes tasting quite different from those in the village. For sweets, a kind of white pudding was brought out. Those in the know said it was rice pudding. My father, who loved sweet, buttery food, liked this pudding a lot. It was too sweet for me. I took a spoonful and that was enough. The pudding was made with rice, sugar, and milk. Later, coffee was given to the adults while the children had lemonade. It was the first time I had tasted this sour drink, and I liked it very much.

When the meal was finished, we heard that it was time to fetch the bride. We went outside. There was a highly decorated bus and two open trucks waiting in front of the house. Some of the women climbed into the bus. The men and a great number of us children filled the open backs of the trucks used to carry goods. This was the most exciting part of the wedding: the caravan going from the bridegroom's house to bring the bride home. The three vehicles carrying adults and children did not go directly to the intended destination—the bride's house—however; it went through all kinds of streets and alleyways while sounding the horns, while people on the open trucks were yelling, "Amen! Amen!"

This was the first time I had ridden in a motor vehicle. Rushing through the narrow streets in the truck, blaring its horn at street corners, was better than my wildest dreams. The local children from Bozkır, recognizable from the clothes they were wearing, were all excited too.

We watched with interest the mock arguments and bargaining, like what sort of special gifts the future mother-in-law would promise to give the bride as gifts, that went on before the bride would come outside to leave her parents' house. Then, when the bride, gorgeously dressed, left her parents' house with a coy expression of reluctance, and, accompanied by everyone's good wishes, stepped toward the bus, a shower of coins and sweets were thrown in the air. For us children, collecting up the money and sweets that fell to the ground was the best part of the wedding.

The wedding celebrations ended and we returned home. Mother described what she had seen at the wedding many times. She was particularly impressed by the experience of drinking coffee after the meal.

In the women's area, Mother observed that everyone turned their coffee cup upside down after drinking their coffee. This must be the custom here, she thought, and did likewise. This was the first time in her life that she had seen people read fortunes from their coffee cups and she enjoyed it. The fortune-teller, a lady from the city, who picked up each of the overturned coffee cups in turn, interpreted the coffee grounds inside the little cup, predicting what would happen in the future of the family of that lady. Mother said that when the fortune-teller woman picked up her cup, she asked, "What did you wish for, sister?"

Quite bewildered, Mother said, "I don't know. I just thought this was the custom here, so I copied you ladies by turning my cup upside down."

The fortune-teller turned Mother's cup up and said, "Oh well, let's tell your fortune too." She must have known that my mother had come from the village and was the mailman's wife. In order to make this little village woman happy, she said, "You're going to be given a great opportunity by the government."

Mother went on telling this story of a fortune in the coffee grounds for the rest of her life. According to her, what the fortune-teller told her came true. Mother declared that the opportunity she wished for was not that her husband should keep his job as mailman. "The wish the fortune-teller told me would come true did so when, three years later, son, you passed the exam to go to the Ereğli; that is, İvriz Village Institute," she said.

For three years, Father went on being the mule mailman, carrying the mail for the Turkish Republic Mail Office in Bozkır. Then, in order to keep it open during the winter, the State Highways Department improved the road between Bozkır and Konya, and Mailman Rahim's job came to an end. For years, he went on telling the adventures, some trying, some dangerous, he had lived through in the winters on the road between Bozkır and Seydişehir. "I carried the mail with my mule for three years," he would say. Children born after he gave this job up were the ones who most loved to listen to stories of his adventures.

The Mule Mailman

Neither foul, wintry weather,
nor floods or fiercest frost,
nor chattering teeth
can stop him on his way.
He is the mailman of Bozkır
in charge of seventy-two villages;
a responsible mailman
with his pack beast, the mule.
He puts on rough shoes
and his gaiters of wool,
winds a scarf
around his throat and his head,
puts a flat cap on top of them all;
with warm fleece and mittens,
takes a forked stick in hand,
walking in front of his mule
without stopping,
finding his way.
Twelve hours to his goal:
mail in the saddlebags,
roped tight to the saddle,
delivered on time
to the Turkish Post Office.

Rahim, the mule mailmen, a postman of the Turkish Republic

Guardians of the Black-Pea Field

1
I Start School

Even if I talked for days about our life in the year 1949, the tale would still not end. I was in primary school. Our instructor was a man called Sergeant Mahmud. Perhaps because he was one of the most well-built men in the village, people called him either "Tall Mahmud" or "Big Mahmud," whichever fit the situation. He had been a sergeant in the military and had taken part in the special instructor training program in 1940. He had little knowledge, but, as he was a terrifyingly strict disciplinarian, he was known as a good teacher. He was addressed as "Hoca," teacher, or Sergeant Mahmud by the villagers. Father was very pleased when I was put in Mahmud's class. The other instructor, Sergeant Hamit, similarly trained, was known among the villagers as a teacher who lacked discipline. Hamit did not beat or belittle his students but, when scolding mischievous students, contented himself by calling them "miserable donkeys."

Both these teachers came from our village. They were responsible for teaching the first and second grades in turn. So whichever teacher was assigned to a child when they started first grade would be the one to teach them in second grade as well unless the child was held back a year. In those days, unless there was some pressing reason, no one repeated a grade. In fact, all the children my age were registered at school when it was Instructor Hamit's year. In September, the head teacher, Mehmed

Kekik, known otherwise as Black Hasan's son, would take a pen and notebook in hand, call the drummer, and begin to register the children. Starting from the lowest neighborhood of Karagaç and attracting the children by the rhythmic beat of the drum, he would write down in his register the names of all the children who were over six years old. The teacher would wait for the children to arrive and encourage them to join in the procession consisting of himself, the drummer, and one of the village watchmen. From time to time, simultaneous cries of "Amen!" combined with laughter made the ever-growing crowd of children about to start school even more excited.

Meanwhile, the mothers who didn't want their children registered that year cajoled the head teacher to put it off until the following year. One would say, "Our daughter is too old. We've gotten her engaged. Before the year's out, she'll be given to a husband. Don't write her down, Hoca." When the watchmen reminded them of the law and the punishment involved, they speedily gave up their requests. But it still happened that some children, such as an orphan girl seen to be without the few coins needed to buy a notebook and pencil, would be passed over by the teacher and the guardian without being registered.

Back in September 1947, when the procession to register the children came near our house in Çat, after going through Karagaç, Ahmetli, Ömerli, and Cingiller, the excitement and uproar had greatly increased. My friends from the neighborhood—Bahri, Vehbi, Abidin, Molla Ali's son Kerim, Sergeant Halim's son Bekir, Kezban's son Ali, and others—had registered and joined the throng. It was our house's turn. When the teacher called out my name and was about to write it down, my mother objected, saying in a brave voice with great authority, "My son is still too young. He can't go to school this year."

Teacher Kekik said, "Very well, Karakaşli," and put off registering me for school that year. However, according to what I had understood from my father and mother's conversations, I was in my seventh year then. It was true, I was undersized and skinny, but I knew that the real reason was that Mother was happy to have my help as a babysitter. My brother Mehmet was still a baby. While Mother was weaving, there was only me to look after him. My sister, Kadın—it was only years later that I learned her real name was Ayşe—was not old enough to look after a child. She was about five and a half, and Mehmet was three years younger. Mother had to see that her three children were clothed and fed, as well as weave the white broadcloth and striped calico. When she was at the loom, setting up the warp threads, winding the bobbins, or doing the washing by the river, it was my job to keep the baby quiet. This meant I couldn't begin my schooling in Instructor Hamit's year.

A year later, in September 1948, a little taller and more developed and well aware of my responsibilities, I began primary school in Instructor Mahmud's class.

2
Hasan Çelik, Monitor

Before starting school, I already knew how to add and multiply small numbers. I used to listen with an attentive ear to my mother counting the warp threads while weaving, and the conversations my father had about numbers and calculations connected with trading. I must have given the right answers to the questions Instructor Mahmud asked about numbers, since before I had been at school a month, he made me the class monitor.

Tall Mahmud, who had a large family, was an instructor, not a real teacher, so he received a very small salary. It was impossible for him to look after his family on that salary. He owned a share of one of the felting devices that turned by using the powerful flow of swift running water. He also had a garden and vineyard that produced enough fruit and vegetables to feed his family.

When I was made monitor, my first responsibility was to take care of the classroom key, and arrived at school early each day to open the door. When school was over, I locked the door and hung the key on a string around my neck so as not to lose it. I also had to check the students who came late to our class and beat their hand with a small stick; direct two to three students to sweep the classroom at the end of the class; and inspect the piece of wood each child had to bring during the winter months, then light the stove. Sometimes I needed to go to the principal's office to get the chalk needed for our classroom.

Every school day, Instructor Mahmud would come to school in the morning, spend fifteen to twenty minutes making us read and recite spellings, then say, "Hasan Çelik, continue doing this. Everyone will read in turn, and everyone will learn the multiplication table, or I'll break their heads." Then he would leave and attend to his own business.

While I was in first grade, I made my friends read and I also played a lot of mischievous tricks. The first-grade students studied in a large room on the ground floor of a two-story building that we called the People's House, built by the villagers. The older kids were right across the river from us, in the primary school for grades two to five, which was also built by the villagers in early 1940s. To cross over the Ulu River, which we also called the Dere River, that ran between the People's House and the primary school, there was Kemer Bridge, built by the Seljuks, or maybe left by the Romans. About fifty or sixty meters beyond the two school buildings, the Dere River joined another river, the Yayla River, and together they flowed down to Bozkır. In order to cross these joined rivers and get to the neighborhoods on the other side, there was another bridge called the Wooden Bridge. In the spring, these rivers would flood. As the incline was steep, the waters rushed downward in torrents of foam. The villagers called this a bird-catching flood. There was no handrail on either the Kemer Bridge or the Wooden Bridge. Our mothers would warn us, "When you cross the bridge, don't walk on the side. Keep to the middle." But for us children, it was very exciting to look from the bridge above at the foaming water rushing below us.

We used to cut the branches of the big willows and poplar trees growing alongside the rivers and make a variety of toys for ourselves. The main ones were popguns, whistles made out of young willow tree branches, whips, sticks for "Hurling the Stick," spinners, and spinning tops. There wasn't a single ball at the school. If there had been, it would have fallen into one of the rivers and disappeared. But almost every boy had a pocketknife. There were about fifteen to twenty blacksmiths in the village at that time, earning enough to support their families. When I was four or five, a blacksmith who came to our house to ask a favor from my father brought a pocketknife as a gift. My father put this under my pillow while I was sleeping. I was delighted when I found it the next morning. At my first opportunity, I went outside, cut a stick, and started to carve it. Of course, I immediately cut my hand. Mother simply pressed salt on the bleeding wound and told me to be more careful; that was all. If you cut your hand and it bled, or hurt your head in a fight, most mothers did not worry too much. Fathers, upon hearing about it, contented themselves with getting angry.

During recess, we children from Çat would get into fierce snowball fights against the children from the neighborhoods of Ahmetli and Karagaç, continuing until our hands were frozen. When we had to move fast, we would take off the overly large plastic shoes on our feet. Because of that, I sometimes played in the snow in my inner leather shoes. Of course, the thin leather shoes got very wet. Later, when I went inside the classroom, I would put them by the stove to dry. I didn't know how long to dry them, so new shoes lasted less than two months. I remember how Father cursed the people who made and sold such bad leather shoes. Of course, I never told anyone at home that I had played in the snow in those shoes and then dried them next to the stove. At such a time, Father would not neglect to scold me, or the siblings who followed as the years went by, saying, "I'm sick of hearing about your feet, your back, your notebooks, and your pencils."

In the spring of 1949, when I was the first-grade monitor in the earthen-floored classroom in the People's House, the fun and games I enjoyed there made me happy, and, quite often, rather than going home after school, I would stay and play. There were many times I was so involved in the game that I forgot to go home. On the days that I was late to arrive home because of this, I felt a little guilty. Anyway, according to our fathers, mothers, and even neighbors, children attending school did not think about working. "Just when they could have been of some use, that cursed school makes our children idle," some fathers would complain. They would mock our schooling, saying things like, "Those who go to school only learn about bugs and birds, mules and donkeys. They don't even know how to say a prayer." When I heard things like "What's the use of what you learn at that school of yours? Sheep, goat, donkey, stallion," I used to get very upset, but couldn't say anything.

As soon as I came home from school, there was always a job for me to do. If there were animals in the stable, they had to be fed and watered. If there was a flock coming home with the shepherd from grazing, I had to go and find our animals. I had to prepare wood for the stove in the evening, chopping it into sticks if necessary, or bring drinking water from the village fountain.

Although the schools were supposed to stay open until the end of May, in the villages, they would close at the end of April. In the spring, planting the fields and gardens as well as looking after and taking care of the goats and kids, sheep and lambs, and cows and calves were the responsibilities given to children, and the National School Authorities gave permission for village schools to close early. After the Children's Festival on April twenty-third, very few of the children who looked after animals, or whose families went early to the summer pastures, would attend school.

3
Will We Go to the Yayla?

Our family had a good breed of cow that year, although in the spring, she had no calf, as either she had miscarried or the calf had died. The previous fall and winter, we had not held on to an animal or even two, such as a goat or a kid. Unlike the other children, we had neither calf nor kid to be a source of joy that spring, and my siblings and I envied our neighbors. We were jealous of my friends, Bahri and Vehbi, who were able to cuddle their lambs. In fact, when the mother of Vehbi's kid died giving birth and one of his sheep miscarried, everyone in the neighborhood admired the way he persuaded the sheep to adopt the motherless kid. When the flock returned at night, it was great fun to see how the orphaned kid, running and bleating "Ma-a-a," found the sheep calling "Ba-a-a," and began to suckle.

In spite of having no calf, our cow had plenty of milk. Mother made a mash with potato, onion, vegetable peelings, or rotting vegetables, putting all these in a large pot, adding water, and boiling them all up together with a little bran. Every day, the cow would enjoy drinking five or six liters of this "vegetable soup." Mother would say the cow gave plentiful milk because she fed her with this watery mash. This plenty consisted of one liter of milk at night and one in the morning. While drinking the warm soup, the cow would relax, and that made the milk flow. My mother would talk to the cow in a rhythmic voice when milking her, and calm the animal with her words. I remember well how my father used to talk in a caressing voice to our mule, the most important pack animal, when loading it. Even though I was a child, I thought it strange that these were the same people who could comfortably scold their children for even the slightest mistake. It must have taken years of experience for them not to grudge any effort in raising and keeping alive the domestic animals that were of such great use to them. All those in their right minds knew the saying, "People who treat their animals badly will pay for it. If you once frighten an animal, especially a cow or a mule, it will not be easy to make use of it again."

Sheep, goats, cows, and calves could not be kept in the village during summer months. The planted crops, the vineyards, gardens, and fields of grass for hay were not there to be grazed on. Those families who had cows with calves would either go to the yayla, the summer pastures, for three months of summer, or would ask a relative or neighbor who moved to the yayla for the season if they could look after the cow. In return, the caregiver would get a half share in the proceeds—the butter, cheese, etc., made with the milk from that cow. Even if it were possible to find an honest person to share your cow with, no one would look after an animal entrusted to her as if it were her own.

The children left in the village during the summer months would be a different problem. Apart from the children of the three or four families who had gardens or vineyards to attend to, the other children would involve themselves in all kinds of mischief. Saying they were going to fish or swim in the river, the boys would dive into this or that garden, steal and eat whatever they found, and do great harm to what they didn't eat. They would stamp on the windfalls under the fruit trees, and grub up the roots in the gardens, saying they were looking for cucumbers, and the plants would wither. They would pick unripe corn cobs and throw them away, and scatter or cut sunflowers or Jerusalem artichokes to make seasonal toys. Observing all this, families with children generally thought it a good idea to go up to the yayla for three months.

4
The Sarot Yayla

Ah, the yayla, the summer pastures of village Çat! For the children of families who could go there, it was paradise. There were no boundaries.

Everywhere was a playground for the children: the mountains, the valleys, the green plains, and the marshy ground watered by the ice-cold water coming from underground springs. The children searched for hollows in the mountain they had not seen before. Those secret places filled the children with curiosity as to what they might hold. It was not enough to play only on the green meadows watered by the springs. The children used to roam over hills covered with vetch, clover, buttercups, thistles, saffron, and other plants; by the rivulets of the steep mountain passes; and through rocky gorges. Very often, they would not think of going home until they felt hungry.

There was also a lake formed from the snow that had melted in the high mountains that surrounded it. The waters of this lake would dry up toward the middle of the summer, partly from evaporation and partly from falling into the depths of the earth in sinkholes, roaring as they fell, leaving an extensive area of level ground behind. The children could roam as long as they liked. After the rains, they would collect mushrooms and toadstools, shivering from the chill.

If you ran for an hour to the foot of the mountain on the other side of the lake, you would come to the yayla of Dere, the next village. Between Çat's summer pasture and Dere's summer pasture, there were green meadows, springs, hills covered with vetch and clover, and mountain passes. The color of almost all the flowers was saffron yellow. First, before the snow had completely melted, came the yellow crocus. The buttercups on the green plains sparkled in the sun like a golden carpet. The clover and vetch on the low hills and slopes of the mountains were yellow too. The pasture was likely called Sarot—which means "yellow grass"—because of this.

In spring, there was plenty of water. Springs burst forth everywhere. The main source of water for our summer settlement was the Head Spring, which gushed out between the stones and rocks arranged by the sacred place at the foot of Çilehane Mountain. So much water flowed from there that the spring could not contain it, and rivulets would gush out in buckets from its sides and corners. There were plenty of other springs around the greater summer pastures, which had names like Exhibition Gusher, Witch Elm Fountain, Kirez Gusher, Blessed-by-the-Teacher Water, and Hümmet Spring. These came boiling out of the ground to leap straight up into the air. Great Spring and Meat Spring were pure cold-water springs that found a way out from under the rocks at the bottom of hills. Gushing water springs could even be found at the tops of the mountains, like Esenek Fountain.

For us boys, there seemed no limit to the places we could explore. We would go to the other side of the mountain simply out of curiosity. We would swim in the gullies between the mountains before the waters of the lake dried up. I still can't understand how we didn't catch a cold, swimming and playing in the icy waters of this lake. My friends Muzaffer, Vehbi, and Bahri knew how to swim. The rest of us tied our long underpants up on each side and, after wetting them, would blow the legs up into two balloons and lie on top of them, trying to stay on the surface of the water.

Bahri and Vehbi lived on Eski Yurt, a private summer pasture belonging to one big family. As they had a lot of animals, they had more work to do than we did. The jobs the children did on our yayla were not considered much of a chore. Those of us who didn't have elder sisters to be childminders helped our mothers by looking after the younger siblings. We had small jobs, like looking after the kids, lambs, or calves, and it was our responsibility to lock them in the small sheds just before the herds came home.

5
Moving to the Yayla

In the middle of April, Mother and Father began to talk about going up to the yayla for the summer. If they went to the yayla and joined the milk cooperative, they'd be able to save up enough butter for the family for the upcoming year. One would not move to the yayla with a cow that did not have a calf. Even if the cow gave plenty of milk, cooperative sharing of milk wouldn't be possible with only a cow. "Cow's milk has little fat in it," they used to say. With four goats, they would be able to join the yayla milk cooperative. Sheep and goats gave less milk, but their milk contained more fat, and therefore was more acceptable. The milk of goats that fed on sweet-smelling herbs such as thyme on the slopes of the high mountains had a much better fat content, color, smell, and taste than cow's milk. After my parents had talked it over, or perhaps because Father had other ideas in mind, they decided we would go to the yayla that summer. The families who had many sheep or goats had already headed to the yayla several weeks earlier. My father did not have the money to buy four goats with kids. Even if he had, he did not like to buy things for cash. If he did, it was only after much hesitation and deliberation. When buying a necessity, it always involved some bargaining, and he nearly always came out of it with a profit.

At that time, there were few goats or kids for sale at the market or in the villages of Bozkır, and those available were sold for a high price. Some of the resourceful villagers would go to the villages of Manavgat and come back with goats and kids. They would sell some of them and keep the rest for themselves.

What was it like to go from the Çat village of Bozkır to Manavgat in those days? Oh, those fathers of old knew! They would sling a sack of provisions on their back and set out on foot along the so-called road-trails created by people and animal feet. They would travel across the mountains, with their lonely valleys, knifelike ridges, and narrow passes, following animal tracks that were sometimes hardly traceable, drinking water from the springs, rivers, and snowmelt. They had the choice of taking one of the merciless passes, such as the Susam, Alaca, or Windy passes, with the danger of freezing to death before they reached the villages of Manavgat on the Mediterranean side of the Taurus Mountains. If they were caught in a blizzard or a rainstorm, they would be lucky to find refuge in a cleft of rock or a cave. The path they had to follow could become unrecognizable, flooded, or covered with mud. For such a journey, they wore only moccasin-type shoes made of raw ox leather. Boots or other shoes would wear out before the traveler was halfway there. Many times, I watched my father cut animal hide to make his own moccasins and the strings for them. In the fall, our villagers used to make the same journey with a mule or donkey for other reasons. Dried fruit—that is, figs—were bought from the Manavgat villages to sell at Bozkır or in its villages. Though Father had often been there for figs, he had never been to Manavgat to buy animals.

This time, it was for goats with kids that Father decided to go to Manavgat. He and my great-aunt's neighbor, Abdal Hacı, had agreed to go together; in my mother's words, "Two madmen had conned each other." Sharing costs and profit, they would buy as many goats with kids as their means would allow, come back, sell some, and share the remainder.

As the weather was rainy and there would be snow and storms in high places, they did not set out immediately—in fact, not before the end of April. First, Father took us up to the yayla. One beautiful, sunny spring morning, we loaded up the mule and the two donkeys with our bedding, our pots and pans, and provisions, and set off on the road to the yayla. Father told us, "On the way, we can collect some dry kindling from the thickets around Akdağ and put it on top of the load on the mule."

My mother, Baby Hayriye swaddled on her back, walked by the mule with encouraging cries, with three-year-old Mehmet riding one of the donkeys, and six-year-old Kadın, sniffling and tearful, sometimes walking, sometimes riding on top of the load on the mule. After they had left, I took the cow's halter with a spare rope tied to it, and set off, too, on my own. I was eight years old then, and it was my job to stop at suitable places along the way and let the cow graze before arriving at the yayla.

The water gurgled along in the valleys we passed through. The cow went in one direction and I tugged it in another, so several times, the boots on my feet got wet before we were halfway there. I thought, I'll stop at the willow trees on higher ground and let the cow graze while my boots dry. Even if not thirsty, no one could pass by Söğüt Spring without drinking its ice-cold water.

When we got on the path to the yayla, the first challenge for people and loaded animals was the muddy trail of Yuvalca Hill. The sticky mud clay grabbed onto the shoes and kept them! The rest of the road was flat until it came to Çamurluk. There were no more dangers after the narrow gorges of Çötü and Dördoluk, except for traversing the length of the running water. Çamurluk was very steep and water continuously oozed out at various places along the road. The road itself was slippery with mud in most places. Care had to be taken when passing there, especially with a loaded animal. When I got there, my family caravan had long since passed the place. The road continued through a small, narrow valley, and then the great Söğüt Plain opened out in front of us.

The spring there never dried up throughout the twelve months of the year. The plain was extensive. It was situated halfway from the village to the yayla, in both distance and elevation. Until the time when they were allowed to move up onto the yayla, the villagers could only come by day to this pasture to graze their animals. The road upward went along the side of this plain. Travelers who wanted to drink the springwater had to step away from the road to cross the wet grass and a small river coming from the majestic mountains in the background. On the lower side of the Söğüt Plain, there was a small area of piled-up rocks, rye grass, and saplings called the Unbelievers' Graveyard. This was the graveyard of a tribe that had lived there many hundreds or thousands of years ago. Our people treated this place as sacred, since there were very old graves of ancient peoples who had lived there long ago, even if they had been unbelievers. Out of respect for the spirits of the long-gone dead, no one cut wood or brushwood, or damaged the plants growing there. Even the children, seeing branches that could be cut to make excellent canes, were afraid that something bad would happen to us if we went in there, and instead went on our way without touching anything. The sweet chirps of the meadow sparrows that went in and out among the bushes in that old graveyard are always in my ears.

Our way led up to Eğirmeç Hill next. When we got to the top, we knew we had almost arrived at the yayla. In the excitement of this, we would hurry over the fairly flat part of Han Dolaylar, even though it was very stony. At this point, it would have been about three hours since we had left the village. At Beşik Kıran—the "cradle breaker"—the narrow crossing to Sergi would be leaped in one stride at the cost of getting our feet and knees wet. All at once, we would find ourselves on the dark green plain of Sergi, bright with yellow buttercups gleaming in the sun. In our joy, we forgot the difficulties we had had since leaving the village, as we went up over Yuvalca Hill; through the narrow valley of Koru, where two mountains seemed to touch each other, across Gerez and Dördoluk Valleys; and up the slopes of Kireçlik and Çamurluk. The surface of this high plain would be scattered with grazing cows that had come there earlier. After we drank a sip of water from the Sergi spring, less than three minutes later, a beautiful green plateau, which we called the Çat Yayla, spread out in front of our eyes. There, the level green area, ten times the size of Sergi, looked divine. This extensive plain was formed by the way the Esenek and Çilehane mountains inclined, and one side was girdled by the ridges of Tuzla. The older folk had very intelligently built stone huts called yayla houses on the lower skirts of the mountain. This was to let the children play safely, and the calves, kids, and other young animals graze on the wide expanse of green grass in the middle of the plateau. It was a very joyful picture of animals grazing and hens running freely and shouting children playing happily, accompanied by the voices of the women gossiping and talking of all things near and far.

That year, we borrowed the yayla house of my older Auntie Haşşa. It was a typical one-room shack with dry stone walls and a shed, situated at the bottom of a slope, at the top end of the plateau, on the way to Big Spring. As the walls were built without mortar, the air, and of course the sound, could freely enter and exit. Food was cooked and bread made over a fire of brushwood. If the hearth didn't draw well, the smoke would not stay inside for long, but escape through the walls. Inside the house, we talked in low voices. If we talked loudly, the passersby outside could hear.

My parents had arrived at the yayla before me, and were busy arranging things in the house. As the floor sloped only slightly, the ground was damp; Mother and Father placed branches of freshly cut spruce on the floor before spreading a sack over it.

Some neighbors who had moved to yayla a week before us came to welcome us, bringing a plate or two of yogurt. We had become very hungry since leaving the village, and so we poured a little grape syrup on the yogurt and ate it immediately. This traditional welcome was one of the sweetest memories of our yayla, especially for us children. After we had finished the meal, my father and seventeen-year-old brother, Hilmi, went with the mule and donkeys to Aygır, the forested area, to collect wood and brushwood as fuel for cooking.

6
The Goats of Manavgat

Three or four days after we arrived at the yayla, my father and Abdal Hacı set off after lunch for Manavgat, the coastal region on the other side of the Taurus Mountains, shouldering a bag of provisions. It wasn't early in the morning, but lunchtime. It was important to find somewhere to stay that first night. The high valleys of the mountains were full of snow, and sudden storms might turn the weather wintry. As it was necessary to go over the pass in daylight, they could spend the first night at a certain mountain cave, or in one of the houses not yet occupied on some other village's yayla. Those humans or animals unfortunate enough to be caught in a storm in the mountain passes of Yelli or Susam would not emerge safely, but freeze to death. Goat buyers in the spring and dried fruit salesmen in the fall had to choose the time to cross the passes very carefully.

When the men from our village set out for Manavgat or Alanya, otherwise known as "the other side," a secret fear would be felt by the women and the children old enough to understand. At the same time, joy would be felt at the thought, My dad will bring us a goat and kids, and dried fruit.

Many years later, I talked with Abdal Hacı. He described to me what he and my father had done when they went to get goats from Manavgat: "My dear nephew, we arrived at the village of Manavgat, a real pain of a place, all stone or rock. The whole place was both rocky and full of scrubby bushes. But the weather had warmed up and there were a number of goats grazing around. At first glance, we couldn't see any fruit trees or cultivated areas, nor any running water, but still, we could see fifty or sixty houses. As we say, 'Why would anyone set up home on the top of a mountain?'

Well, anyway, there was a man Rahim knew, so we went down to his house. We'd been two and a half days on the road in the mountain passes, and we'd finished all our food the day before, so we were tired and hungry. The man welcomed us into his house and, after returning his greeting, we explained what we had come to buy goats with kids. As we were asking if there were any goats for sale in the village, the fellow's wife brought in a tray and placed it in front of us. On it, there was a tub of slushy snow and three wooden spoons. The man of the house said, "Help yourselves."

Oh! Oh! I thought to myself. There was no bread or anything else to eat with it. My friend, a tub full of slush was all there was!

Slowly, slowly, your father picked up a spoon, took a small amount of slush, and put it in his mouth. Then he reluctantly took another half spoonful and put it in his mouth. It was as if he didn't want to insult the owner of the house, you see.

"Hey, man," I said to Rahim, "we've crossed mountains and gone over high passes without getting ill, and now you want to get pneumonia from eating slushy snow? Curses on such friends and such hospitality!" I took him by the arm and we left the house. Cursing and damning the fellow, we walked straight toward the herds of goats we could see in the distance.

Haci and my father found a man who had a large herd of goats, and, after bargaining with him, they bought thirty goats at six liras each. That man filled their stomachs and hosted them overnight. Early the next morning, he said goodbye to these two novice goat traders, warning them not to tire the goats, particularly the kids, by going too quickly or walking for too long.

The usual custom in the villages of Manavgat that earned a living from livestock was to sell the older goats. The villagers would let the kids they intended to sell drink their fill before milking the goats. Their hair became glossy and handsome, so they were able to sell them for a better price. As a result, as my father and Haci began to climb the mountain, well pleased with life, my father said, "Good, we bought goats, which give plenty of milk, and have well-fed kids. We'll easily be able to sell them at our yayla."

Of course, they listened to the herdsman's advice and stopped from time to time to let the goats graze and the kids suckle their mothers. Even so, some of the kids got tired and slowed them down. Our two likeminded friends, who were engaging in the goat-trading business for the first time, became worried, thinking, If we go so slowly, it'll take us a week to get to our yayla. So, from time to time, each one picked up one or two of the exhausted kids and carried them in their arms or on their shoulders. They were lucky it didn't rain, so they were able to get back to our summer pasture in three days.

The Manavgat region had a Mediterranean climate, and, even in the winter months, the animals could find enough green grass to eat. Moreover, in coastal areas, goats gave birth early. The kids they had bought looked quite well grown, and their hair was shining with health. In spite of a tiring journey of three days, the goats and kids made a good show. They were more handsome and meatier than the ones raised by the herdsmen of our village. The buyers on the yayla began to bargain for whichever goat had caught their eye. Some of our neighbors made up their minds quickly and fourteen of the goats on show were sold for ten liras each. Hacı and Father chose in turn eight goats each from the sixteen unsold.

Hacı decided to keep all eight of the goats he had chosen for his family. My mother quietly said to my father, "If we also kept all eight, that would be wonderful," but he didn't listen.

He said, "I want to sell at least three more, four if I get a good price. That's what I'm considering doing." He told the customers, our neighbors, "You can choose three or four more," and the bargaining went on. My father's price was fixed, but the neighbors continued to haggle, saying, "Eight liras is a good price, maybe one might sell for nine."

My mother kept popping in and out of the house, gazing at the buyers with black looks. As the best-looking goats were sold first, it looked as though we would be left with the four or five least productive ones.

7
Rise in Anger, Lie Down in Grief

It was a little late for noontime prayers when Father went into the house to pray. Mother seized this opportunity to speak politely but firmly to the customers who, hoping to buy the goats cheaply, were waiting for my father to give his final answer. "Neighbors, we are keeping the remainder of the goats for ourselves. They are not for sale."

Even though Father was careful to say his prayers according to the given ritual, his ear was always open. When peddling goods with his animals in villages near or far, or saying his prayers, or even when asleep, he always had an ear open to what was going on around him. It was a necessary feature of those who earned their living the hard way. Even while praying inside the house, he could hear the sounds coming from outside through the loosely built rock wall; he most certainly heard what my mother was saying. He got up angrily, leaving his prayers unfinished. Hastily, he walked out, giving Mother a hard kick as he did so. Shouting loudly to the customers, he said, "My friends, all the goats are yours for eight liras each. If you have money in your pocket, give it to me and you can take the goats before I change my mind."

"An opportunity is an opportunity," said the neighbors who had been waiting for a bargain, and immediately all of the goats were sold.

We children looked at each other in dismay. Even my older brother, Hilmi, who disliked being at the yayla, said, "Oh, my God, what's going to happen now?" and sank down on a stone in front of the house.

Father went inside again and swore at my mother, saying, "The yayla is too good for you! We're going back to the village."

After finishing his prayers, and without saying anything further to us, he went straight toward Tombacık, a grassy place with willow trees, under which the men on the yayla used to sit and chat.

Mother, Hilmi, and I—those of us in the household who understood what was happening—were left frozen with fear. My mouth and throat were bone dry, with no spit to swallow even. None of us uttered a syllable, not me, not my mother, nor Hilmi. My childish head was in a whirl and I wanted to hear a word of hope. But none came.

All the goats had been sold, hadn't they, so we would have no joy in being at the yayla. I sat there thinking to myself, How many days are left before we go back to the village? And why did we come to the yayla? I haven't once gotten to go to the hills to dig sweet crocus roots. I wonder if I went to Eski Yurt, would I see my friends, Vehbi and Bahri?

Mother put a little bran in front of our cow before she milked it. My younger siblings, Kadın and Mehmet, were fretful, overtired from playing on the grass with mud. Slung on my back, the baby, Hayriye, was wailing constantly. I tried to distract her by swinging my hips first to the left and then to the right. The baby was certainly hungry. My mother was upset, angry, and also hungry—how in the world could she have milk in her breasts to suckle Baby Hayriye? It was the time of year when those in the village had the least food available. Even the zucchini had not grown yet for cooking. There wasn't even a bunch of green onions in the house, either. Vegetables such as zucchini, beans, peas, potatoes, and onions had been planted only a week before we left for the yayla. There was absolutely nothing to cook in the house except cracked wheat and dried garbanzo peas. At least we always had a little grape molasses, which we called pekmez. Before our own was all used up, my father would always bring back a tin of pekmez he had bought cheaply on his peddling trips, either from the Aladağ villages, which survived by growing grapes and grape products like pekmez and raisins, or from the Friday market. Obviously, it was because he, himself, had a sweet tooth. After every meal he would say, "Bring a little pekmez to clear the taste in our mouths."

In those days, it was not usual for the villagers to buy vegetables and fruit from the weekly market or the stores. Apart from cracked wheat and wheat for bread making, villagers did not eat any items of food they had not produced themselves. Night and morning, we ate plain pilaf, cooked in water with perhaps a little salt. Those houses without cracked wheat were considered poverty stricken. If we had ayran—buttermilk—as well as cracked wheat, we were quite content. We gave thanks if we had bread. Most people ate food such as meat, preserved fried meat, cheese, or halva only at festival times, if then.

My mother slept, at most, four or five hours a night. If nutrition was poor, little milk was produced. Baby Hayriye continually cried from hunger and thirst. When we older children said, "We're hungry," we were used to the half-joking scolding we got: "Remember the days when your stomach was full?" or "Eat the root of the oleander."

The previous fall, my older brother Hilmi, then a youth of sixteen, had wanted to go to Aydın, but Father, saying he was too young and would be put upon there, would not let him go. Father wanted to keep Hilmi with him to help in the peddling trade and acquire a taste for buying and selling and making a profit. Hilmi, however, did not enjoy working with Father. Every job they did together began and ended with curses, and they never stopped quarreling. However, Father did promise Hilmi that, if he helped him that spring and summer, he would take him to Aydın in the fall and see that he got used to working there.

Hilmi was very skilled at looking after horses and mules and, when he wanted to, he was good at using a spade, shovel, or ax. That summer, my father was busy planning how he might keep Hilmi at home and put him to work. He probably came up with several different plans.

My mother's anxiety about the shame we would feel if we moved back to the village could be seen plainly on her face. Not having any goats, and only the meager milk of a calfless cow, was a matter of shame; the yayla women's neighborhood milk cooperative would never accept Mother as a member. Upon returning home so soon, after just leaving for a summer in the yayla, who knew what the poor woman would have had to listen to from the village gossip. What tales of arguments, of insulting names, of who had meddled in someone else's business however many years ago, would go from one tattling mouth to another. This gossip would be heard in every corner of the village, as well as in our neighborhood, and even become the talk of distant, sharp-tongued relatives. There would be no shortage of people asking, "Oh, did you hear, your Fatma became an object of shame at the yayla? I wonder if it will turn out well."

Of course, Father must have been thinking of the jokes and malicious gossip his wife and children would be subjected to on account of their returning to the village so early in the summer. He thought of it, but once the goats had been sold, the deed was done. Father was very familiar with the saying, "Those who rise up in anger will lie down in grief," but he had fallen into such a position—a manure hole—that he could neither stay there on the yayla nor go back to the village. He most certainly swore, asking himself, "How did I get so angry as to get myself into this mess?" Had he gone over the snowy mountains to buy goats in the villages of Manavgat, only to be disgraced at home? How could he get himself out of this situation? However he looked at it, it exactly fit the saying "Like a stick with shit at both ends." Trying to overcome his feelings of helplessness and despair, he told himself, as he always did, Everything comes from God, everything comes from God, so there must be good in it somewhere. He couldn't ignore the situation, however. Father used to blame the devil for his mind drifting off during his prayers, but not even his devil, who never left him alone, showed him a way out.

8
The Black-Pea Guardians

The evening of the day Father sold the goats, my mother's face was still sulky. We children were like orphans who had forgotten how to laugh. My elder brother, Hilmi, hoping to get some sympathy from my mother, kept saying, "Well, I'm off to Aydın to find a job for myself, good or bad."

At noontime that day, after selling all the goats and having threatened once more to take us back to the village, Father left, only to sit all afternoon at the foot of a willow tree, socializing with some men there, and turning things over in his mind. It was well after dark when, refreshed after spending time with some men, he opened the small wooden door of our yayla house and came in.

Mother and I were sitting in silence by the light of the twigs and brushwood burning in the hearth. Mehmet and Ayşe had long since drowsed off. Father started to speak. "Hilmi, my son, go to the village early tomorrow morning, and take a look at our wheat field. Collect a load of wood on your way back."

That means we're not going back to the village, I thought to myself.

Mother didn't utter a sound. She heated up the pilaf left from lunch with some soft flatbread and set them in front of my father, then went back to her corner.

Could I find the courage to say anything? I knew that in such situations, silence was best. Whatever happens, I'll learn about it in the end, I thought, and began to wait quietly.

Father ate a few mouthfuls of food. He looked from Mother to me and Hilmi, then back again to Mother and, as if to torture us, began a lot of meaningless talk. "This year, the lake in the yayla dried up early. The shareholders decided to plant black peas. They made an agreement with the farmers and their partners. Now they are looking for a guardian."

My mother said not a word. I thought to myself, What's it to us what's planted where the lake was?

Father had a share in the grounds of the lake grounds through his first wife, Hilmi's mother. Father's share had been given to a farmer to plant black peas, a plant with pods full of small, round black peas. Father had grown black peas once before on a small, dry field of ours in the village, so I knew a little about them. As they have a short growing season, the shareholders had thought black peas were a suitable crop to plant on the dried-up lakebed. The stalks were also very useful as animal fodder.

I was still curious. Well, okay, but what's it to do with us? I kept asking myself. However, I kept quiet and went on waiting. Either Father would explain it himself, or else Mother, with great skill, would find out from him.

If they were going to quarrel, they should just get on with it. Father, in any case, was like a child. His anger didn't last. The next day, he would have forgotten half of what he had said the day before. In fact, he couldn't stand the strain for long. What had been on the tip of his tongue burst like a bombshell from his mouth: "I took the job of being the guardian for the black-pea fields on the lake ground!"

Mother didn't speak. She just sniffed. She was against it, but in the dim light of the feeble fire, it wasn't obvious. I waited for her to say, "So, what's next?" but she kept silent.

Father couldn't stop himself, and continued, saying, "Tomorrow afternoon, when Hilmi comes, we'll get some wood, cut timber for the roof, and build a small shack beside where the black peas are sown. There's already a ruin there. We'll use the stone from that. If we give it a makeshift roof, it'll last for three or four months, that will do. Hilmi and I will collect the necessary materials, prepare them, and, in two days' time, take them up to the ruin. In a week or ten days, a small yayla house will be ready and we'll move there. You and the children will stay by the black-pea field by day, and Hilmi and I will be there at night to protect the plants from being eaten by the wild, untended animals on the mountain."

The planted area was just in front of the yayla of the village Dere. The job of the guardian was to keep the black-pea field safe from animals and grass thieves. As payment, the guardian was to receive forty havayı (approximately five hundred kilos) of black peas at the end of the harvest.

In spite of all the uncertainties of the day, that night, we went to sleep rejoicing that we were not moving back to the village. The lake was not that far away; from our yayla, you could get to the big sinkholes of the lake in half an hour. I said to myself, I can come back and play with my friends sometimes. We would have a new yayla house near Dere Yayla, where there must be children to play with. It didn't matter that we had no goats. Father said there was lots of green grass to graze there. Our cow would feed well and have lots of milk. Since she had no calf, the milk would all be for us. There was still water in the lower section of the lake, but it would dry up completely in the next three weeks. The water had long since drained away from the level area near the mouth of the Çatal Oluk stream and the Big Cave. Farmers from the Karacahisar village had already begun to plant black-pea seed there.

9
Lucky Man

What a lucky man my father was! Before twenty-four hours had gone by, he had been able to find a way out of the unpleasant situation that he blamed Mother for getting him into. To my childish way of thinking, this business of being guardian by the lake was absolutely Hızır's doing. How was it that just at this time Hızır, the legendary helper of people in trouble, had come to our aid? In a way, we were leaving the yayla, but not going back to the village.

My father went on repeating, "Forty havayı black peas, as much hay as we can gather, and Hilmi and I will gather more wood than we can burn. I probably can take shares in a pottery kiln. That's a profit whichever way you look at it."

This was a really imaginative plan. Maybe he had other ideas in his head, but he didn't tell us about them. In any case, we understood and knew many things without the need of words, even if we were young. I had finished the first year of primary school. I had nothing with me in the way of a book, notebook, or pencil. As we had no calves or kids to look after, my time was my own. I could enjoy myself and go with my friends to where the lake had not dried up to play at dunking each other, or to the head of the springs to collect various kinds of mushrooms, or simply wrestle with one another. It didn't enter my head that keeping watch over the black peas had anything to do with me. At most, my job would only be to keep Baby Hayriye amused while my mother was mowing grass or collecting brushwood. This business of my father being guardian over the black peas seemed attractive to me. It did not affect my siblings, Ayşe and Mehmet, at all. Mehmet couldn't even talk properly yet. My elder brother, Hilmi, was probably happy about it too. To work in a cool place on the high plateau as a guardian was a much better job than going with my father to far-off villages to sell pots, hungry and thirsty, walking at the side of pack animals for hours in the hot sun.

10
Katıran Forest

Just behind the Esenek and Çilehane Mountains, on the other side of the deep valley of Çatal Oluk, was another even higher mountain range. This was part of the Taurus Mountain chain running parallel to the Mediterranean Sea. From the top of Esenek Mountain, one could see the snow on the slopes of these mountains, even in the height of summer. Accumulated water ran down to a lake from the passes the mountain range. A small stream, running from the largest of these mountains by way of the pass known as Çatal Oluk, or "forked spring," watered a large green plain before it entered the lake. This name came from the fact that when the snow there began to melt in the spring, it formed twin springs that were the source of the water running down the upper slopes of the pass. In April and May, well-watered green plains were a paradise for the animals grazing freely there. The horses and mules, animals that were not milked, would be set free to graze in the valleys and on the hills, able to drink water from the springs and rivulets. They were completely free with no herdsman or control of any kind. The horses and mules formed herds, which we called "öğrek." Each of the herds had a stallion as its leader. Set free, if only for a month to a month and a half, the animals were given a chance to graze freely, rid themselves of the parasites on their bodies, and eat green grass. These wild herds knew where the greenest and best-watered pastures were, sometimes roaming great distances in one day. A villager who wanted to find the animals out at pasture would have to search through the various valleys among the mountains.

At first glance, all the cows, young or old, scattered around, grazing on the hills and in the valleys, completely free. Toward evening, those with calves would begin calling them as they slowly made their way toward the homes of their owners. Their milk had increased during the day and their udders were heavy. The one- or two-year-old bullocks and heifers, together with the barren cows, would not return to the house of their owners, but go together, of their own accord, to a level place we called the cattle bed, and, in accordance with their natural instincts to protect themselves from dangerous wild animals like wolves, slept all together there. Regurgitating and chewing their cud there until morning, at first light, they would once more leave together to scatter and graze at will.

It would not be entirely wrong to say that, in general, all the mountains and hills surrounding the Sarot Yayla were bare. The ground had an overall covering of vetch, sage, dwarf corncockles, Rose of Sharon, and woody plants like crooked juniper and the astragalus with its crescent-shaped flowers. Together, these prevented the soil from eroding in the rain. Only a small portion of the high ground behind the almost-bare hills and mountains was black in appearance. That place was called Katıran, after the Taurus cedar that grew there. This was a sweet-smelling variety of conifer that grew easily in high places. The tree had a very symmetrical appearance, and was very resinous, so woodworms did not eat it. Maybe because the wood had a loose grain and broke easily, or because, as it came within the boundaries of Pabuççu village, it was well protected; for whatever the reason, this was then a virgin forest, untouched by the merciless axes of the villagers.

According to the sayings and stories of our grandfathers, these mountains were at one time covered with the trees from which beams and joists were made. The forests, which had flourished for hundreds, maybe thousands, of years on these mountains where little rain fell, had been cut down and destroyed. Immediately above our Çat Yayla was a single juniper tree, many centuries old, which had survived, uncut, growing among the rocks. Our ancestors had considered this tree sacred, and called it a shrine. If only all trees could be regarded as such!

The slopes where the cedar trees grew were quite close to the blackpea field. Though there was no road, it was only an hour's walk away. My father and my older brother, Hilmi, worked for a week, taking our mule and donkey by night to the forest to cut down trees and bring the logs back to the place where they were building the yayla house. Every night, they cut down four trees, and, after pruning the smaller branches, would bring the thicker branches back, loading them two by two on the donkeys, and dragging them to the ruin that was to become a house. As they knew it was forbidden to cut down any kind of tree in the forest, they covered the cut logs they brought back with mud and hid them among the grass and bushes. So no one would see them, they began and finished all the work under cover of darkness. After enough wood had been shaped in readiness, they built four low walls with stone from the ruin, covering these with a roof of closely packed fresh juniper branches and mud. Before ten days had passed, Father and Hilmi came back, saying, "Our new yayla house is finished." The next morning, we loaded our bedding and stuff on the pack animals. Ayşe walked along, crying and sniffling. Mehmet was carried at times by Father, at times by Hilmi. With Baby Hayriye swaddled on Mother's back and the cow under my control, we moved to our new yayla house by the black-pea field.

The new house sat on a small hummock facing the black-pea field. A little wider than the shacks in the yayla, it was a kind of one-room shed with a makeshift door made of a sack, which was draped across the doorway.

There was a stream, two feet wide, running just below the house. On the other side of this was the newly sown black-pea field, about one hundred and fifty to two hundred meters wide, and five hundred to six hundred meters long. The shoots were only just beginning to show, and the ground looked black rather than green. On the other side of the field was a hill, entirely covered with stones, going toward the Aygır Gap. On the right side of the freshly sown field was the place where the lake had recently drained away and been replaced by mud.

Between the end of the field and the stony hill was a fast-flowing stream and some marshy ground, immediately behind which rose a high rock above which the yayla houses of Dere village could be seen. To the left, on our side of the field, the plain below Çatal Oluk Pass, stretching as far as the eye could see, was scattered with animals grazing here and there all over the valley.

We settled into our shack at once. It would be a problem to keep our cow out in the open on her own without a calf. We tethered her near the house, feeding her with grass cut from places where it was plentiful. The cow quickly grew used to this abundant source of food and continued to give us a liter of milk, morning and evening.

At first, being a guardian did not require much effort. As there was plenty of wild grass around, not many animals raided the black-pea field. If one did, we drove it away with stones and curses. This job seemed like good fun to me when it first began. I used to run at times to chase the bullocks and heifers and then go by myself to explore interesting places near the field. I used to frighten the frogs in the marsh, hunt for the nests of the pigeons seen flying among the rocks, and look with admiration at the water disappearing into sinkholes. I used to murmur, as if talking to myself, "I wonder where that water disappears to? Or is there an empty space beneath? The water makes a noise as it goes underground, so there must be an empty space there."

The largest of these sinkholes had a cave, opening directly into a huge rock next to the Dere Yayla. This was called the Cattle Cave. In June, I learned why it was called this. In the noontime heat, gadflies attacked cattle grazing in the fields and bit them to suck their blood. In order to escape from the pain this caused, the cattle were maddened into action. In other words, they rushed hastily into a dark cleft or shade for refuge. A cow, heifer, or bullock tormented by these gadflies would enter this cave and hide there until the afternoon became cooler.

11
Treasure on the Dry White Hills

My so-called enjoyment of chasing the cattle and wandering around freely soon began to tire. Father and Hilmi, for one reason or another, were always busy doing something. The bare, stony hills opposite us were not as barren as they seemed. The rocky slopes were so steep that neither mule nor horse could climb them, but upon going, axes in hand, to look at them, one could see the dry stumps of the juniper trees that had once grown in the clefts of the rocks there. These stumps, left from trees cut years before, had not rotted away, but whitened under the sun like the rocks around them. Seeing these juniper stumps still preserved after many centuries, Father rejoiced as if he had found treasure. All day long, he and Hilmi worked together, piling up the logs they cut from the stumps, which could be used for roofing in the village. My mother was expected to come and carry the logs on her back down to the level ground below. In accordance with the village custom, "A man doesn't carry a load on his back, that's a woman's job." My father insisted she do it, but for once in her life, Mother retorted, saying sensibly, "Hey, fellow, take a look at yourself and then look at me. I'm not even half your size. It takes strength to climb down these rocks with a load on your back. It would be hard for me and you're much stronger. If you want to finish the work quickly, then you carry the wood with me. It won't do you any harm, but Hilmi's still young, so don't let him carry it all." Since there was no one to see him and joke about it, my father agreed to do such "women's work." The two of them carried the logs down the steep hillside together.

On other days, they cut the grass growing around the planted field and dried it. My father and Hilmi spent some nights stealing more trees from Katıran Forest. Since the older members of the household were busy all day, it became my job to scare the animals away from the black-pea field, from before dawn until dusk. At night, Father or Hilmi would go from time to time to see if any animals, such as camels or mules, had come to the field, and drive them away.

Every other night, during the darkest hours, Father and Hilmi would take the wood and logs they had prepared beforehand and transport them from the yayla to the village Çat, an eight-hour round-trip trek. No one from Dere or our village of Çat could know what they were doing. No one must complain to the foresters. The real reason Father had agreed to be the field guardian was clear: to illegally gather wood for the house he was planning to build back home in the village. With Hilmi's help, Father continued to secretly store up logs for another month or two.

Father secretly moving lumber in the dark of night

Meanwhile, May had passed and the June heat had begun. A month without rainfall had made the surroundings very dry. The green grass covering the hills and valleys slowly turned yellow and then withered away. The black-pea field was kept watered and grew strong and green, from a distance attracting the eye like a sparkling emerald. As the animals had only the dry steppes and countryside to search for food, their hunger made them raid the field both day and night.

12
My Legs! Oh, My Legs!

Without any hope of seeing or playing with them, I had long since forgotten my friends in our village yayla and the Eski Yurt. I kept running from morning to night, driving away the calves, kids, sheep, year-old donkeys, bullocks, and camels that invaded the field on all sides. My feet were bare. The ground all around was soft. I constantly stepped in and out of mud or into water up to my knees, getting wet as I did so; over and over again, the mud dried on my legs until, by the time evening came, all the skin there was cracked and sore. When I went home in the evening, my legs were unbearably painful. In order to soften the dry skin, my mother would rub my legs with salted butter. At first, this would sting a lot, but then it soothed my pain. As soon as I had filled my stomach, I would curl up and fall fast asleep. Seeing the suffering I endured made my mother moan about what had caused us such hardship.

From time to time, Mother would go with Father to the village. She would walk for at least four hours with her child on her back. When they arrived, she did whatever work was necessary in the summer—hoeing the vegetables and watering them, making bread for the household, and preparing food for the workers at harvest time. At such times, Hilmi would stay back and look after us. He was quite good at managing things. When my mother wasn't there, he even milked the cow. However, he was unhappy about many things in his life. When he was forced to work, he would get angry and swear loudly. He loved tormenting any animal or child near him, or anyone he thought he could frighten. For this reason, whenever my mother left us with him, she never went without a backward glance. We were treated badly every time, especially my sister, Ayşe.

Toward the end of July, the hills and valleys where animals had been grazing had dried up. The only green thing left was the black-pea field, and we were troubled by all kinds of animals and insects. The animals increased their attacks of the field, just like bees rushing to a juicy spleen hung outside a butcher's shop. The wretched creatures didn't even give us time to say, "Let's sit and have a mouthful of food." While I was chasing animals away on one side of the field, I would see two heifers stripping the black peas on the other. They would manage to run away before I could reach them. Some of them became expert thieves.

My eight-year-old self, chasing away hungry calves all day long

July and August passed by, filled with our merciless attempts to drive the animals away. At the beginning of August, most of the families of the villages of Dere and Çat, who had been in their respective yaylas, left the yayla and returned to their villages, and so there were fewer marauding animals.

Just when we thought we were going to have an easier time guarding the black-pea field, the Yörük camels and horses made a habit of coming there. My father and Hilmi realized that they couldn't deal with these animals by simply driving them away. They resorted to catching some of them and tying them to stakes in the ground. Father planned to charge damages to the animals' owners before releasing them. The animals were difficult to catch. By then, Hilmi had searched for and caught our mule, which had been grazing freely. Using our mule, Father and Hilmi would direct the nuisance horses toward a narrow, rocky canyon hemmed in by mountains on each side. As there was no way of escape, it was then possible to catch them. One time, three strong Yörük men showed up and tried to take back the captured horses for free. Father threatened to shoot them, and so they paid a little fine, like a kilo of dried cheese.

All summer long, I had no friends to play with. A young man named Nurlubey, Hilmi's friend from our village, and his younger brother, Kerem, were with us, but only for two weeks. Hilmi told Nurlubey, who had been working on construction in the village, that they could secretly cut down trees in Katıran Forest. During the day, when the two friends went to do this, Kerem and I would play together. Both of these boys were orphans, without either father or mother. Kerem was the same age as me. One day when we were playing in the sand, I saw a louse crawling on Kerem's head and told my mother. The poor child's clothes had not been changed for months. When my mother looked Kerem over carefully, she began to cry. He was covered in lice. My mother stripped him and gave him a thorough washing, then she dressed him in some of my old clothes while she washed and boiled Kerem's clothes.

13
Yogurt on the Yayla

In spite of all the troubles and pain, my life as a guardian was not all bad. I have many happy memories. A young woman called Ceren Ayşe from the Dere Yayla would say to me, "Hasan, don't beat my calf." During the early days when there were not many animals raiding the black-pea field, she twice took me to her house and offered me bread and yogurt. Lifting the cover off the cauldron full of yogurt, she carefully drew the cream on top to one side, then put the yogurt underneath onto moistened flatbread and placed it in front of me. What delicious food that was!

It was the first time I had been to Dere Yayla. As a yayla, it wasn't much of one. Between the simple rock cabins, there was only stony ground. It wasn't green like the Çat Yayla, but the view was still very beautiful. It gave me great pleasure to see, all in one glance, the blue-green lake, the valleys and hills stretching away to the Çatal Pass, and the level plain of Meyre Spring, behind which the high Çilehane, Katıran, and Akdağ mountain peaks rose so majestically.

Once, two camels got a taste for visiting the black-pea field. We got tired of chasing them away five or six times a day. We used to play a game, catching the more docile ones and bringing them to their knees. We tied their front knees tightly together so the animal couldn't get up. We didn't want these animals to die of hunger, so we fed them with dry grass. Whatever happened, we hoped their owners would come get them.

It was normal to see camels grazing freely on the mountains of our Sarot Yayla and the neighboring yaylas. The yaylas of the Antalya villages were in the higher valleys and pastures of the Taurus Mountains rising up behind us. We called the people who lived there, who subsisted entirely on their livestock, the Yörüks. The names of the Yörük hamlets nearest to us were Hocalı, Sülek, Namaras, and Taşbaşı. Our Yörük neighbors fed herds of sheep and goats on these pastures. Their yaylas were six to seven days' walking distance from their own villages of Antalya, near the coast. The Yörüks kept camels as pack animals for their move to their summer pastures. While they were on the high pastures, they sold their products, such as cheese and butter, at the Bozkır market, only one day's walk away, and bought everything they needed there throughout summer. They would buy wheat from the Bozkır Market, have it ground at the watermill in our village, load the sacks onto their camels, and return to their yaylas. Ever since we were small children, we had seen Yörük camel caravans coming and going along the road past our yayla on their way to and from the market.

The day after we had tied up the knees of two docile camels, a Yörük youth came. He had a four-liter crock of yogurt in his hands, which he had brought as a present from Hocalı, his yayla. "Please forgive our camels," he said. As by that time, our cow had little or no milk, the yogurt was a very welcome gift and we set the camels free. The Yörük youth went away happy. The young man had walked three hours from Hocalı to where we were with the crock of yogurt in his hands, but he was happy to have gotten the camels back so cheaply.

Those camels came back one other time. I was pleased by this, knowing what would happen. The young man once again came to fetch his camels, bringing us an offering of delicious yogurt.

14
Why Some People Don't Eat Onions

At the beginning of August, the only food we had to eat, either at our guardian's hut or at our house in the village, was bread. Our cracked wheat bulgur, cooked as pilaf, was finished. From time to time, Father and Hilmi would go to our small vegetable garden at Kayadibi, pull up the onions that were going to seed, dig up some potatoes, and bring us zucchini and beans. Little by little, our stomachs were getting used to having no pilaf. Potatoes and onions mixed with a bit of butter and eaten with flatbread was quite tasty. However, as the weeks went by and we had only onions with a few potatoes and zucchini, we really began to miss our cracked wheat pilaf. For at least two months of that summer, almost every food Mother cooked was mainly onions. It is likely for that reason that neither Mehmet nor Hayriye would eat onions when they grew up. Little Mehmet must have become sick of eating onions, cooked or not, day after day. My mother's milk must have smelled of it, because even Baby Hayriye smelled like onion. Even when they grew up, if any dish was cooked with onions, both Mehmet and Hayriye refused to eat the cooked food, just eating the flatbread instead. Naturally, until they became young adults, both were scrawny and unhealthy.

Toward the end of August, Father or Hilmi would sometimes bring us a saddlebag full of sour summer apples, fresh grapes, and pears from our trees in the village. The taste of the fruit we ate that summer, even if it was squashed, rotting, or unripe, is still sweet in my memory.

15
A Dead Donkey is a Clean Donkey

From time to time, the farmers who had half shares in the black-pea field would come and take a look, bringing us presents, like cooked meals, green vegetables, potatoes, onions, or zucchini. Once, a donkey belonging to one of the visiting farmers died. With difficulty, we dragged the body to a place far from our hut and left it in the open. Lying in the sun all day, the body began to smell. Thousands of flies flew around the corpse like a swarm of bees. The next morning, I woke early and found strange, long-necked birds as big as sheep clustered around the donkey's corpse, quarreling with each other as they ate the rotting flesh. I was fascinated. When I went nearer to get a good look, they flew up into the air and began circling slowly around. Most of the donkey's flesh had been eaten, and the bones could be seen. When I went further off, the birds returned one by one. Advancing cautiously toward the corpse, they hopped on and tore at the remaining flesh with great appetite, leaving only the bare skeleton. When open, the wings of these birds were more than a meter across. Those impressive birds I saw that morning were vultures, nature's wonderful garbage collectors.

16

What Kind of Rope is This?

Whenever I was chasing after the animals invading the black-pea field, my brother Mehmet always wanted to follow me. Although he was only three years old, he was very brave and loved to name and curse at the animals in his lisping tongue. One day, when I was going to chase away a bullock that had come into the field, Mehmet came after me. I would drive the bullocks away by throwing small stones at them. As I was coming back, Mehmet bent down and seemed to be pulling at the ground. When I got closer, I saw that he had hold of something like a rope and was tugging at it with both hands. When I was near enough to see what it was, my heart jumped into my mouth. What he was holding on to so tightly was the tail of a snake. The snake was pulling from inside a molehill, and Mehmet was pulling from outside. I quickly made him drop his hold and we immediately ran away.

17
My Tooth! Oh! My Tooth!

"Are you pulling a tack from the donkey's hoof, Uncle?"

One day at the beginning of August, one of my teeth began aching enough to make me cry all night long. Father said to my mother, "Tomorrow morning, you and Hasan take the mule and ride to the village. There, the blacksmith Ankara'lı knows how to pull teeth."

My tooth went on aching all night. Early the next morning, Father helped Mother onto the mule and I sat behind, holding tight to the high wooden back of the saddle. In places where the path was very steep, I got off and walked. When I got tired, I clambered up again. My mother continued to ride. It was really quite difficult for her to get on the mule with a child on her back. She needed a mounting block at least a meter high to do so.

When we got nearer to the village at the Keklik Falls, I got off and held the mule's head. Putting her foot on a stone at the side of the

Mother, with Baby Hayriye on her back, and me—Hasan— going to the village to see the dentist

road, my mother was able to dismount. At that time, apart from a very sick woman being taken to town, it was not considered proper for a woman to ride a donkey, mule, or horse inside the village. Only at weddings did the bride and her close friends, her attendants, with their faces covered so as not to be seen, mount horses and form the wedding procession.

When we got to the village, we tied the mule up in the stable and put some hay for it in the manger. My tooth still ached. Without any delay, we went straight to the forge of the blacksmith, Mehmed Barut, known as "the man from Ankara." Choosing the smallest of his tongs, Master Mehmed told me to keep my mouth open wide. Then he asked, "Which tooth is it, my son, this or that one?" touching in turn each of the teeth I pointed to. When he found the aching tooth, he gripped it firmly with the tongs and pulled it out with great force. I remember shouting "Aa-aah!" and seeing blood spurt suddenly from my mouth. The blacksmith/dentist pressed salt into the gap where the tooth had been. "Get well soon, my child," he said. "By tomorrow morning, you'll be feeling fine."

I felt as if the whole of my mouth and chin were about to crack. The pain was terrible. It surpassed the throbbing pain of my rotten tooth. After the salt was pressed into my mouth, a strange, salty taste suddenly became mixed with all my pain. All at once, not only did the violent pain stop, but the constant pain in my tooth had gone, and I was overjoyed.

When we got home, Mother said, "Hayriye's sleeping; you stay here at home with her. Before evening comes, I'll go to Kayadibi and dig up some potatoes and onions," and, after picking up an empty bundle and a hoe, she left the house. As I couldn't go far from the house, I walked as far as the edge of the flat roof of the hay barn and looked in wonder toward the Ahmetli neighborhood opposite us, at the gardens and vineyards and the mountains surrounding the village. I hadn't been in the village for more than three months. Everything had changed so much, I couldn't believe my eyes. It was as if all the trees had grown taller and spread out, shading everything around them. Swallows were skimming through the air around me, reminding me of the vultures at the yayla. I looked toward the neighborhood opposite ours, to the houses in which my mother's sisters, my aunts Hatçe and Rukiye, lived. I had really missed my grandmother, Kirez Ebe, who lived in the Karagaç neighborhood at the back of the opposite hill.

As I looked around, right and left, Mother arrived with the vegetables she had picked. "Son," she said, "the ground is as dry as a bone. I had difficulty digging up the potatoes and onions. Tomorrow morning, before we go up to the black-pea field, let's get up early and water our vegetables at Kayadibi."

Our stomachs were empty. We chose some of the small potatoes and onions from the garden and boiled them quickly. Too impatient to peel them, we wrapped them in soft flatbread and ate them like that. As soon as darkness fell, we spread a coverlet on the floor and went to bed. Trying to remember the various turns and bends of the narrow water channel and how it crossed to the other side of the valley over the Yayla River to reach our vegetable patch at Kayadibi, I fell asleep.

18
Geriz: The Bridge Over Hell

My mother woke me up early before the sun had risen. "Come on, Hasan, get up. Let's go and water Kayadibi while it's still cool. Before it gets hot, we'll take the road back up to our hut by the dry lake."

The only places in Çat convenient for growing vegetables were small, level areas along the banks of the rivers running through the valleys among the steeply rising mountains. The river ran at a level two or three meters below that of the gardens, so a channel was dug upstream from wherever a garden needed watering, and the water diverted through this into the gardens. The owners of the gardens would divert the water to flow down a smaller channel from the top into the chosen plot. As these channels were made to run almost level along the ground, from time to time, they needed attention. Normally, repairs were carried out in the springtime. The garden owners would choose a date and, with spade and hoe, go together to get the job done easily. During the summer, if further attention was needed, the owner would take a small hoe and do what was necessary to make the water flow more quickly.

In the case of our garden, the water needed to irrigate through with a narrow channel from the Ulu River, then snake along the foothills and

Geriz: Bridge over Hell

cross high above the Yayla River before reaching the gardens, which were a couple meters higher than the river. This was done by means of a structure called a geriz, a long, narrow, hollowed-out tree trunk, like a one-sided open pipe or a long canoe, which carried the water from one side to the other. As this pipe was narrow and parallel to the ground, the water in it moved very slowly. After many days or weeks of carrying the water across, mud, sand, and twigs would collect on the bottom of the geriz. As the water level rose, it would overflow and fall into the river more than twenty meters below. At such times, there wasn't enough water flowing across to water the gardens, and the geriz would need to be cleaned. One had to step into the geriz with bare feet, bend down and very carefully throw handfuls of the mud and stones collected there into the river below. It was only about a foot wide and one and a half feet deep, so it couldn't be cleaned by anyone large. For one thing, their feet would be too big, and, for another, they would be afraid of falling into the gorge below. Those for whom watering wasn't urgent would shrink from facing such a danger.

That day, when my mother came to water our garden, she found very little water was coming through the geriz. In order to finish the job quickly, she decided that I should clear this geriz, the narrow water canal in the sky! I had cleaned the Kayadibi geriz once the year before, so I knew what to do.

Children are both brave and foolhardy. At least, that was true in our village, for both boys and girls. With our feet in this narrow channel, we would crouch down and, crawling like ants, hold on to the side with one hand and scoop up the mud and stones and throw handfuls of debris into the gorge below. In one of the many stories we listened to as children, we heard very often of how souls crossed the hairsbreadth Bridge over Hell into Eternity. I imagined this bridge to be like the geriz carrying water to our Kayadibi gardens.

19
Fed Up

As time went on, it seemed as though our job of being Black-Pea Guardians would never end. In the middle of August, our stocks of food had almost run out. The elders talked among themselves, saying, "There's at least another month before the black-pea field can be harvested." We were all fed up of being on a mountaintop with no neighbors to talk to. We were tired of eating the same food—flatbread and boiled potatoes with onions. Even that didn't always fill our stomachs. Father and Hilmi, in particular, whose jobs involved a lot of physical work, had great appetites. My mother was often the last to eat. While she was busy with the baby, we would finish the large bowl of hot food placed in front of us. Once, she couldn't stand it, and had to say, "Hey, eat a little slower and leave two bites for me." The oldest two stopped as if she had offended them. It wouldn't be wrong to say that my mother's stomach was never full.

Even though the place we guarded was high up in the mountains, during July and August, the days were very hot. There wasn't a place with sufficient shade under which to set a cloth for breakfast unless we went inside the hut. My elder brother, Hilmi, then a young man, didn't want to be there any longer, not only because he was fed up with the work he was doing, but also because he wasn't with the other young men in the village. By that time, he and Father had carried many loads of wood and logs down to the village. Father was a man who didn't know when to stop. He tried to persuade Hilmi to stay, saying, "Since we have to be here on the mountaintop another month, let's find logs in Katıran and take them to the village to burn in the kiln."

One morning, Hilmi wrapped up some dry flatbread in his pocket handkerchief and, cursing, exclaimed, "I'm fed up of being here. I'm off to Aydın," and started walking toward the village. Father ran after him, pleading with him. An hour later, they both returned. We never found out what Father said to persuade him to stay. They worked together for another two or three days. Even though Hilmi still wanted to leave, and repeated, "I'm going to," a few times, Father managed to get him to stay with us and help him for another month.

20
The Black-Pea Harvest: Hard Work and Sorrow

Karacahisar was a village of fifty to sixty families. It was very close to the foot of Aygır Mountain, and only an hour's distance from where we were. Villagers from there were shareholders in the black-pea field. Toward the end of August, they began to come every other day to see if the black peas were ready to be harvested. At the beginning of September, they decided that the pods were full enough to be harvested and that work could begin. After giving the shareholders in our village notice of this, the peas were scythed over three days and left to dry in the sun. In one area, the peas were still green, but it was decided to cut them down, too, with the thought that, as it might soon start to rain, at least the stalks would be saved.

We had one week left of being guardians. We just had to wait for the bundles of peas to dry. We children were overjoyed when we heard that, as soon as the harvest was over, we would return to the village. Farmers began to harvest the crop with two pairs of oxen and two sledges. This allowed one pair to rest from time to time. Acting as a weight, one farmer would stand on the sledge, the base of which was studded with flints, as he guided the oxen over the dried pea stalks to thrash them. At the same time, another farmer, pitchfork in hand, would turn over what the sledge had thrashed.

The most valuable part for the shareholders after processing was the saman. Saman is the finely shredded hay that is left after separating the grain. This hay is very nutritious for animals in wintertime feeding. The resulting peas from the harvest were of less use to them. In return for watching their field, the shareholders promised my father forty sacks of peas from the harvest; that was the original deal.

21
Thirty-Seven Sacks of Peas

Winnowing took one and a half days. The stalks with the pods were piled into a long, thin heap, waiting for a favorable wind to blow to separate the peas from the pods and the stalks. The farmers' luck held good. One day, a wind blew through the heaps all day long; the peas were completely separated from the pods and dry stalks. They began to measure the peas using a giram, which was a metal bowl that held around three kilos. This was a quarter of the weight of a havayı, and the crop weighed only thirty-seven havayı, or around about four hundred and fifty kilograms.

My father watched the process anxiously. He couldn't stop himself from saying, "I was promised forty havayı of peas," and asking, "What are you going to do now?"

One of the shareholders brazenly said, "What can we do? That's all God gave us."

Some of the other shareholders said, "Let's split the cost of three havayi among the shareholders and let everyone pay their share."

In the end, most of them agreed on this alternative. The payment was to be 125 kuruş per share, but no money came from their pockets. They all brushed the matter aside, saying, "I've no money on me at present." Even later, when we asked them to pay us, no one gave us a kuruş. We didn't get any money from any of them. They passed by us without a care, simply saying, "I guess you did not guard the field enough." We eventually let it go and forgot about it. Having survived on the mountaintop without any real harm, we didn't look behind us.

At the end of harvest, the shareholders took a lot of the straw, which they divided up into sacks, and each shareholder was allowed to fill four of these. Each of them stuffed the sacks they brought as full as possible. The well-built men skilled at this job pressed the straw down so hard that their sacks weighed twice the normal weight. Only a mule or a camel could transport such heavily stuffed sacks. In those days, Yörüks would come with their camels and transport the farmers' loads for a fee. Even if the bean field hadn't produced a great deal that year, all the shareholders were delighted at having gotten hold of very nutritious fodder for their animals.

22
Back to the Village

Father and Hilmi took three days to carry the sacks of peas and the loads of hay that had fallen to our share back to the village. At last, the time to empty the hut and return to the village had come. Father decided to take the beams and logs off the roof and carry them back to the village. "We'll leave it for today," he said. "Tomorrow, Hilmi and I will come and strip the wood off the roof, load it onto the pack animals, and bring it to the village." We were very happy to hear him say, "Children, today, we'll take you back to the village."

Pallets, quilts, pans, plates, the tin tray, and all our other possessions were loaded onto the animals. Mehmet was put on the back of one of the animals. With Hayriye on Mother's back, all of us, children and adults, set out along the road to the village. Two hours later, halfway home, Father suddenly dove into the brambles growing alongside the road. A little later, he reappeared out of the bushes with a bundle in his hand. When he opened it, it was full of fresh grapes. He gave each of us a bunch. We ate these grapes with great appetite. He admitted the truth: when he'd come back from the village the day before, Father had hidden the bundle to make us happy. We children talked over and over again of the surprise our father had given us.

23
Exactly Fifty Years Later

I prepared the first draft of this black-pea story on April 5, 1999. I sat down after breakfast and wrote until I finished it in the evening. At that time, I did not have a Turkish keyboard on my computer, so I wrote it without using the Turkish letters ö ü ş ç ı and ğ. My aim was to finish it as soon as possible.

A week or so earlier, I learned that, a month before, my mother had had a stroke and lost her ability to speak. I arranged to have my lessons at the university covered so I could fly to Turkey to see her. I'm going, but what good will it do her? I thought. I wondered how to get her brain working again. Suddenly, this story of the black-pea field came into my head. I decided that if I wrote this story, which had happened exactly fifty years before, during possibly the most trying part of her life, in as much detail as I could remember and read it aloud to her, it could be of some use.

My mother had been living alone in the village in our family house. She had been able to see to her most essential needs. When my sister Hayriye and her husband, Abdurrazak, heard that my mother had lost her ability to speak, they decided to look after her, and took her to their house in Antalya, the city on the southern coast, just on the other side of the Taurus Mountains from our village.

When I got to Antalya and saw my mother, she couldn't speak, but simply made moaning noises. Her face showed whether she was feeling happy or uncomfortable. While in my sister's house, I found a quiet time to sit for half an hour, four or five times every day, and talk one-on-one with my mother. Without tiring her too much, I would read this story for ten or fifteen minutes and then take a break. While listening, my mother would sometimes smile, or sometimes wrinkle up her face and make groaning noises as if to say, "No, that's not what happened, it was like this." I realized that what I was doing was helping.

My other siblings who came to visit her were either babies or hadn't been born when the story took place. They became interested in the story and began to read it. My sister Nuriye, in particular, made joking remarks to Mother while reading it. My mother would make noises or shake her head, trying to show she agreed or disagreed.

I finished reading the story to my mother during the two weeks I stayed in my sister's house. Toward the end of my stay, although not fully in control of her voice, my mother would try haltingly to say a few words. Before flying back home to America, I advised my sisters Hayriye, Nuriye, and Fevziye, the youngest, saying, "Go on talking with Mother about events and memories that might annoy her or make her happy."

Two months later, my mother had regained her ability to talk enough to speak a few words on the telephone.

A Threat of Divorce by Sharia: If the Fish Doesn't Know It, the Creator Will

"Uncle, uncle, come and rescue me! Please come! Uncle, uncle! Come and rescue me, please!"

In the darkness of dawn, I woke to the sound of a woman's screams. As though I hadn't heard, I drew the quilt over my head and snuggled closer to my sister, Ayşe. She was three and I was six. We slept on the floor on the same pallet.

The shouting continued. "Uncle, uncle! Please come and rescue me."

Without taking my head out from under the quilt, I looked toward the hearth, from which crackling sounds were coming. My mother had gotten up from the pallet she shared with my father and was lighting the fire with twigs. She was rocking the cradle at the same time. That meant Baby Mehmet had woken up.

The tearful voice continued crying outside the door. "Uncle, uncle! Please rescue me!"

Father had been away from home for some time. It seemed he was tired after returning late from peddling his goods. Without opening his eyes, he called to my mother, "Look and see who that is, and what they want at this time of day."

Mother replied, "Husband, I know that voice. It's Cayneser's girl, Anakiz. She must be in trouble."

Lifting the latch, she opened the door a crack. "What is it, Anakiz? What's your problem, my friend?" she asked.

"The Yörük swears he'll divorce me. Tell my uncle to talk to him."

In order to calm Anakiz down, Mother said in a soothing voice, "Oh, my dear girl, would anyone divorce a wife for nothing? And is divorcing a wife so easy? There's the government. There's the state. Let's see, now, what's troubling Hussein Aga?"

"Last night, he came home from Aydın. He'd sent me some money while he was working there. I bought a room and a stable next to our house with it, as they seemed cheap. I didn't spend the money here and there; I saved it up. I bought the room and the stable we needed, thinking the man would be happy. I told him about this as soon as he came home. Instead of being happy, the fellow went wild. First, he shouted and then he screamed. He hit me a few times. I'll tell you what he said next:

What will I do with a room?
What will I do with a stable?
I'm a handyman,
a man who can make for himself
what he needs.
A house, a stable,
a shed for straw or wood,
whatever's needed!
Go back at once,
return, and get the money.
I don't need house or stable.
All I need is a bit of land
to plant potatoes, onions;
two or three feet of land,
raised earth with running water.
Get out!
Give back the room and the stable.
You bought it . . . you can sell it,
whatever shit you like!

Don't come here again
unless you get the money back;
with God as my witness,
and by his Sharia law,

thrice three times to make it nine,
I will say, 'I divorce you woman,'
and we will be divorced forever.

"That's how I was left out in the cold. Uncle Rahim, will you please talk to the Yörük? Maybe he'll listen to you, Uncle. My neighbors heard the commotion; Kerim the Wrestler and Şükrü the Smith tried to persuade him not to divorce me, but the Yörük would have none of it. Uncle, please rescue me. I've nobody else but you."

While my mother was at the door listening to Anakız's troubles, my father, who had not woken up for the early-morning prayer, quickly performed the ritual prayers he had missed. Hastily, he put on his leather inner and his rubber shoes, then said, "I'll go and talk with that madman, Yörük Hussein, and see what I can do."

In a gentle voice my mother said, "Go, talk to him, but don't press him too far. He's the kind of man, once he gets angry, there's no knowing what he will do." She warned him over and over again, saying, "What's more, when he first came to our village, you said he was a killer who had come from his own village to seek refuge here."

"All right," my father said, and left, with Anakız following him to her house in the upper neighborhood.

Yörük Hussein was one of the fifty to sixty men in the village who seasonally traveled to Aydın province to find work. He was a skillful builder of walls. From time to time, these migrant workers sent money by post to their wives and children left behind in the village, and to their mothers and fathers if they were still alive. They did not often write letters to their loved ones. "What's the good of a letter with nothing in it?" they would say. The letter would contain greetings and inquiries about their health, but they wouldn't want to write if they couldn't say, "I posted you such and such an amount of money."

When Father had left the house, I asked Mother, "Why does that woman call my father 'uncle'? Is she a relative of ours?"

Mother put more twigs into fire and then put a pot of cracked wheat porridge on the trivet to cook. She took Baby Mehmet from his cradle and, while giving him the breast, told me the whole story of Anakız.

Anakız had lost her father and mother at an early age and became an orphan. This little girl who had no brothers or sisters was taken in by her aunt Asli, a neighbor of ours known as Tall Asli. Asli, who had no children of her own, had lost her husband in the Great War, and lived alone. This aunt who raised Anakiz was penniless and needed help from the neighbors. Of these, my father's family was the one that helped most in raising this orphan child. They had watched over Anakiz as she grew up. That's why Anakiz called my father "Uncle."

When Anakiz was a young girl, two young strangers called Emin and Hussein came to our village. As they had come from a far-off village of a Yörük tribe, everyone began calling them Yörük Emin and Yörük Hussein. Our villagers grew to love these two hardworking, diligent, and well-mannered brothers. The old aunt who had looked after Anakiz for so many years, and her neighbors, in particular my father's family—that was, my grandfather and grandmother—all helped Anakiz get married when Yörük Hussein asked for her hand. My mother finished her story by saying, "That's why, although we're not related, Anakiz comes to us to kiss your father's hand and celebrate with us at festival times. Yörük Hussein may be called a friend of your father's. Maybe he will make that obstinate man listen to him and not destroy the orphan's home."

Half an hour after leaving the house, Father came home with a gloomy face. Before my mother could ask, "What happened?" Father, obviously upset, began muttering bitter complaints about Yörük Hussein.

"We accepted this mountain Yörük into our village, we helped him to marry orphan Anakiz. We did all we could to help them set up a good home. That mean-hearted, obstinate fellow refuses to listen to a word I say. Whatever argument I bring up, the man goes on repeating, 'If my money comes back, she can come too. Otherwise I'll divorce the woman. If what I want isn't done, I can't and won't take that woman back.' I left Anakiz weeping and crying without stopping. I talked to Doyduk Mehmet, who sold Anakiz the room and the stable; he swears he bought a donkey with the money, and says, even if he wanted to give the money back, he doesn't have a penny in his pocket. Right now, I don't know what to do," Father said.

"God forbid this young woman in despair do herself harm, my dear," said Mother anxiously. "The rivers are in full spate at this time," she murmured.

Father shouted, "Stop, woman, don't let Satan hear you!"

"Wouldn't the government interfere in the divorce of a woman with a child?" Mother asked, spreading a cloth on the floor. "Isn't it a pity for the poor woman?"

Our cracked wheat pilaf had been cooking since the time we got up. We sat down to our morning meal. Father finished filling his stomach first and got up. "If we report the news to the officials, it won't go down well. It doesn't seem like Yörük will change his mind. If we force him to, I'm afraid an accident might happen," he said.

"Look here, my man," said Mother. "As they say, 'Many are the blessings that fall on one who helps an orphan.' Can we wriggle out from under this if you take the room and the stable off Anakiz's hands? Maybe later, either Cemil or the blacksmith from Ankara whose houses are next to them will find a reason to buy them from you."

Father told her he had been thinking the same thing, and so he went to see Yörük Hussein again. Anakiz, who had been sitting during all this, crying outside on the doorstep, ran after him.

About an hour later, Father returned. He had talked with Yörük and promises had been made.

"Hussein, my friend, take back your vow. Give up divorcing your wife. By next week, I'll find the money and bring it to you. I have about two hundred kilos of dried figs on my hands, which I brought back from the other side of the mountains. I'll soak them and wrap them up in kilo and half-kilo amounts and sell them at the Friday and Seydişehir markets till there's none left, and get the exact amount of money needed."

Yörük Hussein accepted his offer and said he would give up divorcing his wife Anakiz for the time being. My father kept his promise. One week later, he had the money needed to pay for the room and stable. They were of no use to us, as they were too far from our house. We locked them up and they stayed empty for more than a year before Cemil bought them for the amount of money we paid for them. We heard later that, after three years, Yörük Hussein went back on his word and bought back the room and stable from Cemil for exactly twice the price.

My father did this, and many other good deeds like it, without expecting anything in return. Sometimes, the one who benefited, instead of reciprocating the good turn done to him, would behave in a churlish and ungrateful way. Then he would sing this ditty to his children as a lesson to be remembered for the rest of their lives:

*"Everyone does good to good people;
it's the brave one who does good to the bad.
I did a good deed,
throwing it into the river;
if the fish doesn't know it,
the Creator will."*

PART THREE

The Village That There Was

Basketmaker Ali's Fountains

Double-chinned Ali was one of our nearest neighbors. Our doors were opposite each other. The street between us, really an alley, was too narrow for a loaded donkey to pass through without difficulty. Although they weren't relatives, I called Ali "Ali Emmi" or "Uncle Ali," and his wife "Havva Abla" or "Aunty Havva." Ali Emmi earned his living by weaving wicker baskets, panniers, and trugs. He was my father's age or maybe a little older. This neighbor of ours always looked serious and never put his nose into other people's business. Both Havva Abla and Ali Emmi were very fond of my siblings and me. Havva Abla had a particularly sweet way of talking with children. "Mind you, don't throw stones at my chickens," she used to warn us often.

The basketmakers used the fresh shoots from the willow trees along the river to weave baskets suitable for carrying by hand or on the shoulder to prevent the fruit or vegetables they were carrying from getting squashed. The panniers were used mostly to carry straw, the dry roots of vegetables gone to seed, or even the piled-up manure from the stables. Our village was surrounded by rivers and streams on three sides, and willows loved water and grew quickly; there were enough trees for ten or fifteen basketmakers to earn a living. The villagers from the surrounding area, which was mostly arid, got their baskets from the basketmakers in our village.

A pannier, a type of basket that could hold forty or fifty kilos of fresh grapes, was a deep basket that a donkey, horse, or mule could carry for a long time. This kind of basket was woven from the long, thin two-year-old branches of blackthorn, a shrub that can grow in dry places and could be woven into a dense, pliable material. Blackthorn branches bore pitiless thorns. It was difficult to cut with any old knife, but the village blacksmiths made knives for basketmakers that were very suitable for cutting blackthorn. Even with such special tools, the basketmakers' work was hard. Each blackthorn branch had to be dragged through the bushes after being cut and cleaned of thorns, then there was a great price to pay for splitting each branch into two or three lengths. The basketmakers' hands used to run with blood. They often cut their fingers, and the fingers that remained intact would thicken or be pitted with unsightly callouses. Not all basketmakers made this kind of basket.

The women and young girls knew best where to find thickets of blackthorn on the mountains. During the first weeks of spring, young blackthorn bushes would burst into shoots that turned into leaves. The clustered leaves of the blackthorn would act like a magic food or medicine, giving life to sluggish, wasted bodies, starved of the vegetables they had longed for during the winter months. The tender blackthorn leaves had a sour taste. It was a good remedy for the lack of vitamin C they had suffered for so long. The villagers believed it would bring them better health, and rejoiced. The blackthorn leaves were not gathered one by one. Using the thumb and middle finger, the gatherers would neatly twist and gently pull off a cluster. There was always a thorn beside every cluster. The finger that it pricked would run with blood. The best time to pluck the blackthorn leaves was just after rain. The thorns softened when wet and did less damage to the hands plucking the leaves. Some smart girls missed the fresh blackthorn leaves so much that they couldn't wait for it to rain. They carried pitchers full of water from the stream and sprinkled water over the shoots to soften the thorns so they could pick the leaves as soon as possible. The blackthorn leaves they filled their bundles with were eaten in a variety of ways—raw, as a salad, as a pilaf with cracked wheat, or made into soup. These resourceful women would dry the extra leaves they had collected but didn't eat straight away, to store and use in the winter.

In the places where blackthorn bushes were plentiful, they provided shelter for birds and small animals. They usually grew on bare mountain sides where they were the first refuge for rabbits, foxes, tortoises, and other rarely seen creatures. The blackthorn flourished, with white flowers that opened after the rain and branches that became covered with tiny fruits. These dark blue berries were as big as barley grains and provided food for small creatures all summer long.

Ali Emmi was known in the village as the most hardworking maker of panniers, apart from his older brother, Halil Emmi. A basket he made could be used for years. He would get orders months before the grape vines were harvested. He'd take the orders then, as he needed a lot of time to search the mountains and thickets for the materials he would cut and drag home. Self-made moccasins on his feet, a small saw in hand, he would patiently trek over hills and mountains where the blackthorn grew, cut the blackthorn branches into suitable lengths, and pile them onto his donkey to be carried home. He had no idea how to cheapen his work, and never tried to. His reputation was such that it was said, "The baskets Crazy Ali weaves are as strong as bone."

Basketmaker Ali

Ali Emmi would stack the branches he had cut and trimmed in the mountains in a shaded place at the entrance to his house. He would prune the blackthorn branches he had chosen with such care, and then split them in two, lengthways. I loved to watch silently while Ali Emmi was doing this. He would start weaving the basket, whether a pannier or a trug, from the base. He would choose a split branch for both density and flexibility. He laid the spokes down in what looked like a spider's web, then started to wind the very first crossing line with a circular motion, supporting the frame with the toes of both feet. Holding a knife or blade in his teeth, he would begin the process of weaving. He wouldn't say much, but sometimes asked me, "My lamb, pass that long spoke to me, will you?" and I would give it to him. I would feel as though I was helping him, and this made me glow with pride.

Ali Emmi and Havva Abla had no children. They used to say, "What can be done? Allah didn't give us any."

His elder brother, Halil Emmi, who had fought at the Dardanelles in World War I, and his wife, Ümmügüssün Abla, had no living children either. "They were born and died, born and died. Allah did not give them life," they mourned. They went on complaining in this way until one day, a baby girl was born to them. They called her Durdu, meaning "the one who stayed." Durdu began to grow up as the only child of both the households, and the joy of these sweet, elderly neighbors made the whole village happy. Like the rest, my father and mother were happy for their neighbors. They had not wanted to show too much love for their own children in the presence of a childless woman. They had been reluctant to do so, thinking, It will seem like boasting and upset the neighbors.

It was not unusual for the villagers to pity the helpless. They pitied a married woman who could not bear children. If a farmer's ox died, it was a cause for pity. Not to be able to afford to sacrifice an animal at the Feast of Sacrifice was considered a pity. Likewise, a person who couldn't find a cure for an illness of a member of his family, or a girl of fifteen who was abducted and forced to be wife to someone, always aroused pity, as did orphans.

I imagine many villagers pitied Ali Emmi and Havva Abla for not having their own children. However, neither Ali Emmi and Havva Abla felt "less" or "incomplete" because they could not have any children of their own. They certainly did not show any jealousy toward other families. Havva Abla, especially, always showed her love for us children by helping us out whenever possible. When my father was out on his rounds and my mother was at the summer pastures of the yayla, we children were left in the village to water the garden. We would say, "Havva Abla, please wake me up tomorrow before dawn," and go to sleep without any qualms. If we came from the fields with a loaded donkey, we would ask her for help, saying, "Havva Abla, come and help us unload."

When children began to do little chores, parents would often give them responsibilities, as well as tasks beyond their capacity. However unfeeling this may seem, the tasks imposed on children at an early age taught them the need to work, and gave these small creatures self-confidence, a taste of freedom even, as well as encouraging enterprise. When Havva Abla saw we were struggling to carry out the jobs given to us by our fathers or mothers, very often she would come and help us.

It was the year I started primary school. When Ali Emmi, sitting in the shade of the overhang preparing his spokes as usual, saw me coming home from school one day, he called me over. Whenever I saw Ali Emmi sitting and weaving one of his baskets, I loved to go and watch, so I went straight over to him. Without taking his eyes off the branch he was shaping, Ali Emmi asked, "Come, my stout support, tell me what you learned in school."

I showed him the words and pictures in my alphabet book and talked about multiplication tables. He looked randomly at one or two pages, then he asked what the words meant. As he listened to me, he wrinkled up his face. After a while, he said, "My lamb, I love you. But what you read to me was all about things like plants and flowers, sheep and goats, mules and horses. What's the good of that? If you read about them, what difference does it make? Oh, I wish you were learning to recite prayers, so that when I die, you could bless me with a prayer."

Like all village children, I hung my head. I couldn't answer back to an older person, no matter whom, and I didn't.

I loved Ali Emmi and respected him more than my real uncle. Ali Emmi knew I would listen to him in silence and liked the way I didn't interrupt for any reason. But this time, he was upset. His face was serious. It was different from the way he looked when he was paying full attention to the work in hand. He started to murmur complainingly to himself. Something had certainly happened to grieve him. As he went on speaking, his voice became muffled. He started making a trug. Without heeding that I was near him, he went on working and talking to himself.

You poor basketmaker, Crazy Ali!
Making excuses
to scorn what this small child
has read and learned.
What about yourself?
What can you yourself do?
In order to earn two crusts of bread,
you spend a day on the mountains
cutting branches until evening,
hungry and thirsty
then work for twelve days,
to weave two or three trugs,
a couple of panniers.
Will it always be so?
Nonstop, this life, this toil.

Filled with blind breath?
No child, no heirs.
When death comes,
no one at all,
not one to say a prayer
for you, when you are gone.
In this fleeting world,
why all this effort
to feed a greedy gullet?
Poor, wretched Ali!
Trug and basket Ali!
To come into this world,
and leave it as
a basketmaker.
Of all your work
what will you leave behind
when you are gone?

Ali Emmi talked and talked, his voice becoming tearful. It was as if he was in great pain. Even though I didn't fully understand what he was saying, I listened without speaking. I waited to see what he would do. First, Ali Emmi put down his knife and handsaw. He left off working on the basket he had just begun and stood up, telling me, "Off you go home, my lamb." He went toward his own house. He came out with a mattock and spade, swinging them both onto his shoulder. Then he went off along the road to the yayla.

A little while later, Havva Abla came home from watering her garden and asked me, "Have you seen Ali Emmi? Where's he gone to?"

I told her he had taken his mattock and spade and gone up the road to the yayla.

"Goodness gracious! We don't have a vineyard or a garden on the way to the yayla. Why did he go there, I wonder, that mad fellow of mine? Can he have gone to cut wood or something on the mountain? No, that's not it. The donkey's tied up in the stable. And what would he do with a spade to cut wood?" she said anxiously.

This is how Ali the Basket Weaver started to become Ali, the Water Diviner.

That day, Ali Emmi, shouldering mattock and spade, walked for one and a half hours along the road to the yayla. It was uphill most of the way. Sweating in the midday heat, he didn't even think of being tired. At the place called Kireçlik, on the road to the yayla, there is a steep, rocky slope above the lower valley of Dördoluk and before coming to the plain of Söğüt Spring. There, right on the path to the yayla, was a small area of the road that, winter or summer, was always muddy. Water, seeping from a crack in the rocks even in the hottest, driest summer, dampened a patch of earth a few steps wide. Most of those who came and went along this road knew this as the place where wild bees and butterflies came to drink.

When Ali Emmi came to this damp patch that he remembered from seeing before, he took his mattock and spade and began to dig a ditch on the upper side of the road without doing any damage. The earth was stony and covered with fast-growing, prickly brambles and bushy shrubs. Ali Emmi, with his customary diligence, continued digging the ditch until after time for afternoon prayer. Then, as evening was falling, shouldering his tools once more, he returned home.

In answer to the questions that his wife, Havva, and brother, Halil, had as to why he had left his basket unfinished, where he had gone, and what he had done, he described the work he had done there. He had made up his mind. He said that his main aim from then on would be to work only for the benefit of others.

"I will dig up the mountain until I find where the water seeping away at Kireçlik comes from. Then I will lay pipes from the source as far as the road and make a fountain just above the road so the water doesn't spill over. If I find sufficient water, I'll make two outlets. I want the trough to be a wide one. Even if in the drought of the summer, the water only comes drop by drop, it will collect in the trough. Travelers, beasts of burden, the birds, and the wild beasts will drink the water there and bless me. Maybe the travelers who drink from the fountain will say a prayer for me. Our food will be a crust of bread. We have a garden to sow onions, potatoes, and salad greens, and a big enough vineyard. Havva and I will get by. I don't want to work for money anymore. From now on, going as a day laborer or making baskets is not the work for me."

Since they saw that Ali Emmi was quite determined, his wife and older brother simply said, "Well, if that's what you've decided, let's see you do it."

Ali Emmi worked for three months on the ditch he had begun to dig in the unyielding ground at Kireçlik. Those coming and going from our village, the Akpınar villagers who used the same road, and the Yörüks who passed with their camel caravans every week in the summer on the way to the Friday market, were all amazed to see one man working away for days, all by himself. It aroused the curiosity of the passersby to see him working away as if to pierce the heart of the mountain.

When Basketmaker Ali's intentions were made plain, the passersby began to show their appreciation and admiration of him. Travelers along the road no longer passed on after just greeting him with good wishes for his work. They began to bring him small, simple presents such as food, or a new or little-worn shirt, or new underclothes. Those who understood his needs began to supply what he needed of their own accord. One of the villagers said, "Ali, my master, I've a good steel pick at home. I haven't used it for years. Come and I'll give it to you this evening. It'll help you remove the stones." One of the potters offered, "Uncle Ali, I'll make the water pipes you'll need and have them ready for you." Another neighbor who counted himself better off than most said, "Brother Ali, when the time comes to make the fountain and the trough, I can get you five or six bags of cement." One of the blacksmiths said, "Master Ali, when your mattock wears out, leave it at my forge. I'll repair it for you."

Ali Emmi would say thank you for the gifts or promises of whatever kind, and take what was offered, saying, "Your good health, may it never lessen." If he received more than he needed, he would share with his neighbors who had nothing.

Even the August heat could not make Ali the Basketmaker slacken his efforts. During the grape harvest, he laid the water pipes, covered the ditch, and began the work of concreting. Somewhere, he found a long iron pipe and gotten the blacksmith to shape it as he wanted. He built a wall for the fountain and put a long concrete trough in front of it. Before the first snow fell, Ali Emmi completed his first good work, the Kireçlik Fountain.

One of Basketmaker Ali's fountains

Without waiting for spring to come, Ali the Basketmaker began to seek out and find places where water seeped into the roads, first on the way to the yayla, followed by other distant areas of the village such as Çötü, Dördoluk, Irmasan, and Alan, from which roads stretched to the furthest fields or pastures. Using his experience from the first fountain, he worked hard to drain the water from roads and footpaths, which usually stayed muddy all year, and channel it into useful fountains.

By this time, Basketmaker Ali Emmi was known in our village as Ali the Expert Water Diviner. He never turned down the requests of the nearby villagers who heard of his skill and dexterity in finding water and making fountains. He made a great number of fountains on dry roads and footpaths. Everyone around knew and respected him as Ali the Expert Water Diviner from Çat. He went on making fountains near or far, on mountains and plains, until the end of his life.

Gypsies

1
Circumcision

In my childhood, the Romany, or Gypsies, were called the Abdals by the people in our region. Later, I learned that Abdal signified nomadic peoples who moved from place to place as a way of surviving for reasons of economy or philosophy. This was in the era before villagers began to migrate to the big cities. The Abdals would supply useful goods and services to the villagers, who earned their living by sowing and planting, harrowing and harvesting, and raising animals and produce. Despite providing often essential services for very modest sums, the gypsies were not much trusted by the villagers, who became nervous whenever the gypsies were around; they were more careful of their goods and children at such times.

The gypsy men, women, and children were hard workers. Most of them were dark-skinned and had beautiful green eyes. Apart from their interesting headscarves, the women's way of dressing was little different from that of the village women in the area.

"Rather die than get a bad name," the saying goes. It was said that these strange people had once gotten a bad name, though no one knew when or how this prejudice toward them came about. Many were insults and cruel sayings about gypsies: "the Abdals are thieves," "the Abdals have no religion and no beliefs," "if you sleep with a gypsy, you will never get clean, even if you wash until the bricks beneath your feet crumble," "don't make a hasty decision at a time when a gypsy divorces his wife."

Deep in my memory is an event concerning the Abdals. I was probably four years old. In the lazy days of summer or autumn, the village boys of the same age used to play a game called Barefooted, Pumpkin-Headed. It was played with pieces of stone, big or little. We joked among ourselves as we played this game, then we stopped to listen to the increasingly loud sound of pipe and drum. When we looked in the direction of the sound, we saw four strange men, two playing a tune, and the other two shouting an announcement, like town criers.

It wasn't long before we understood what was happening. These were the Abdals who had come to circumcise the boys whose time it was—which, as luck would have it, was around age or four or five. When we learned what circumcision meant, we ran away like scared cats. Climbing on to the high roofs of our houses, we began to watch what was happening with apprehensive curiosity.

The first "victims" were the boys whose fathers were at home. The father would step out of the house with his son, and situate himself, holding the child. Any nearby villagers would gather and watch, having been drawn outside by the music. Each father promised the child crying on his lap, "Son, I'll buy you a collarless shirt, half boots, lokum (Turkish delight)," and other such gifts. The pipe and drum continued playing a popular folk melody. Suddenly, beguiled by the music and the caressing words, the boy left off crying, if only for a minute. One of the circumcisers expertly caught hold of the child's hands and feet, the other circumciser, one hand holding the penis tightly between two sticks, swiftly cut off the foreskin with a razor. The child roared with pain, drowning the sound of pipe and drum. Those watching cried with one voice, "Amen!" and clapped their hands. After the wound had been sprinkled with salt, the child crept into his father's arms, his father hugging him tight as he took him home.

Accompanied by the music, the two Abdal circumcisers circumcised with the same dexterity and expertise every child placed ready on his father's lap. They used the same two sticks and razor over and over again without ever wiping or washing them. When my friend Muzaffer's turn came, his father, Niyazi Emmi, put him on the circumciser's lap, saying, "My son will be a man." Muzaffer was circumcised, but did not cry out. Then the old Abdal circumciser gave Muzaffer two slaps on the cheek. His cheeks burning, Muzaffer began to cry.

"Ha! That's right, son, cry. Otherwise, God save us, it'll bring bad luck!" the circumciser declared as he gave him back to his father, and the villagers cheered.

The Abdal circumcisers went on with their work until there were no more boys in our area left to be circumcised, other than the boys like me who were hiding on nearby rooftops. Accompanied by the musicians, the circumcisers left for the nearby Uluyol neighborhood to find more boys, before night fell.

"What a good thing Father wasn't home so I escaped," I rejoiced. At least, that's what I thought at the time.

When evening came, Mother said, "Go to the guesthouse and see how many guests there are."

When I got there, I saw the Abdal circumcisers sitting and talking.

"There are four of them," I told my mother, not telling her who they were.

The guesthouse was a responsibility left us by my grandfather Ali. For that reason, it was our duty to take the evening meal to traveling salesmen, master craftsmen, or other kinds of strangers who were there to spend the night. My mother prepared enough cracked wheat pilaf, bread, and ayran, which is like buttermilk, for four people. We took it together to the guesthouse.

The circumcisers expressed their satisfaction, saying, "Live long, sister, the blessings of the departed be on you."

After I had gone to sleep that evening, my father came home from wherever he had been working during the day, a far-off field, the market, or from his peddling journey. Before he reached home, he learned that the circumcisers were at the guesthouse. He paid them a short visit, taking them a basket of straw for their animals, and, after they had promised to meet him early the next morning, returned home.

When I awoke the next morning, Father said to me, "Come, son, let's see if our guests have gone. If not, we must take them some bread." Then he took my hand and off we went. The guesthouse was nearby and we were soon there.

The circumcisers had only just gotten up. "Our work here is finished," they said. "Should we go to Dere or Kozağaç next?" they asked each other.

The oldest of them said to his apprentice, "Let's attend to uncle's business first."

The apprentice asked me, "What's your name, son? My, you're a handsome one." He took my hand and sat me on the circumciser's lap. With the same speed, he took off my underpants, or şalvar, my mother had sewn, and uncovered my legs. Before I knew what was happening, he cried, "In the name of God," and an agonizing pain shot through me. I began to cry. I didn't understand what had happened. But I must have peed on the old man's hand and clothes as he said, "Well done, my son. You've pissed, that's good. That means your wound will soon heal. You're a man now."

My father hugged me, saying, "My son, my brave little bull. Come now, I'll give you a whole comb of honey," and he took me home.

The honeycomb Father gave me was the size of his hand. I went on crying and eating my honey. What was done, was done. And with what injustice? I wasn't crying just because it hurt. Yesterday, my friends had all been circumcised ceremoniously to the sound of a zurna, the high-pitched reed flute, and a davul, the large drum, while the people watched, clapped their hands, and said, "Bless the deed, Amen." The music of the pipe and drum had given the village a festive mood. Not a zurna nor a davul had been played for me. There had been no neighbors to clap their hands and wish me well. All I got for being circumcised in the silence of the morning was half a honeycomb. And I wasn't even old enough to understand why I had been subjected to such pain.

That was my first encounter with the Abdals. For a time, whenever I heard the word *Abdal*, I would run and hide from fear.

Three or four months after the circumcision, five or six of us were playing on the grass at the yayla, the upland pasture, when we saw a file of two men and three or four women coming toward the Oba, our summer village there. An elderly neighbor who had been watching us play said, "Children, go and hide. The Abdals are coming."

It would be wrong to say we all scattered. Some of us shouted, "Uncle, we've been circumcised!" Others, "Uncle, my willy's been cut!" We all streaked toward Çilehane Mountain behind us and began to clamber up it. Stopping when we got to the upper slopes, we started looking to see whether the Abdals had gone or not. Our protective mothers, thinking the gypsies had scared us intentionally, went and scolded the unfortunate Abdals. In fact, they weren't circumcisers, but tinsmiths.

My circumcision was not the only unforgettable encounter I had with the Abdals. Another even more comic event happened years later when I was thirteen. But I'll get to that in a bit.

The village children learned a lot about the outside world by observing the goods and skills of Abdals and other traveling peddlers who came to our village. Most of these people with unfamiliar clothes seemed so foreign to us. Abdals, who sold their services for a living and whose pack animals carried goods we didn't have in the village, would come and go according to the season, to barter their goods. These strangers would price their goods according to the barter method. Sometimes they'd manage to sell unnecessary trinkets, like machine-made tops for boys and smooth little stone sets for girls for Five Stone games, but mostly they sold very necessary goods that we could not easily access otherwise. I enjoyed silently watching for a long time the tinsmiths and saddlers who came to our village. The tools and the materials they used attracted my attention. Peddlers selling small items useful around the home were loved best by the women and children. What didn't they have in their bags? Without spending money, one could get a notebook in exchange for an old pair of woolen socks, sewing needles, or a bodkin, or a reel of thread for a dish of cracked wheat.

Most of the sellers brought the special products of their own area. Peddlers from the forest villages brought spools made from bark, gum arabic, resin, rolling pins, tongs, and even kneading troughs and round tables for rolling out pastry. From Akçapınar and Bahatlar came the special white clay needed for making whitewash and for boiling up grape syrup. The Pabuççu villagers came to collect hides. The Yörük people brought butter, soft cheese, goat hair, and wool. The peddlers from the villages of Manavgat brought dried figs, pomegranates, blueberries, and carob beans. Fish came from Yalıhüyük. Tahtacis, or woodworkers, from far away, came to our village to saw planks from great poplar trees cut into usable sizes. Village life depended significantly on the skills of visiting craftsmen, such as saddlers, tinsmiths, musicians, and entertainers. Gypsies provided such services.

Gypsies led a nomadic life, going to different places at the time of year when it was possible to get work. They roamed in groups of three, five, or more families, traveling with a caravan of pack animals, donkeys, horses, or mules carrying their tents, bedding, and tools. They chose where to go according to the climate and produce of the area. They used to come to our village and its surrounding areas in summertime, rather than in the winter months when it was cold and snowy. Large caravans would divide into two or three groups and make separate camps, pitching their tents on different nearby meadows. Wherever they found work and earned money, they would then camp for a few weeks, one or two kilometers outside the village near a fountain, running water, or a well. The men would do the work they were good at in front of their tents, to showcase their craft. Having proven their expertise and skill, they would obtain permission from the village authorities to enter the village. Tinsmiths, saddlers, and musicians were allowed to work in the village for a limited time during the day.

Bir sadaka ver ağam, bacım,
Bakayım falına yavrucuğunun,
Kısmeti iyi çıkar ağam, bacım!

Two Gypsy women singing, asking for alms, and offering to tell fortunes

There were no restrictions on the work of gypsy women. They would come to the village in the morning, two by two, an older woman with a younger one, and go around each house in turn till evening came. Stopping outside the outer door, they would sing a tuneful ballad and beg for alms. The owner of the house, man or woman, who opened the door, believing it was bad luck to turn away a beggar, would give the gypsy woman whatever came to hand. Food, such as a piece of bread, a handful of cracked wheat, or an onion, would be tossed into the goatskin bag the Abdal women carried on their shoulders. Following this, they would offer to tell a fortune.

The greatest skill of the Abdal women was fortune-telling. The village women believed that these women had the power to see into the future. A young village woman's greatest wish was for her child's future. In the hope of learning what was in store, and in accordance with what was predicted, mother and grandmother would be very generous toward the Abdal fortune-tellers.

Abdal fortune-tellers would take dried flower seeds or fruit of different plants from their girdles, and chant jingles such as "Open, fortune, I say, open!" and scatter the different grains. Then they'd exclaim, "Look! You see, don't you? Your fortune will be revealed," giving the person hope. If you opened the door to an Abdal woman, it wasn't enough to say, "I don't want my fortune told, my good woman, go away!" She would use every kind of persuasion to convince you to let her tell your fortune.

One day, two Abdal women begging for alms knocked on the door of a neighbor's house. The owner of the house, Uncle Hönker, opened it. The elder of the women said, "May your day go well, mister. Give me alms and give joy to the souls of your ancestors."

Uncle Hönker gave each of them a round of flatbread.

In a beguiling voice, the same Abdal woman continued:

For the love of your ancestors' souls,
give me your alms again, Uncle.
I'll look at your fortune, too.
May all you wish for come true!

Although Uncle Hönker replied, "I don't want my fortune told. Good cheers go with you, sister," the Abdal woman went on with her sales pitch:

> Uncle, I see you're a bachelor.
> Sit down and I'll tell you your fortune;
> does the future shine brightly before you?
> I'll know by a look at your palm.

When she said this, Uncle Hönker teasingly answered:

> Hey there, my black-haired sister,
> you're right, I'm an unmarried man.
> Please do me a favor, I beg you,
> find a wife for me, quick from your clan.

The Abdal woman cried in turn:

> Ugh! Save us, dear Mother! Hey, man,
> do you think we are that kind of folk?
> What you wish for never could happen;
> our bed is the ground, we're in a bad mood,
> at night, our dogs also lie down without food.

With this retort, the two Abdal women scurried off into the distance.

2
How the Gypsy Women Outsmarted the Peddlers

Let's go back to the comic and embarrassing events I mentioned before. One happened in my thirteenth year, and I've never forgotten what the gypsies did to us.

My father liked to take a companion with him when he went on his rounds as a peddler. I was at boarding school then, but when I came home for the summer holidays, I would work with Father the whole of the time. That June, we had decided to go with a few of the neighbors to the villages of Kozağaç and Karabayır to pick apples. These apples were called summer apples. When it started to get hot, they would ripen, but drop soon afterward. Unless they were collected in time and sold quickly, they would rot. The people of these two villages, where such apples were plentiful, liked to sell the apples from their orchards wholesale to those who earned a living as peddlers. At the Friday market of Bozkır that week, after talking to several men from two apple-growing villages, Father and the neighbors decided to go to those villages to pick and buy the apples from their orchards. Early Saturday morning, our neighbors, Hasanoca, Medali's son Kemal the Blind, and Berduş's son Hacali, left for Kozağaç with a donkey each, and my father and I left for Karabayır with our two donkeys. We all set off together. As the animals had nothing to carry, we were able to ride at least half the way, and arrived in Karabayır an hour and a half later. My father found the villager he had spoken with at the Friday market. After agreeing on the price per basketful, we went to his orchard, shook the trees, filled our sacks with the fallen apples, and paid for them. Loading our donkeys with the sacks of apples, we returned home toward evening.

We had to get the apples we had collected off our hands within two days, at the most. If the apples stayed in the sacks any longer, they would turn brown, become tasteless, and be impossible to sell.

The next morning, taking advantage of the coolness of the early hours before dawn, we loaded the sacks of apples on our animals, and set off in the dark. We were going to the villages that produced grain for a living, to exchange our apples by bartering them for whatever the villagers had in the way of wheat, barley, and garbanzo peas.

In villages where grain and cereals were produced, the only fruits were melon and watermelon. These juicy fruits were a joy to eat in the heat of summer, but they did not ripen until late July. In the long, hot days of June, it was the duty of peddlers like us to satisfy these village farmers' desire for fresh fruit. So that evening, our apple-seller group decided they would go to the Seydişehir villages of Lower, Middle, and Upper Karaviran, which were within one or two kilometers of each other. Calculating that the road there would take six hours, we set off two hours before dawn, driving our apple-laden donkeys in front of us.

We peddlers liked to set off very early in the day at dark. The villages we had to pass through along the road—in particular, the larger ones,

Dere and Ahırlı—were peaceful then. We could come and go without encountering the morning bustle.

The first five hours of the journey passed uneventfully. We had passed through Dere after forty-five minutes. When we reached the dusty red plain called Kızıldüz, dawn was breaking. Before the sun rose, we had gone past Ahırlı. At the level ground near Sandı, we joined the Bozkır-Seydişehir stabilized road. From then on, the road widened. There we had to pay more attention to our animals so that they did not damage the wheat and barley being grown for fodder in the fields at the edge of the road.

While encouraging the pack animals along, I did not interrupt the elder apple sellers in their discussions as to which village to go to first. While doing my duty of driving the loaded animals, I walked with my head full of dreams. The road came to the edge of Soğla Lake and ran for a considerable distance along the shore of the lake. On the other side of the road was the Çarşamba Canal, carrying water to the plain of Konya from Beyşehir Lake. The word Soğla, or Suğla, refers to the fact that in some years, the lake water either receded or dried up completely. We noticed that day that the lake was quite low. The land left behind by the receding water was very fertile. The villages bordering the lake would divide the land according to the number of family members, and use it to plant garbanzo peas. The bright green fields of new shoots, and the lake itself, extending as far as the eye could see to the high mountains beyond, were reflected in the still waters of the lake. On the right side of the road, the muddy waters of the canal flowed so slowly that, unless you [or one] looked very closely, they seemed to be stagnant. Water-loving willows formed a green line bordering each side of the canal.

The Akkise Bridge over the canal gave way to a shortcut to the road to the village Karaviran. This road was a very narrow pathway, on each side of which were fields of wheat and barley. Even though we had to take greater care of our animals to see they did not damage the crops in these fields bordering the road, we chose this way in order to save time. Having come with our loaded animals without any difficulties along the Bozkır-Seydişehir Highway, we had almost reached the turnoff at the Akkise Bridge, and our goal lay only an hour ahead of us.

Just then, we saw a long caravan of pack animals coming from the opposite direction. Father and his friends recognized it as a Gypsy caravan. The caravan was composed of many people and loaded pack animals. In order not to be on the same road at the same time, the apple sellers decided to hurry and reach the turn at the Akkise Bridge to avoid meeting with the caravan. We started to drive the animals as fast as they would go.

We were able to turn off the main road to cross the bridge without meeting the gypsy caravan. As we were going a little more slowly across the bridge, three or four women ran after us crying "What's in your packs, uncles?" When they heard we were carrying apples, they turned toward their caravan and shouted, "They've got apples! Shall we get some?"

The gypsy caravan continued along the highway without slowing down. Once over the bridge, we took the footpath to Karaviran. The number of women following us increased. They came up to us and said with great persistence, "Come on, uncles, sell us some apples! We want to buy your apples."

My father and his friends said to each other after a short calculation, "If we can sell at least a hundred kilos to such a big caravan, we can off-load the rest at our destination by evening, and return home earlier." They called a halt and unloaded their packs, almost covering the footpath as they did so.

Those who came to buy apples were all women, young or old. There wasn't a man among them. What's more, they came in ever-increasing numbers. Each apple seller opened one of his sacks and displayed the contents. Some of the gypsy women said, "Please, uncles, give us one. Let's have a taste." Without waiting for my father and his friends to say, half reluctantly, "Take one, then. If you don't like it, don't buy," each of them had snatched up an apple and started eating it.

As Father was, so to say, an experienced salesman, he immediately took out his scales. He weighed out three kilos from our sack for his first customer and tipped them into her skirt she held up like a bag. When her skirt was full, the gypsy woman said, pointing to an elderly woman, "Uncle, my mother-in-law will pay," then she ran off to join the caravan.

The other peddlers warned my father to sell turn by turn from the apples in their sacks too. After that, my father began to weigh out two or three kilos from the other sacks. When it came to the business of paying, the women pointed out other women as responsible for that. While the women were making sure that the amount they asked for was being weighed, almost all of them, saying, "God bless you, uncles," would devour one or two more apples.

In all of this commotion, it was my duty to hold the halters of the pack animals to prevent them from damaging the crops in the wayside fields. In my childish way, I enjoyed watching the goings-on. I was happy, thinking, They'll finish selling the apples today; tomorrow, we'll return home and I can play with my friends. I can swim at the Gürlevik Falls pool or I can go with them to the yayla, the summer pasture.

Our apple sellers, confident they would get their money, went on weighing out apples, trying their best to persuade the chorus of women around them to buy. When four or five of the women went off together after filling their skirts, the men began to panic a little. Father stopped and said, "First, let's get the money for what we've sold, and then we'll start weighing out apples again."

One of the women called out, "Don't you worry, brother, I've got the money here," pointing to her bosom.

Kemal, the youngest of the peddlers, said, "Let's see! Is the money there?" He put his hand on her breast to feel for a money-fold or something.

One of the women intently urged Father, "I'm fixing a wedding, Uncle. Weigh me fifteen kilos," and opened the goatskin bag she was carrying.

But Father reacted quickly. "I've weighed out a lot of apples, sister. Let's have the money now, and then I'll go on with the job."

The same woman asked, "Will you change a gold piece, Uncle?"

Shocked, my father and his friends said, "We don't have the money to change a gold piece. You must give us coins for the apples."

Then the woman who had filled her bag with the apples she said she would buy emptied them all back into my father's half-filled sack, saying, "Gold's all we have, Uncle," and the other women all followed suit. Having emptied their skirts, all the women hurried off at a trot toward the caravan without a backward glance.

Our "experienced" salesmen stood, turned to stone. Ten or fifteen kilos of apples had gone from each of the sacks. Four grown men and a child were robbed in broad daylight, in front of our very eyes. Within an hour of the villages where they had hoped to sell their loads, the fruit of two days' hard work, they had been tricked out of their apples by the women. The four peddlers cursed the Gypsy women at length and loudly. But those women had long since gone far away.

My father groaned. "I weighed exactly sixty-five kilos of apples, and my arm hurts. Should I be more upset about that, or at being robbed by those hussies?"

Even Hasanoca, the calmest of the peddlers, complained again and again, "The Abdal women won! They all beat fools like us!"

Kemal, the youngest of them, tried to make the others laugh, saying, "I've come off best of all, I think. I got to fondle the woman's breast, to see if it was true when she said, 'The money's here.' Her breast was full and firm, the hussy."

Not one of the others smiled or said, "Good for you!" With long faces, they began to tie up their half-empty sacks.

At the beginning, the peddlers had been happy to sell to the Gypsy women. Not one of them had said to another, "My friend, you sell your apples and good luck to you. I have no flour left at home. I need barley and wheat, not money. I'll go on to Karaviran and exchange my apples for grain." Now they were all angry and they had no one but themselves to blame.

After loading our apple sacks onto the donkeys, we journeyed for another hour and then separated to go and sell in the three Karaviran villages as planned earlier. Father and I unloaded our apples in Middle Karaviran. One of the other two peddlers chose Upper Karaviran and one Lower Karaviran. Upon coming to a village, a peddler couldn't sell his goods for the price he asked for. He had to bargain. We bargained with the few old people who had not gone to work in the fields, and determined what should be exchanged for our apples: four kilos of apples for one measure of wheat, three for a measure of mixed grain or garbanzo peas, and two and a half kilos of apples for one measure of barley. In those days, it was considered unlucky to use scales to weigh the grain to be exchanged, so bowls ranging in size from small to large were used. The smallest one, cylindrical in shape, would hold from one to one and a half kilos, according to the type of grain. Once the bargaining was done, everyone, old or young, man or woman, began to bring a certain amount of grain and take their apples without any fear of being cheated. We couldn't refuse anyone, whoever came. My father didn't turn anyone away who wanted apples, even if they brought things to eat such as flaxseed, poppy seed, or eggs. We sold our apples so as to please the villagers of Karaviran. Sometimes even children were happy to get a kilo or half a kilo of apples in return for a small dish or plate of garbanzo peas.

1950' lerde,
Bozkır ve Seydişehir yörelerinde,
hünerleri ve kurnazlıklarıyla,
köylere hizmet götüren bir Çingene Kervanı

*A Gypsy caravan in the 1950s
going to serve the villages of Bozkır and Seydişehir*

As there was no guesthouse in Lower or Upper Karaviran, after finishing selling their apples, and before it got dark, our friends who had gone to the other villages came to Middle Karaviran. Together we all ate the meal of flatbread, cracked wheat pilaf, and ayran offered to us at the guesthouse. The older apple sellers said, "Let's sleep for a while in front of the guesthouse. We'll take the road home early in the morning." But not one of them spread out an empty sack to lie on. When one of them said, "Friends, we've already been robbed and made little profit. If we set out now, we'll be home before morning," they all decided to start off at once. They didn't want to be seen by neighbors upon arrival to our village.

Loading the animals with the grain we had obtained, we started out along the road. My father lightened the load on one of our donkeys. "Son, you're the smallest. If you walk a bit and ride a bit, we can go quickly. But hold on tight, don't go to sleep and fall off," he said.

The apple sellers kept up a conversation all the way home. Perched on the donkey, I held on to the saddle tightly with both hands and listened, half-awake, half-sleeping. They talked of exciting journeys they had previously experienced with their pack animals. From time to time, they would exclaim, "How come we were cheated by those Gypsy women?"

As we journeyed along that night, it was decided that nothing should be said about it to anyone in the village. They knew how people would joke about it if anyone were told. All of us kept our promise. We even kept it secret from our families. But for years, we remembered this experience and whenever we saw one another, we would say, "Hey, remember that time we sold those apples?" and laugh about it.

Sixty years have passed since then. My father and our other apple-selling neighbors have gone and departed this life. I am telling this story for the first time in their honor. Maybe their children, grandchildren, or great-grandchildren will read this and smile like their ancestors did.

Grass Thieves

Every summer, many families of the village Çat moved to Sarot Yayla, the summer place in the highland pastures, for three months. It was a wonderful place for children and animals, but it brought a lot of hardship for adults, especially for the women, who had to constantly be on their toes to look after the animals and children. If you asked their husbands, they would say, "While the wives are enjoying the fresh, cool air of the yayla, with almost no responsibility, we are leading a dog's life in the village, or are away peddling, or working on the plains of Aydın." If you asked a wife at the yayla, she would say, "The yayla is the most grueling place for women." And indeed it was. When I was a child, my mother told me a story of just how awful it could be.

At the yayla, a woman and her children would live in a windowless, flat-roofed stone hut with an earthen floor, in a little village of similar huts, called "the Oba." To fill her children's bellies, she would cook meals of cracked wheat over a fire of twigs and logs. If the family had the means, they would buy a few goats with kids and bring them to the yayla. The woman would have to milk the goats twice a day. For most of the day, their goats stayed with a herdsman who looked after the cooperative's animals. Twice daily, this herdsman would bring the herd from grazing and bed the animals down near his hut for an hour or two, at the edge of this little village. Each woman would have to go, bucket in hand, to find her goats from among the thousands of animals for the first milking, and go through the same struggle in the afternoon for the second milking.

The evenings would present another problem. If the woman had a cow, and the cow had a calf, she had to find it before its calf did, otherwise the calf would suckle till there was no milk left. And what if the cow didn't come home from grazing? Normally, a cow with a calf, forced to leave the Oba early in the morning to go graze all day freely in the hillsides and meadows, came back for its calf before dark. If a cow was late, it had to be found before nightfall. She might worry, I hope the cow was not eaten by a wolf! She would walk all around the huts till she found it. Once the cow was found, it was milked, but the work would not end there. The cow's milk and the goats' milk had to be put together and delivered to the partner in the cooperative. Careful track had to be kept of the contributed daily milk, by dipping and marking the level of the milk on a new dry stick each time.

When it was that woman's turn to collect the milk from her partners after three or four days, the milk had to be boiled, cooled, and made into yogurt with the utmost care. Milk that was boiled in a cauldron that had not been cleaned of the previous boiling's sediments would curdle, and all her efforts would go to waste. During those three or four days, she had to churn the milk to separate the butter from ayran, or buttermilk. Part of ayran had to be sent to the village for the husband and close relatives. The excess ayran had to be turned into keş, a nonfat cottage cheese, or slowly cooked with cracked wheat and later dried to make tarhana, a cereal suitable for making soup in winter.

The children's food, clothing, and injuries were other problems. They played all day on the muddy ground with bare feet and uncovered heads. By the time they came home, their legs were sore and blistered. Their mother would have to clean them up and rub salted butter onto their legs. If they screamed with pain, she'd let them; she knew the salt would cure the sores.

The next day, in the half-light of dawn, she would milk the cow and let the calf suckle, then drive the cow away from the huts toward the hills and valleys where the cow would graze freely all day long. After the morning milking of the goats, the herdsman would take the herd, with the help of the sheepdogs, to graze where the grass was greenest. The kids of the family goats had to be joined to the separate herd, which has its own shepherd. The woman would let her calf feed on the grass alongside the huts so it learned how to graze. After combining the morning's milk and taking it to the cooperative partner, coming back home, and thinking of sitting down a little, a neighbor would come along. "Hatma, dear, I've no wood left for the fire. Come, let's go to Aygır Forest to collect kindling together. I'm afraid to go alone," she would say. There's no way out, the wife would think. I must go because I may need her help myself in a few days.

The two women, each with a rope four or five arm-spans long tied around her waist and with a small ax in her hand, would set off on the road to Aygır. They would have to walk two or three kilometers to find dry kindling in the woods. They'd go barefoot or wear cheap galoshes made of black rubber. They would choose their firewood, some dry, some still green. Binding the branches together with the rope, they would heave the bundle onto their backs. Upon bringing it home, they'd spread it out on the roof of the hut. If one of them had an infant to suckle, she'd carry it on her back while they did all of this. On the way home, with the bundle on her back, she would carry the infant in her arms. If she had a six- or seven-year-old child, she would take the child with her. Returning, the infant would be carried on the child's back. Many times, I carried my baby sister, Hayriye, back home from the forest of Aygır.

A lucky woman would have a resourceful husband. He would provide a stock of wood to burn the first few weeks. He would go to the forest and cut down bushes and kindling, load them onto the donkey, and pile them up in front of the hut. A husband would often not sleep at the yayla, but return to the village the same day. Before leaving, he would admonish his wife, "Daughter of Halil, when the firewood's finished, go with someone and bring back half a bundle or so on your back. If I can, I'll come and give you one or two more loads. If not, you must provide firewood for yourself."

As you may have noticed, a husband at that time did not call his wife by her name. He would begin by saying, "So-and-so's daughter," then continue, "My girl, go and set the table," or, "Girl, my back's itching. I haven't changed my underclothes for a month."

Some families in the village owned mountainous areas, suitable for gathering grass and weeds, and cutting firewood for the coming winter months. Other families who didn't have such land kept only the animals they couldn't do without. For a household with children, it was an absolute necessity to keep a cow, however good or bad. Every woman wanted to have a little milk, yogurt, and ayran in her house. Every family had to keep a donkey, as well. A donkey was necessary to carry saddlebags and implements, wherever you went, in or out of the village, to the mill, the market, or to a garden or vineyard. A donkey's staple food was hay. If the gleanings left after the wheat and barley had been harvested could be bought from the yayla, this would be mixed with a little hay and given to the animal. It was essential to provide hay as well as the thorny plants dug up from the mountains as winter fodder for the cow. In families who had no property from which to gather grass, the wife would be expected to find at least a little winter fodder for a donkey and a cow. These women would go to the forest to find what plants the goats and sheep had not devoured. They would bring bundles of these home on their backs and spread the plants out on the roof to dry.

Well, after a herd of two thousand sheep and goats had passed over a meadow, any green plants left could not be pulled up one by one, let alone cut with a sickle. The women had to go deep into the thick forests where herds of goats could not go, and find weeds growing among the rocky places there. This was such a torturous job that their hands would bleed and their knees would be bruised. It was incredibly painful to walk down the mountain with loads of greenery on their backs.

At times, when the women at the yayla went to the forests to forage for green plants, their eyes would light on bright green pastures in the distance. Their faces would take on the kind of look of a hungry cat eyeing a piece of liver hung on the hook in a butcher's shop. However, those pastures were the property of Karacahisar village. My mother, as she told me this story, said, "A right-minded woman would not have the audacity to think of going and stealing someone else's grass. But does Satan ever rest?"

Haspe, one such young and strong wife on the yayla one summer, was talking to her neighbors, Arefe, Haşşa, and İlmas. She was trying to persuade them, by hook or by crook, to do what she wanted. "The goats never go to the slopes on the other side of Aygır Forest and it seems there's a lot of grass there."

Early one morning, after milking the cows and sending them off to the mountains, and having given the milk to their cooperative partners, the four young women tied their sickles to the ropes at their waists and set off on the road to Aygır. When these four women reached Aygır, which was a deep valley bordering two neighboring villages, Karacahisar and Çat, they plunged into the forest where the trees grew too thickly for the goats to access, in the hope of finding untouched grass and weeds in narrow crevices. However, they saw that either someone had gotten there first, or the goats had eaten everything up. There wasn't even a handful of greenery left. They continued on through the forest until suddenly it ended and they came to a meadow with piled-up stones around the edges. Without listening to Arefe, who said, "Oh, this must be somebody's property. Let's go back," the others took their sickles and began to cut the best-looking clover in the meadow. Knowing the sickles might clink if they struck a stone on the ground, they cut the stalks from the center of the grassy area.

Arefe looked on in amazement as her friends slashed like lightning through the plants. She didn't know whether to join them or not in this meadow to which they were strangers. "I'm a God-fearing person. I'll cut some young branches off the forest's oak trees until they've loaded up," she said to herself, and began not only to cut the oak branches, but to pick the thin grass hidden at the bottom of the juniper stumps.

In order to collect enough for a load, the other three women swiped the clumps of clover vigorously with their sickles. Suddenly, three young men appeared, running rapidly toward the three women. Each of the young men caught one of the women, pushed her down on top of the clover, and sat on top of her, leering at her with rage. Weeping and crying, the women begged, "Don't do it, big brother. I did something foolish; don't you do the same." But these three young men had their way with each of the three women in turn.

The fourth, Arefe, had wandered off looking for grass and, without uttering a sound, was secretly watching what was going on. Eventually, the three young men let the women go, saying, "Come now, ladies, cut as much grass as you can carry, and be off with you. May it be a blessing to you. Come again tomorrow, the next day, too, if you like, and steal as much as you want."

They ran off into the forest and disappeared. The three women, Haspe, Haşşa, and İlmas, cut a plentiful amount of grass and loaded it onto their backs. On the way back, they walked along, talking in whispers among themselves about the size, shape, and behavior of the young men who had raped them. A little later, the fourth woman, Arefe, appeared in front of them, laughing cruelly, and saying, "I saw it all. But I swear to God, your secret is my secret." İlmas knew Arefe meant no such promise, but was in fact threatening to expose them. The cruel truth of village life at that time was that when a woman was raped, it was considered her fault; she was shamed and ostracized, if not criminalized.

İlmas, known for her cunning mind, quickly strategized how to convince Arefe to help protect them. "Look here, sister, we'll share what we collected with you. We'll split the fodder we collected into four parts and top up our loads with as many dry twigs as we can find. Then, if anyone asks when we get back why we loaded ourselves up with sticks as well as grass, we can say we didn't find enough grass, so we picked up some dry kindling on the way."

The other two brave women, Haşşa and Haspe, who were terrified of the village gossip, agreed with this suggestion immediately. Arefe was happy with the situation, as she had gained a full load without any trouble. The four yayla women returned to their yayla huts, huffing and puffing under their loads, three of them with unimaginable pain.

The husbands of İlmas, Haşşa, and Haspe were back home in the village, working on their respective occupations as blacksmiths, millers, peddlers, and vegetable growers. They did not have to travel all the way to Aydın, Söke, or Manisa provinces as day laborers. What if I am now, God forbid, pregnant? they worried. My husband never comes to the yayla when he is busy ... What if ...

With thoughts like this, each of the three heroic women went to their partner in the cooperative to beg for the loan of a small pot of yogurt and hid it away behind the pile of bedding, without the children noticing. That night, each of the three women lay down on the pallet placed on the floor, but not one of them could sleep. It seemed the morning would never come. As soon as dawn broke, each of them milked their respective cow and drove her up toward the mountain meadows. Each of them asked a nearby neighbor to pick out the family's goats with the help of a child, to milk her three or four goats at milking time, and deliver the milk to the cooperative partner's house, and to mind her small children for a while. Then, each of them made a bundle of the yogurt she had borrowed as a present for her man, and left the Oba before the sun got up.

It took three hours to walk from the Oba to the village. As they took to the road, our three heroines supported each other. Together, they planned what they would say when their husbands asked why they had come to the village without any warning. Each had an excuse ready:

"Man, the cracked wheat was finished," "I came to wash your clothes, man of mine," and "I came to put brushwood around the peppers, eggplants, and tomatoes that I planted three weeks ago." They thought up many such believable stories as they walked along. It was imperative their husbands not discover that they had been raped.

Each of the three women tried to calculate whether they could have gotten pregnant the day before. All three were thinking of the well-known saying: Can the ocean catch fire? It might happen. One must make sure that the unexpected didn't! If they were able to lie with their husbands when they reached the village, the women knew all their anxieties would fly away. Of course, they were not pleased at having to get up early and go to the village, bundle in hand, and suffer the ups and downs of the rocky road as if they had nothing else to do. But they had no choice. These traumatized women believed themselves to be at fault because they had stolen the grass. Each of them silently swore to herself. Never again! Curses on the grass I took, and on the wood too. Let the husband who keeps a donkey take care of the hay and the saddle himself.

And so one summer's day, three young husbands got to lie with their wives in broad daylight. And on that very same day, their wives, İlmas, Haşşa, and Haspe, said, "I cannot trust the neighbor to keep our children safe at night," and returned to the yayla before it was dark, flying up the road and taking only two and a half hours for a three-hour journey.

For the rest of their lives, they kept what had happened to them on that meadow a secret. Somehow, my mother had heard the story. These brave mothers, who were only trying to provide for their families, believed they had been punished for being grass thieves, punished with unimaginable trauma. As I think of them again now, I pray for their memories.

Stampede

The freedom of the yayla, the Sarot upland pastures, very much needed by animals and children alike, could sometimes bring about an unexpected, if comparatively small event. A young heifer or bullock grazing alone on the mountain might be eaten by a wolf, or a mischievous young boy playing on the hills among the rocks might fall and break an arm or leg. Our people were used to dealing with such events in their lives.

What the people living on the yayla for three months every summer were most afraid of, especially mothers of young children, was a stampede. They would tell the story of a young girl who was trampled by a stampede and lost her mind. The name of this lovely young girl was Sedef, and she lived for years without developing in either mind or body. Mothers were not afraid that their children might hurt themselves by falling from high rocks. They were not afraid their children might drown when swimming in the small lake, full of water at the beginning of the season. They were not even afraid of their children being bitten or kicked by one of the Yörük camels when they tried to mount it or collect camel hair to make into balls. But every mother was afraid of a stampede, and scared their children, warning them of this dangerous happening.

Stampedes came at great speed, like a train without brakes, unseen, like the natural disaster of a mountain flood after rain, and were more dangerous than an angry mob of infuriated, vengeful people. A stampede came and went with such swiftness that before a spectator could ask, "What's happening?" he would be rolled over like a cylinder and trampled upon. There was no hope for a person to whom this happened. They might survive, but in great pain.

It was pointless to say, "I wonder if there will be a stampede at the yayla this year." It would certainly happen. It was very fortunate that stampedes usually took place on the hills or valleys, and rarely happened within the Oba, the grouping of huts where the people lived. The time of day, place, and direction of the stampede, however, could not be known. An experienced person, looking around carefully, might hear a stampede in the distance and take precautions.

One evening in the middle of the year 1950, a young woman named Halime, whose family had come to the Sarot Yayla for the first time, was trying to find her two children. Either she didn't hear the stampede or she didn't recognize the sound. Without realizing what was happening, she found herself being trampled by hundreds of hooves. Her nearest neighbor saw this and began to shout, screaming, "Neighbors! Gülkadın, Anakiz, Menevşe Sister, come quickly! Halime's been run over by a stampede!"

Boğarsak: Stampede

The neighbors ran and found the young woman on the ground, covered in blood. Shouting "Oh, my God! Help us quickly!" their voices echoed over the whole plateau. By chance, there were two men at the yayla who, seeing the situation, said, "The woman's alive. We must take her to the hospital in Konya," and sprang into action. They took two support poles from the three-legged churn used for separating butter from the yogurt, and wrapped a carpet around them to make a stretcher. Laying the wounded woman down on the stretcher and tying her safely onto it, they attached the poles at the head of the stretcher to the saddle of a donkey. The ends of the stretcher trailed on the ground

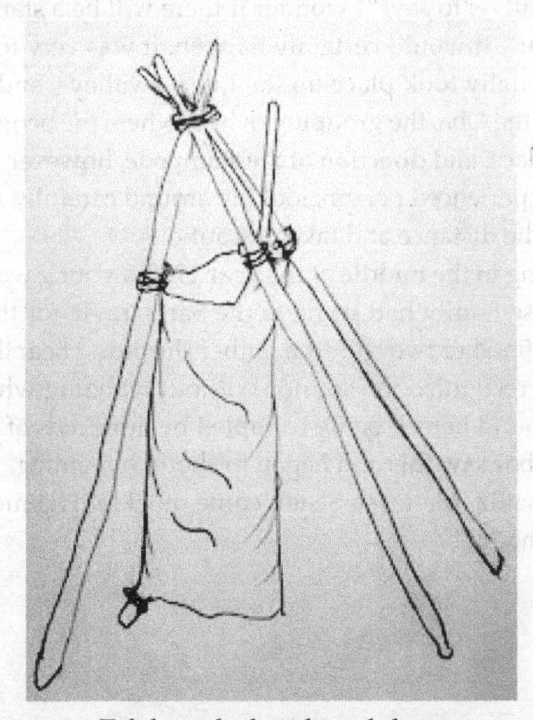

Tuluk yayık: three-legged churn

as they walked down the narrow, stony path to Bozkır, arriving there about midnight.

The jeep they hired there reached Konya State Hospital before morning. The patient was still alive. She needed an operation immediately, and this was done. Meanwhile, the resourceful villagers who had brought Halime to the hospital in time sent a telegram to give her husband, Ibram, news of the event. He had been at work hoeing the cotton fields on Söke Plain when the accident happened. Upon hearing the news, and after seeing his wife in the hospital, Ibram went to the yayla and took over the task of looking after the children and the animals that needed milking, helped by the wives who were his neighbors. Two weeks later, almost well again after a successful operation and good aftercare, Halime was able to return, first to the village, and then, the next day, to the yayla to be with her children.

While Halime was in the hospital, Ibram had prayed for her to get better and had vowed to offer a sacrifice. A week after Halime returned, a huge cauldron stood bubbling from morning till noon, right in the center of the Oba. Ibram slaughtered a well-fed young billy goat as an offering. The meat was cooked in the cauldron and served with pilaf. Everyone on the summer pasture was invited to the meal. The meaty cracked wheat pilaf was piled onto trays, and placed onto low tables. Everyone sat on the grassy ground around the tables and enjoyed the delicious and special meal. Halime and Ibram went around saying, "God bless you," to their neighbors, and thanked those who had helped her and looked after the three children, left all on their own when she had been injured.

In those days, there was no state, local, or village institution or office to give people first aid. In an emergency situation, the people of the villages acted as one body to do what was necessary. Whenever they heard of anyone dying, for example, the young men would take pickaxes and spades and go to the cemetery to dig the grave at the family plot. When there was a fire, they would run with pitchers in their hands to bring water from the Uluçay River. And although from time to time, they argued and fought with each other, whenever a disaster or emergency happened, villagers from Çat would join together and help whoever needed it.

Stampedes did not happen in and around the village of Çat, but only at the yayla, the upland pastures. Upon arrival at the summer pastures, all the nonproductive cattle were left free for the season, according to tradition. These cattle were two- to three-year-old heifers, uncastrated bullocks, and barren cows. They would wander over the grassy hills and valleys, grazing at will. In other words, for up to three months, until the hills and valleys became dry and barren, these animals lived a free life, responding only to the promptings of nature. A natural, instinctual wish for protection made them form small groups in the evening in a suitable flat place where they had been feeding, and spend the night there side by side. That place was called the cattle bed. At first light the next day, they would go to their favorite grazing places.

The promptings of nature were strong. Young animals were full of hormones coursing through their veins. In the life of every heifer, a time came when one such hormone made her blood boil like a cauldron. Her hot blood would overwhelm her, and the young animal would give off a powerful scent. No human or even animal could smell this, with one

Tufran yayık: Pottery churn

exception: the bullocks. It was such a piercing scent that it would draw the young bullock like a magnet, even if the heifer was grazing on the other side of the mountain from him. The smell compelled all the bullocks grazing on all sides of the mountain, whether low or high. This scent, created by nature, directed the bullocks to turn in the direction it came from. This hunger was not something they were conscious of. All they wanted was to find that scent. First, the nearest bullock would find the heifer and try to mount her. To prevent this, the heifer would run swiftly away. Then the number of bullocks after her would increase. Three, five, fifteen, thirty, forty—the number of bullocks might become more than a hundred, each of them running faster and faster after the heifer. Each of the young animals would run to the limit of its strength and speed in order to be the first to reach the heifer. In accordance with the law of nature, the heifer would increase her speed, and the herd of bullocks would chase faster and faster after her, forming a powerful stream, heedless of any obstacles. This was a stampede.

Those who heard the thundering hooves and the bellows issuing from the mouths of these stampeding animals were lucky if they could find a place to run to and hide. People or animals, big or small, all those who couldn't run and hide, were in danger of being crushed. The stampede could continue for about an hour before the strongest and speediest of the bullocks caught up with the heifer, held on to her with his front legs, and, with his hind legs still running, managed to couple with her. This coupling happened so fast that, within a very short time, that mysterious scent pervading the air dried away and was gone. Then the tired animals, no longer conscious of the scent, would realize how hungry they were and each one scattered to its chosen grazing place.

After this event, the heifer was pregnant. This was good news for its owner. It meant that the following spring, the family would have a cow with a calf. There would be milk for the baby, however little. If any milk remained, some of it could be taken to make yogurt. The yogurt could be watered down and shaken in a large vessel to make ayran, buttermilk, as an accompaniment to plain cracked wheat pilaf.

Herdsman Mustafa

1
The Yayla Tradition

Two important factors prompted the Çat villagers to go to the yayla every summer. One factor was being the owner of either at least one milk cow with a calf, or five or six goats with suckling kids. The second was having several children that didn't have the strength to work at anything in the village. If the first factor didn't hold, especially if there wasn't at least one cow with a calf, the second did not matter. Although the summer pasture had fresh air and was safe for children, if there was neither milk nor yogurt for the family, it was simply a mountaintop.

Even if a family with many children hadn't kept a cow during the rest of the year, in the spring, whatever money they had would be used to buy five or six goats with kids, and then they would migrate to the summer pasture. No family wanted to go there without a cow to milk. However, in the spring, even if one had the money, it was very difficult if not impossible to find a cow with a calf to buy. The cow was a family's source of milk and yogurt, and no one would sacrifice it just for money.

Choosing the day to migrate to the summer pastures was an important decision. It was the duty of the muhtar, or the village headman, an elected official responsible for the major affairs of the village. This was affected by how much snow there had been in the mountains in the winter, the amount of rainfall in the spring, and how high the grass in the valleys had grown. It was necessary to check that the grass had grown to the proper height before the day could be decided on. It was usually a day in the last week of April, or the first week of May. The day the village headman and his advisers had decided on would be announced to everyone by the village watchman. He would climb onto a roof from which he could be heard by most of the villagers. Cupping his mouth in his hands to direct the sound, he would turn first one way and then the other, shouting the same words in his loudest voice:

"Hey there, people! Listen well! Next Saturday is the first day for going to the summer pastures. Anyone going before Saturday comes will be punished. Don't say you didn't hear."

On the mountain, there was no need to herd the cows. The milk cow would lie down in the evening in front of the house. The calf and the goat kids would be shut up at night in a small shed. Early in the morning, the owner of the house would let the mother suckle her calf for a few minutes. This would relax her muscles and make it easier to milk her. After being milked, the milk cow would be allowed to suckle her calf for up to five minutes, until the udder was dry. At this point, the cow would be hungry, as by morning she would have digested all the grass eaten the previous day. So, the house owner would shut the calf away with the goat kids. The cow would be reluctant to leave her calf, so the owner would drive her off into the meadows. It was the same for all the cows at the yayla summer pasture. The cows wandered slowly over the mountains and valleys, grazing until evening came. When the cow had eaten her fill and her udder had become uncomfortably full of milk, she would make low mooing sounds, and return to find her calf. Her owner would milk her, and then she would be allowed to nurse with her calf, just like she had in the morning. After being milked, the cow would lie on the ground near the house, chewing her cud and digesting the grass she ate during the day.

Goats did not know how to get back to their owner's house after they finished grazing in the mountains. It was the goatherd's task to take them from the plateau to graze on the mountains and in the valleys. The goatherd's greatest help was a son, if he had one, and two or three dogs. These dogs would protect the herd from wolves while they grazed on the mountains by day or at night. After the herd spent the night feeding where grass was plentiful, the goatherd would take them back to the plateau just after sunrise. There, he would make them lie down in a convenient spot. This was to prepare for the first milking session. With their bellies full, the animals would rest and relax. One by one, their owners would come find them and milk them, collecting the milk in tinned copper pails. For the first month after the move to the summer pastures, the kids would be allowed to suckle from their nannies while they were being milked. After the first milking was done, the animals, relieved and refreshed, would be taken back to graze once more. When the herd had left the pasture, the goatherd in charge of the kids would collect them and take them to graze at a different spot than their mothers. As the owners allowed the kids only a short time to suckle, they would still be quite hungry, so, gradually, they would teach themselves to eat grass.

After grazing again until the time for afternoon prayers, the nanny goats would be taken back to the pasture on the plateau, and settled down. Just as in the morning, the owners would come find and milk their goats, then allow the kids to suckle for a short while. One couldn't even say "allow." The kid was not allowed near the nanny before she had practically been milked dry. Then the poor kid, its belly empty, would suckle for a minute, swallowing greedily. When the milk stopped coming, the kid would attack the nipple with its nose and mouth, like a boxer.

Before darkness fell, with the help of one of his sons and the dogs, the goatherd again would take the herd to graze where he knew the grass was plentiful. The kids would be shut up in the shed for the night.

2
Herdsman Mustafa

The first herdsman I remember was Mustafa. Fifty to sixty years old, Mustafa was a short man with four grown-up sons and a daughter. He and his eldest son, Mehmet, were night herdsmen. Two other sons, Kerim and Ahmet, would graze the animals during the day. Hasanali, his youngest son, along with Mehmet's daughter, Emine, and wife, Leyla, would milk their own herd of twenty to twenty-five goats and process the milk.

The goatherd would choose which of the male kid goats to raise and feed without having them castrated. It was the responsibility of a goatherd to provide a small herd of healthy billy goats to breed from at the fall mating of the village goats. Every year, some of these billy goats would be replaced by younger ones. Young kids whose mothers gave the most milk would be chosen for breeding purposes. The male kids of mothers who did not produce as much milk would be raised for a year and then castrated. When the young billy goats were castrated, the man would give a testicle to each of us children, as we watched him with great curiosity, and say, "Here, son, get your mother to cook this. Eat it to give you strength." We would be very happy. All the energy from the castrated animal, now lacking male hormones, would go to making its body meatier. These animals would be raised and sold to a butcher. The herdsman's fees—the money he earned each season for watching villagers' animals—was his main source of income. This would be supplemented by the sale of his own castrated billy goats.

The women of our village would say of Herdsman Mustafa, "He's a very clever herdsman." He knew each one of his flock, numbering a thousand to fifteen hundred goats according to the season. He could tell you who each one belonged to. He would advise the owner if a goat was ill or if it was well fed. If it was ill, he'd suggest giving it additional wheat bran to eat. The herdsman also knew how to bandage and treat a broken leg, should a goat or kid happen to break one for any reason.

3
The Herdsman's Drenching

In the middle of June, it began to get hot. When it hadn't rained in the mountains for some time, grazing would not be so plentiful, and in many places, the grass would become yellow. The more experienced women who had lived on the yayla over many summers, began to talk among themselves, repeating the jingle, "Soon the season will turn, and the milking is done only once a day."

One evening as usual, Herdsman Mustafa and his son Mehmet took the flocks to graze in the mountains during the night. My mother and her neighbors said, "Tomorrow we'll drench the herdsman." We children went to sleep, wondering how a grown man could let himself be drenched.

The next morning, the flock did not arrive at the usual time. The women who knew the situation did not worry. The sun rose. Some of those who were inexperienced asked each other, "What happened to the flock?"

According to tradition, that day was the day when the season turned. It was the day when the night was the shortest and the day the longest of the year. At noon on that day, the flock could be seen in the distance. The two herdsmen and their dogs were walking slowly behind. The flock was going toward the place where the animals were accustomed to lying down. There, forty to fifty women were seen standing in a row with a bucket in each hand, waiting for the herdsmen to pass. As the herdsmen approached, each woman shouted at the top of her voice, "Where's the milk from this flock?" and poured cold water over the head of each herdsman as she did so.

Young Mehmet jumped this way and that to avoid being soaked. Doing quite the opposite, Herdsman Mustafa walked on calmly without breaking a step, as if the bucketfuls of water being poured over him were a gift from heaven. Drenched to the skin as he was, he continued on his way, smiling all the time. After the last woman in the row had emptied her bucket, our herdsman calmly walked on to his house. The women who had poured the water, and the women and children who had only watched, also returned to their homes.

An hour later, each of the women who had soaked the herdsman walked toward his house with a bundle in her hand. Leaving it at the herdsman's door, she returned to her home. The women who had not soaked the herdsman watched the proceedings, half-admiring, half-envious, talking among themselves, saying, "Oh dearie, I wish I'd soaked the herdsman."

"My friend, that's the trouble. If you don't have a gift for the herdsman, you can't drench him. This is the custom handed down from our forefathers."

"But that wild young herdsman, Mehmet, ran and ran and reached home without getting wet. That made me laugh a lot."

"The flock will only have one sitting today; from now on, for the rest of the summer, we'll only milk once a day."

"God willing, if I come to the summer pastures next year, I'll come prepared and I'll soak the herdsman too."

"I love this custom of our summer pastures!"

Meanwhile, Herdsman Mustafa's house was filled with lovely presents of various kinds, like kilos or half kilos of tea, sugar lumps, coffee, pies, buns, grape juice, scarves for his wife and daughter, pairs of socks for the sons, and shirt lengths for himself. This was the way they expressed their apologies and good wishes, as if saying, "Forgive us for drenching you. You look after our flocks so well, we know we'll always need you."

4
Death by Lightning

One year later, the folks of Sarot Summer Pastures lost their beloved herdsman, Mustafa. It happened at the beginning of May. Some of the people had come to the summer pastures a week before, and others were just arriving. A cloudy sky had turned to rain. That night, Herdsman Mustafa and his son Mehmet had been grazing the flock. Just as they were leaving Çilehane Mountain and walking slowly to bring the flock down back to the pastures, a bolt of lightning struck. Herdsman Mustafa and five of the goats died immediately. Ten or fifteen goats escaped slightly singed. From the front of the flock, Herdsman Mehmet saw what had happened and, bursting into tears, ran toward the Esenek Pass rising up behind the plateau. He shouted with all his might, "Hey, everyone! Come here quickly. My father's dead!" Those who heard him shouted in turn to inform everyone who was on the plateau that day.

We had come to the summer pastures only the day before. My father was there too. The village imam, San Hoca, was there as well. About fifteen of the men ran together toward Esenek Pass. The woman and children all waited anxiously on the yayla plateau. About half an hour later, people were seen coming down slowly in the pouring rain. The men had gone up without anything to carry a body down on. After considering what to do, three of the strongest young men decided they would take turns carrying the body on their backs. When the procession reached the crowd on the meadow, it was my father who was carrying Herdsman Mustafa's body. Tall and strong, my father was always willing to do what he could to help whenever anything like this happened.

There was no usual burial place on the mountain. Either no one had died there before, or the dead body had been carried down to be buried in the Çat village cemetery. In accordance with his family's wishes, Herdsman Mustafa was buried on a slope of Tuzla Hill overlooking the summer pastures. A large stone found among the rocks made an impressive tombstone.

The villagers of Çat continued their age-long custom of migrating to the summer pastures. Old and young, they all went on telling the story of Herdsman Mustafa. For many long years, Herdsman Mustafa's sons carried on doing their father's work. The years came and went. First, Çat village stopped being a village. It became the township of Çağlayan and a municipality. The time came when no one kept a cow, or four or five goats, and eight or nine hens. The summer pastures of the yayla became a sweet memory for those who remembered the place as it had been; for the younger generations, it was a place of natural beauty where they occasionally went to have a good time. The simple dwellings located there became neglected and fell into ruin. Those who had the money began to build concrete houses there, as a place to go and relax.

Herdsman Mustafa's grave is the eternal watchman over the Sarot Summer Pasture. Even today, this herdsman still lives on in the hearts of the people who come and go there.

The Honor of the Village

1
Soğla Lake

Soğla Lake occupied a large area between the townships of Seydişehir and Bozkır. On the western side, the steep Taurus Mountains rose up abruptly. On the other shores, where the land sloped gently upward, was a wide plain densely covered with fields and gardens. On this side, there were villages, some right by the lake, others at a distance of five or six kilometers from the shore. The settlements of Yalıhüyük, near the larger town of Bozkır, and Gökhüyük, near the small city of Seydişehir, were right on the shore of the lake. The people of these two villages earned their living not only from the fish and the reeds from the lake, but also from the narrow strip of land along the edge used for agriculture and farming.

Near the lake, from between one to five kilometers away from the shore, there were other villages, some small, some larger. The villagers of Yalıhüyük, Sandı, İldoğan, Aliçerçi, Ahırlı, Meyre, and Akkise, which were attached to Bozkır, and Kissecik, Taraççı, Akçalar, Bağra, and Lower and Upper Karaviran, which were attached to Seydişehir, all earned their livelihood from agriculture. The land available to be cultivated in these villages was small in proportion to the population. For a villager who plowed using two strong oxen or a pair of horses, every inch of ground was precious. So much so that a farmer would not allow anyone, not even a brother, to overstep the boundary of his field by even a centimeter. So it was that quarrels over these boundaries, however seldom and however disastrously they might end, were never lacking.

There was no river or stream to feed the lake. It was situated in a hollow in the surrounding land, which was filled with water from the rain that fell especially during the fall, winter, and spring. In years of plentiful rain when the lake was full, small waves would rise as high as the doorsteps of the houses in Yalıhüyük village. Then, the expert fisherman of Yalıhüyük would be overjoyed. They would fill their sacks with a great number of freshwater fish they had caught in the lake and load them onto their donkeys before traveling to villages only a day's journey away and bartering them for the local produce. From my childhood, I remember the fisherman from Yalıhüyük coming with loaded donkeys to sell fish in our village of Çat, even though we were eighteen kilometers from the lake. My mother and the neighboring women would exchange dried green beans and pickled thorn apples for a good amount of fish. In those years, the people of the surrounding villages ate their fill of fish.

One interesting feature of the lake was the sinkholes that occurred on the Taurus Mountains side of the lake. At different times of the year, the level of the lake used to drop by one or two meters from the water that flowed through these sinkholes, and also from natural evaporation. In years when little rain fell, the water dried up in the summer, leaving a long, completely level area of land around the lake. At first, this land was thick mud. A thin layer of silt, shining like a mirror, made the land very fertile. It was said that, when the weather warmed up, one could see, by looking closely, that the plants grew and matured within a few days in this damp, fertile layer of soil. The people believed that the lake receded because the earth sucked up the water.

In some spring seasons, the lake waters receded early. When that happened, the people of the villages near the lake made use of the exposed land, according to an age-old system that had been agreed upon. This land was no good for growing wheat or barley, which needed a long season in which to ripen, but was excellent for growing things like garbanzo beans or other produce that matured in a shorter amount of time. The villagers living near the lake worked day and night to plant garbanzo beans, melons, watermelon, and sunflowers on this narrow strip of fertile soil. This custom wasn't followed every year. Sometimes, the exposed strip was too narrow. However, the people of the villages neighboring the lake were still happy. For those with little earnings, any bit of fertile soil was a welcome opportunity. In the fall of such years, there was an increase in the number of weddings celebrated.

2
Fertile Soil: If Blood Drops, Life Will Flourish

In the early 1950s, rainfall at Soğla Lake had been low for several years, and even in winter, the lake was not full. In the spring, the waters dried up early and very quickly. A very wide, level area of fertile land appeared as more than half of the lake dried up. This area of cultivated land gave such a rich harvest that the villagers could not help saying, "If blood dropped on this land, life would flourish." Garbanzo beans, in particular, made a very good profit. These could be harvested much sooner than wheat, and could be sold for a much higher price. In such a year, the people in the nearest villages to Soğla Lake regarded themselves as wealthy.

In the villages, news of events, good or bad, that happened in the general area of Bozkır, became known very quickly. The itinerant peddlers who came and went to villages close to the lake, other villagers who observed the increased sales of the merchants at the Bozkır Friday market, and those from other villages who were invited to weddings at these villages saw their wealth and exaggerated their observations in their conversations. News of these riches spread, and envy increased among those who did not profit from this land. Their thoughts led them to make statements such as: "We are also citizens of this state. Since the land of the dried-up lake is state property, we want to profit from its fertile soil too." Their dissatisfaction increased. The folks in villages neighboring those nearest to the lake wanted to make use of this soil, too, especially the nearby mountainous villages, which were landless—they had little to no land to cultivate. My home village, Çat, was one such village. Our people sent delegations first to the provincial governor, and then to Ankara. Each delegation had the same request: "Since the lake ground is state property and our village is poor, we want a little share in this property too."

The issue was taken up by government officials who knew that throughout history, arguments and fights among neighboring villages for border infringements, even for areas such as meadows and yaylas, which were suitable only for grazing herds of animals and not for agriculture, had gone on. So, the government decided to allot a reasonable number of shares to those landless villages who had applied at that time.

An area of bare earth 350 meters in width and stretching as far as the waters of the lake was the share given to our village of Çat. This was divided into strips lengthwise, according to the number of the persons in the village at the time, so each person's share was a thin rectangular plot twelve centimeters wide, and as long as the distance was from the receding lake. It was not at all convenient, of course, for a family to walk three and a half hours to cultivate the long, thin strip of earth belonging to them. The share owned by my family of seven people, for example, was eighty-four centimeters wide.

Çat was situated among almost barren mountains, and only five or six families owned a pair of oxen and made a living from farming. These farming families collected the shares of other families in Çat, and agreed to farm the ground assigned to Çat, in return for a half share of the produce.

Even after shares in the land had been given to villages like Çat that were far from the lake, the shares of those villages next to the lake were still very large: each person's share was two to two and a half meters wide. Some lakeside villages, however, were very displeased at being given a smaller share than the previous year. The only unhappy village that resorted to violent action to remove the grievance, however, was the lakeside village of Yalıhüyük.

The piece of land 350 meters wide assigned to Çat village lay along the edge of the one belonging to the villagers of Yalıhüyük, who had been cultivating this strip for several years. They were against it being assigned to the distant village of Çat, so they took steps to regain it. One night, they drove their animals onto the land planted by the Çat village farmers and tore the crops to pieces. Faced with this antagonism, our farmers tried to lessen the harm by keeping watch over their land at night.

The road joining Bozkır to Seydişehir ran past near Yalıhüyük. Throughout the year, many peddlers from Çat used that road on their peddling trips. Their pack animals were mostly laden with clay pots. Peddlers passing along that road began to suffer attacks from the

Yalıhüyük villagers. These villagers used to hide along the roadside and suddenly, without warning, began to throw stones from a distance at these peddlers and their pack animals. These attacks were mainly carried out by children from Yalıhüyük.

My father and I were among those who suffered from this stone throwing. It was the year when I was between second and third grade of primary school. As soon as the holidays started, I began to go with my father and help him on his peddling trips. Throughout the year, my father would go alone with his mule and a donkey. In the summer, however, he would get another donkey, and, with me to help him, increase his sales.

3
A Hail of Stones

The rising sun had not yet begun to warm our backs. We had left our village that night, walking alongside our animals, and we hadn't yet been able to warm ourselves. At last, the sun broke over the eastern horizon. As the sun got higher, its heat caressed our backs and comforted our bodies. We were walking along the stabilized road from Bozkır to Seydişehir. There didn't seem to be any motor vehicles coming or going, not even a wagon drawn by two oxen. We walked without a care in the middle of the road. Although there was no need, from time to time as I went along, I called encouragingly to the mule loaded with the bigger pots, which had been entrusted to my care. Otherwise, I enjoyed looking at the greenery all around me and the clear, blue sky. Ever since we had left home, my head had been busy with the dreams I had conjured up in the night.

All around us shone the green of the planted fields and the white and purple blossoms of the opium poppies that adorned other fields, large or small. When I narrowed my eyes and looked at the fields of opium poppies, they reminded me of the colorful dresses made from brilliantly shiny artificial silk that our village girls wore at Bayrams and weddings. My father trusted me, but as he drove two donkeys loaded with pots in front of him, he broke into my dreams, calling, "Son, take care. The mule's load is heavy. Keep it to the side of the road. A truck or an automobile may suddenly come without any warning." I was so mesmerized by the sound of the hooves of the pack animals striking the stones and the loud snorts made from time to time by the animals as they tried to shoo flies away from their noses that I didn't hear him. My thoughts were busy with my friends at the yayla. "I could have been with my friends Muzaffer, Vehbi, Bahri, and Tayyar who are all together at Esenek digging up bulbs to eat. Or we could be swimming away from the sink holes in the yayla lake," I murmured to myself.

As our road came nearer to the Yalıhüyük meadows, the bright blue waters of Soğla Lake could be seen in the distance. "Dad," I asked, "how much bigger is this lake than the one at the yayla?"

My father was not given time to reply. A hail of small stones began to fall on and around us. A few of them struck the pack animals' loads. I heard a small pot crack. Fifteen to twenty children were throwing stones at us without stopping. In order to keep my head from being hit, I crouched down at the side of the loaded mule as I walked along.

"Hasan, you keep on driving the animals," my father said, and with a tremendous shout of "Hey there!" he sprang up, then faced the children. In the same loud voice, he shouted, "Come, let's see what you're made of, you fish-brained spawn! I'm going to make a Yalıhüyük cemetery right here!"

Taking a huge bone-handled pocketknife from his belt, he held it in front of him as if it were a rifle he was aiming at a target. Upon seeing him do this, the children ran helter-skelter off into the distance. I went on driving the animals at a smart pace. When my father thought the children had scattered far enough, he rose and ran to catch up with me. Then we continued on our way together.

The children didn't do much damage to us in this first attack. They only broke two small jugs and a bowl. Later, when we stopped for a rest and examined everything more carefully, we saw that a stone had hit a large earthenware jar wrapped in a bundle on the mule's back. The stone hadn't broken it, but it had made a small dent.

All year long, my father traveled this road at least once a week, taking pack animals loaded with pots to sell at Çalmanda village or its high pastures, the Uluören Yayla. Every kind of pot was made in our village and, like my father, many other peddlers would load these pots on pack animals to be taken and exchanged by barter in distant villages. All our neighbors in our part of the village earned a living through this type of peddling trip to many different villages of the Bozkır, Seydişehir, Hadim, and even Çumra townships.

4
The Governor and the Village Headman 1

The same stoning my father and I had undergone was experienced by many of our villagers, with more damage. Some of them reported the event immediately to our village headman, the smith Mehmet Mengene, also known as Çatal, or Çatal Kafa, which meant "forked head." Others didn't complain, but made the unfortunate events they had experienced a subject for conversation at their evening gatherings in the coffeehouses and discussed it with their neighbors. Mehmet Mengene had long before realized the seriousness of the situation. He went to the Kaymakam, the governor of Bozkır, and told him of the complaints that had been made. The governor coolly replied, "Go, find, and arrest the guilty parties, Headman. Bring them to me, and I'll give them their punishment."

Headman Çatal came back to the village disheartened. He called the village council together and said, "Friends, it's for sure that this man they call the governor has had his pockets filled. He didn't even listen to our complaints. Tell all our peddler neighbors who have business that way, and the farmers who plant our land there, not to go there alone. They should protect each other and go in groups of twos or threes."

In the weeks following the village headman's warning, my father and I agreed with our neighbors that we would go together when we went peddling in that direction. We started to go on our trips particularly early at night in order to pass by Yalıhüyük very early in the morning. This way, we could pass Yalıhüyük land without becoming targets for an attack by the children. After selling our goods, we would arrange to return home together in the dark of night. At the same time, our village farmers started to go by twos and threes to plant the fields at Soğla given to our village by the government. But damage, even if not significant, still continued to be inflicted on our farmers.

5
An Inexperienced Peddler

Osman, who lived in the Cingiller sector of our village, was the young son of Tecel Mehmet Ali. At this time, Osman's family was in a dire situation. He decided to peddle a donkey-load of pots in Karaviran village before the coming holiday festivities called Bayram. Either he hadn't heard what had happened to other peddlers recently, or else he trusted in his youth and courage. Whichever, he loaded his donkey with pots, including easily sold pitchers, basins, small bowls, small jugs, and small vessels used for mixing ayran. As he couldn't leave the village early, when he came near Yalıhüyük village, the sun had been up for over an hour. As Osman was urging his donkey on, dreaming of the sales he would make, suddenly, hundreds of stones began to rain down from overhead. Osman tried to urge the donkey to go faster, but the donkey was loaded and couldn't hurry. The hail of stones broke many of the pots tied to the saddle. Becoming even more savage, the children started to target Osman with their stones. Some of these hit him on the head and injured him. His face dripping with blood, Osman decided to return to our village with the donkey. He untied the pots and was throwing the broken ones away when a stone hit him in the face. Crying, he abandoned his load, got on the donkey, and galloped back to our village. When he got home, his father and the neighbors, together with the injured Osman, went straight to Headman Çatal's smithy to register their complaint.

Being headman was not profitable. Çatal was a man who earned his living by working as a smith. Producing the material from which he made knives, pruning shears, and other instruments involved a lot of work. From morning till night, he swung the hammer in his forge, blowing the charcoal on the hearth with bellows to make the iron red hot. He was one of fifteen to twenty-five smiths in the village who earned a living for their families this way.

When Headman Çatal saw the injured youth, he immediately stopped what he was doing. That evening, he called a meeting of the village council. They knew that many of the migrant workers would be returning from the cotton fields of Aydın to the village for the coming Bayram celebrations. They decided to hold a meeting of the whole village in the open space in front of the big coffeehouse on the day before the Bayram, known as Arefe. All the men of the village aged eighteen and older were ordered to be at this meeting,

Each evening, for the two days before Arefe, the night watchman, Kipik, made a public announcement: "Hello, hello, fellow villagers! Give ear to me and don't say you didn't hear. On the afternoon of the day of Arefe, there will be a meeting in front of the forges. All the men here in the village must attend."

This public announcement was made in three of the neighborhoods: Çat, Ahmetli, and Karagaç. The inhabitants of the neighborhoods of Ömerli and Cingiller could easily hear the announcement made in Çat, as they were situated in the valley just below.

The village Çat, in February 1964

6
The Honor of the Village

Calling all the men of the village to a meeting on the day before Bayram was not a good sign. Most people had not heard what was going on or were busy preparing for the festival. Many of the migrant workers who had gone away to hoe cotton had only just begun to reach the village. It was a tradition for everyone to be at home for Bayram to spend it with family, children, and relatives. Everyone enjoyed keeping this tradition, particularly the young men who went to work far away from home.

Dawn broke, and the day of Arefe arrived. Çat, the largest neighborhood in the village, was perched on the edge of the Erenler Mountain facing the east. It was halfway in shadow soon after the afternoon prayer time. The men of the village began to assemble on the wide, sloping area around the coffeehouse and the forges. They found places to sit in the shade in front of these two buildings. Those who couldn't find chairs sat on the ground. Everyone began to ask each other, "What's happened? Why are we meeting?" Upon seeing the headman, Çatal, sitting in the shade of a tree on the level area in front of the forge of Lame Abdullah the Smith, the assembled crowd knew the matter was a serious one. A little while later, Kipik, the watchman, announced in a loud voice everyone could hear, "Neighbors! Your attention, please! The headman will speak to us."

The headman got to his feet. He bent forward to look at the latecomers for a minute or two. Even those who were whispering among themselves turned their heads toward him. Our headman, Mehmet Mengene the smith, began to speak, his voice trembling slightly:

"Neighbors, friends, I have called you here on this special, holy day for a very serious matter of an extremely private nature. My friends, let everyone take good heed of what we are about to discuss and decide on here, and let no one mention even a word of it outside the village. Not a word or a whisper of it must be heard in our neighboring villages, nor by the officials and shopkeepers in Bozkır. The honor of our village is in question. It is very important. Before we begin the discussion, I'd like us all to make a promise."

Holding up the Koran, he asked in a strong voice, "Friends, do we all swear on the Holy Book, on the souls of the dead, and on our children's lives that we will not breathe a word of this matter to anyone?"

All the inhabitants declared with one voice, "We swear!"

The headman again asked, "Friends, do we proclaim the holy word Şart to keep this promise?"

"We do!"

The headman continued. "Friends, neighbors, as some of us know, for quite a long time, the villagers of Yalıhüyük have been harassing the farmers who undertook the planting of the land at Soğla given to us by the government. We told the farmers to deal with the problem by going in groups. When the farmers were not around, the Yalıhüyük villagers damaged the growing crops. We closed our eyes. We told the farmers, 'Whatever happens to the property, look after it yourselves.' A lot of our neighbors who earn a living by peddling go to distant villages to sell pots, of course. Some of them do business with the villages toward Seydişehir. The children from Yalıhüyük injured our peddlers by throwing stones at them from a distance and broke or damaged the pots and vessels loaded on the pack animals.

"I made this known to the state authorities—that is, to the governor. Yes, neighbors, I went to Bozkır and visited the governor in his office. I told the governor, word for word, about the attacks made on our merchants passing by on the road near Yalıhüyük, and the events that took place at seedtime and harvest on the land given to us at Soğla. I said, 'Our people are asking the government to help them protect their lives and property.'

"Friends, do you suppose the governor replied by saying, 'Of course, Headman. I will immediately call the headman of Yalıhüyük and give the necessary warnings.' Did he? No, he did not!

"Friends, you will not believe it when you hear what the governor's answer was. My friends, this is the exact answer the governor gave me: 'Headman, go, find, and arrest the guilty parties. Bring them to me and I will give them their punishment.' As the governor was not interested in actually investigating the complaints, presumably, the other village boss is bribing him."

The crowd, listening attentively to the headman, began to murmur. Many said quietly and some shouted out, "That means the Yalıhüyük villagers have filled the rascal's pockets," and cursed the governor in colorful language.

The headman went on. "The village council and I have listened for weeks to your complaints, especially from those who have suffered harm. I warned the peddlers who go that way to do business, 'Don't go alone. Set out early from the village. Take care not to get into conversation with people from Yalıhüyük.' Of course, some listened and some didn't. There are those with heads on their shoulders and others who are foolhardy youths. I can't give them all warnings one by one. Finally, one of those who went on peddling trips suffered more than just damage to his property. They broke the load of pots this young man was setting off with to sell in Karaviran, but what is worse, their stones hit him on the head and his face became covered in blood. After saving himself with difficulty, the young man was seen by me and our friends on the village council. Naturally, we were as upset as his father and mother. After hearing of this last event, my friends, I now feel it is necessary for us to protect the honor of our village. Yalıhüyük isn't even a third as big as we are. Who is giving them this courage? Are we always going to be afraid of these villagers who used to come here with their unsaddled donkeys with their loads of half-rotten fish to sell to us, these fish-heads who bring their grain to our mills to be ground into flour?"

The people all shouted, "No, we're not afraid of them!" and added their favorite curses.

Headman Çatal continued. "Friends, our aim is to teach the people of Yalıhüyük village a lesson, without causing the death of any of them or any of us. It would be a good lesson for them if we did as much damage as possible to the fields planted with what is most important to them. We're not thinking of doing anything to darken our reputation for courage, such as attacking a man on his own or picking a quarrel with anyone, or attacking their village or their yayla. Our aim is to ruin their crops one night when they don't expect it. Now let's hear what anyone has to say about this."

A neighbor who was a peddler stood up and said, "Headman, three days ago I was passing by Yalıhüyük. Their opium poppy fields are just beginning to seed. They'll soon begin to scratch them and collect the opium juice from them. The village gets most of its income from that crop. I'm saying let's go to the fields at night and slash the poppies with our sickles, daggers, and swords. A damaged opium head isn't worth a penny. They won't have any opium to sell to the government or any seeds to get oil from. This way, we'll cut their throats."

Headman Çatal approved of this idea, and asked for fifteen or twenty volunteers from those who had been sergeants during their military service. These were to be the leaders, and form teams made up of their nearest neighbors in the village and their relatives and friends. Everyone in the teams was to come after lunch the next day—the first day of the Bayram—and gather in front of the People's House, bringing with them every kind of implement they had at home that was suitable for cutting grass, plants, or bushes. They were reminded once more of the need for it to be done at night in absolute silence. They would not use the roads, either going or coming. They would walk with extreme silence through woods and fields far from the road.

In order to make sure that the collective action they were about to take would remain secret, they were reminded that they had sworn the Şart-oath, and agreed to keep their promise. It was certain that everyone knew the punishment for breaking the Şart-oath. Everyone knew that, by both religious and traditional laws, the one who broke his promise was considered to be divorced from his wife. Even if, for the good of his children, he wished to remarry the same wife, in order to do so, the punishment was very severe: the divorced woman had to marry another man, sleep with this new husband at least once, and then, if she got divorced from him, her former husband might marry her again. Of course, no one in their right mind would want to suffer this disgrace.

Before the meeting broke up, Headman Çatal added, "Friends, let the leaders talk things over with their teams and make the necessary preparations. Don't say anything about this at home. Tomorrow is Bayram. Don't let the village as a whole say or do anything to make our family members and older people unhappy or afraid. Join in the Bayram prayers and then go to the cemetery to ask for a blessing on the souls of those who have passed on, just like every Bayram. Make the children and the visitors who come to celebrate the festival happy. Enjoy the Bayram feast and eat your fill. After we go into action, it may not be possible to eat anything again until the following morning. Come now, may everyone celebrate the Bayram well and happily. I'll be waiting for everyone in front of the People's House after lunch tomorrow."

7
An Unforgettable Bayram

On the morning of the Bayram, everyone got up early. Just as they had the previous Bayram, fathers, and even their young sons under the care of adults, rushed and got ready for the Bayram prayer in the village mosque.

The mothers were thinking of everything to be done at home—cooking the Bayram meal for the family, the animals in the stable to be fed and watered, Bayram clothes for the children, and of course, the visits to be made to their own mothers and fathers. It was the same every Bayram. But that morning, most of the mothers were deep in thought. However hard they tried, they couldn't conceal their anxiety. There were some who neglected the tradition of not giving chores and duties to their children on Bayram. Others, uneasy in their minds, didn't dress their children in their festival clothes. It was impossible not to hear the whispered doubts that passed among the women who were close neighbors. "Let's just see tomorrow morning come, safe and sound," many women murmured. Their husbands must not have been able to keep things to themselves during the night, and the air was full of the smell of fear, fear that said, "Is this Bayram going to be a deadly one?"

The Bayram prayer felt much longer than the previous prayers to many young people. At last, the imam recited the final prayer, saying, "God Almighty, give us all a happy and healthy Bayram day and Bayram night," and, after saying "Amin"—"Amen"—the congregation quickly dispersed. The boys did not want to leave the men or their fathers, and went excitedly with them to the village cemetery to sit at the head of the tombstones, saying prayers for the souls of their dead, and wishing each other a happy Bayram before returning. According to custom, after returning from the cemetery, the adults filled their pockets with a kilo or two of colorful candies bought from the candy sellers who had set up stalls in front of the People's House. The children who came forward and said, "Grandfather, Uncle, happy Bayram," were very pleased to be given one or two candies, and everyone went home with rapid steps.

When my father and I came home from the cemetery, he was happy but agitated. Our neighborhood had a special and enjoyable Bayram

*A group of menfolk of a neighborhood of village Çat
at the Bayram community breakfast*

tradition. We would eat our Bayram meal on the roof of the guesthouse with our closest neighbors. As usual, my mother prepared the meal and my father helped her get things ready. Father and I carried a round copper tray filled with two dishes of food and some whole wheat bread up to the roof. As if everything was normal, we gathered on the roof as had been the custom on previous Bayrams, together with the men and boys from the neighbors' families, each bringing a copper tray filled with food. First, five or six of the grown-up young men took the dishes of food from the trays and placed them on one side. Then, young or old, all the men sat down cross-legged around the trays. Each dish was then offered in turn, according to a specific order. The group of young men who served while the other men sat down and ate were all volunteers. For a young man who had just left off being a boy, it was a great honor to be one of the servers. After everyone at the tables had eaten their fill and gotten up, the servers quickly ate the food in the one or two dishes they had reserved for themselves. Finally, everyone on the roof hugged and kissed each other, with emotional wishes for a happy Bayram. Whenever I had the opportunity to find myself in the village at Bayram time, I always loved being part of this tradition in my neighborhood. In this village where there was no level ground, these traditional Bayram feasts held on the flat roof in the fresh air, laughing and joking with our elders, were for us children a sweet and unforgettable memory.

After everyone had finished wishing each other a blessed Bayram, some half-cryptic sentences such as "We were to be ready after lunch, weren't we?" escaped from their mouths as people went homeward with their empty trays. Father and I also took home our empty dishes and tray. At home, father insisted we all sit down at the table. He wanted to eat a few more mouthfuls with my mother and my younger siblings. What did this eating together signify? It signified a parting. It was the kind of meal always eaten whenever anyone left to go as a migrant worker to a faraway place, or to do his military service.

8
How to Go to a War

After we had eaten, my father took off his Bayram clothes and put on the clothes he wore on workdays: baggy trousers, a vest, and a long-sleeved collarless shirt—the clothes worn in the fields or on the mountain. He took a lantern in his hand and went to the inner room, a windowless place left to us by my grandfather, and took up a sword hidden behind water pots and storage vessels. He then filed it for some time with a whetstone to remove years of rust and sharpen the blade, then he covered it in a piece of cloth before putting the sword inside his waistband so it was hidden as it hung down his left leg. Finally, he wound around his waist the woolen sash he wore, winter and summer.

After lunch, the men, who, like my father, had gotten themselves ready at home, began to gather in front of the People's House. We didn't pay much attention when, from time to time, they said to children like me, who only half understood what was going on, "Off you go, you rascals, go and play. Celebrate the Bayram with your relatives." We waited, curious to see our fathers and elder brothers depart.

Meanwhile, the women and girls were perched on the very edges of the roofs, as if about to fall off them, watching what was going on below them. In very low voices, my mother and the neighboring women murmured, "Good luck to the menfolk. God willing, tomorrow morning they'll return without harm."

Headman Çatal once more warned the hundreds of strong men ready for action. "Friends, neighbors, young men! Be sure to remember that our aim is not to go to extremes. Do not go into the village. Don't even go too near it. No one must be injured in any way. Our duty is only to do as much damage as we can to their fields and vines. We'll take to the woods and fields. We will not pass through any village. The younger ones must listen to their elders who know the way and the area. We expect everyone to return by sunrise tomorrow. I am the person responsible to the government if any inquiries are made. Go now, and may your task be easy."

Our fathers and elder brothers sped away with silent footsteps, first plunging through the cemetery at the foot of the mountain opposite the village. When we saw them again, they were climbing the broad slope between Karin and Kızılkaya, looking like a file of ants darkening the hillside. This moving shadow was almost lost to sight as it reached the top of the mountain. A little later, no movement at all could be seen.

9
No Spunk Left in a Coward

While the men of the village were climbing to the top of the opposite mountain, a few men left behind were quietly heading back into the village. Noticing these men caused a sudden uproar among the women watching from the roofs. "Oh, you shameful cowards! Jackal's sons, you are shameless, disgraceful cowards! And you, traitor Bekeleli, shame on you too! You cowards! You have sound arms and legs! Do you think you are the seed stock of this village?"

"You steal whatever you find in the village gardens, vineyards, pastures, or fields, you slowpoke thief, Seydali! How dare you appear among honest men! You coward! Was it you they chose to spread your spunk throughout the village?"

"Isn't this what our forefathers told us would happen? There are bulldogs who defend their homes, and there are bulldogs who shit in it."

The cowards who were the butt of these and other insults and shaming remarks ran as if about to piss in their pants, and reached the safety of their homes with difficulty. For years afterward, these five or ten cowardly villagers always hung their heads and looked at the ground when passing through the village. Other nicknames, such as "traitor," "asshole," and "bastard," were added to the ones they already had. Nobody called them this to their face, but many people guffawed whenever these words were spoken.

On the night the men of the village went on their campaign, we children went to sleep without a care, but it can't be said that our mothers slept a wink. Every woman went to bed anxiously asking in her own special way that her husband or her grown-up son would return safe and sound. Some of the words that went through their heads were murmured like prayers, others more like curses, and others sounded like sobs.

> *Sons do military service*
> *and fulfill their days;*
> *some wearing uniform,*
> *sergeants, master sergeants,*
> *come on, leave to the village*
> *and make us happy.*
> *Your man goes to Aydın,*
> *goes to hoe cotton there.*
> *You rejoice, thinking*
> *when a letter comes,*
> *there's money there.*
> *But what's this? I ask you!*
> *May the seed of those*
> *who made this happen*
> *dry up to nothing.*
> *On this special holy day,*
> *the rascals spoiled our Bayram,*
> *made it taste like poison.*
> *Hızır, come and save us!*
> *Hızır, protect our men,*
> *grant them come back to us,*
> *all of them, safe and sound.*

10
The Second Day of Bayram Is the Best

On the second day of Bayram, the women got up early and fixed their eyes on the peak of the mountain opposite. I was asleep in bed with my two siblings when a sound from outside woke me up. I recognized the voices, one calling, "Good morning to you, Karakaşli," and the other replying, "And to you too, Hatmetçe," as those of our neighbor, my friend Bahri's mother, and that of my own mother. They were both on their second-floor balconies, which were like extensions above the entrance of their houses, leaning on the guardrails. Their eyes were fixed on Karin Hill and the nearby horizon as they exchanged greetings. I got up, rubbed my eyes, and went up to the roof of our house. I also began to look at the high mountain.

Following the pink flush of dawn, the first rays of the sun made the peaks of the surrounding mountains look extra attractive, as if they were wearing colorful hats like the boys during Bayram festivities. Just at that moment, I seemed to see a black shadow or two in the distance, between Karin and Kızılkaya. I shouted from the roof, "Mom, I see them coming!"

Hearing me, other women called, "Where? Where?" and scrambled up the rickety ladders made of thin pieces of wood, climbing to their rooftops. They began to look intently at the distant slopes of the opposite mountain outlined by the first light of the sun. Just then, they saw, between Karin and Kızılkaya, dark shadows like those of clouds coming slowly downward. The anxious looks of my mother and the neighbors faded and gave way to soft murmurings as they watched their men come into sight.

Before long, before the sunlight had fully reached the village, the men, who the night before had set out on their campaign, entered the village quietly and quickly dispersed to their homes. After snatching a mouthful or two of food, each of them threw himself down on his bed. A great number of the men spent the second morning of Bayram sleeping until noontime.

After lunch, they continued making Bayram visits to relatives as though nothing had happened. No one said, "We cut the opium poppies and smashed them to smithereens; some of us trampled on the vines and others on the gardens." What they had done was to remain a secret. In spite of everything, they were all worried, wondering whether, tomorrow or the next day, the government or state officials might come and punish them.

11
Music Is Food for the Soul

It would not be an exaggeration to say that on the third day of the Bayram, nothing worth noting happened. To allow the children to enjoy one more day of wearing their clean Bayram clothes, their fathers and mothers got up early to tend to the animals in the stable themselves. During Bayram, animals themselves had a holiday from carrying loads, and donkeys or mules were taken out of the stable to be watered at the nearest stream. The fathers cleaned the stable floor and filled the manger with straw and hay, doing what they could to give the animals another day of rest.

The mothers, after milking the cow at home, drove it toward the village herdsman. Keeping cattle in a closed stable all day was bad for them, and so herdsmen did not get a holiday during Bayram, but the women who took their cows to the herdsman did not neglect to give him a small present.

The third day of Bayram was when the children spent the whole day visiting their relatives in different neighborhoods of the village. After kissing their elders' hands in the traditional manner, they were happy to receive a present and play all day long.

In the early afternoon, the band collected in front of the big coffeehouse and began to play lively tunes. The music could be heard even in the neighborhoods of Ahmetli, Ömerli, and Cingiller on the other side of the valley. A great number of people, old or young, began to stream toward the coffeehouse. Those who found chairs sat on them, and those who didn't swayed right and left, listening to the music. The big coffeehouse owner, Musa, brought out several bundles of wooden spoons. "Hey there, my brave fellows, do justice to the tune," he said, handing out spoons to those who loved dancing. The son of Gök Mehmet, Deli Abdullah, and Küpeli, Karabela, and other young men known to be good dancers, took the spoons without any hesitation and began to dance enthusiastically to the tune of "Aslan Mustafa," followed by many other songs. The musicians continued playing tunes one after the other, and accompanied them by singing the words in their best voices.

The band consisted of Sergeant Ali on the violin, Blind Kerim on the banjo, Ali from Ankara on the saz—a traditional three-stringed long-necked instrument—and another player who kept time on the drum. No electronic amplifier was needed for everyone to hear the music played and sung solely by instruments and voices. This was before the village had electricity. The sweet music of the strings could be heard even inside the houses through the open windows. The sound of the spoons clicking in time to the rhythm of the tune and the dancers was so inviting that even my father, who, like Headman Çatal, seldom went to the coffeehouse, came there that evening. They were given places to sit by the younger men.

With words such as "This Bayram passed in a peaceful way. May we all live to see the next one. Bless you and good night," another Bayram passed without any accidents or misfortune.

Well, tomorrow was another day!

12
The Governor and the Village Headman 2

The following day, everyone went back to their jobs in the field or the yayla, garden or vineyard, and the potters and smiths also went back to work.

That afternoon, two gendarmes with rifles on their shoulders came to the village by foot. These gendarmes passed by Kanlı Kaya, the Bloody Rock, and stopped in front of the mill near the People's House. They asked the miller for directions to the home of Headman Mehmet Mengene. The young man grinding flour there said warily, "Come, elder brothers, let me take you to the headman's forge," and placed himself in front of them.

The headman invited the gendarmes, who had walked to the village on foot from Bozkır, into his house. Ayşe, his wife, offered the gendarmes tea. Following that, she cooked a cracked wheat pilaf and filled the gendarmes' stomachs.

As if nothing had happened, the headman asked the gendarmes, "Well now, young lads, there's been no incident of any kind in the village. Why have you come?"

"The governor wants to see you, Uncle Headman," they replied. "You're to come to the governor's office either today or tomorrow."

The headman said, "You've walked a long way with those heavy Mausers on your shoulders. You must be tired. It wouldn't be right for you to hurry back. Let's say you couldn't find me until it was evening. It's like that in the villages—during the day, everyone is out on the mountains or in the fields. Stay here tonight and rest. Tomorrow we'll go together to the town. Today I'll take you to one or two of the beautiful places in our village. We'll eat and drink at the source of the springs, go by the place where partridges are plentiful and try our hand at shooting them, and have a little fresh air as well."

The gendarmes accepted this invitation with heartfelt thanks. That night, they slept in a spare bedroom of the headman's house.

The next morning, Headman Mehmet Mengene took Potter Hasan Kiremit, one of the members of the village council, with him and they went with the gendarmes to Bozkır. They went straight to the governor's office. The governor admitted only the headman.

"Headman Mehmet Mengene, my man, yesterday, the headman of Yalıhüyük village came to me to complain about you. On Bayram night, your villagers swooped down on their village and destroyed the crops in their fields."

Coolly, the headman said in answer, "My very esteemed governor, sir, the people of my village Çat are valiant and honorable. They respect law and order. You go find and arrest the guilty and bring them in. If they are my villagers, I will give them their punishment."

Enraged, the governor rose to his feet. He remembered the irresponsible words he had said to this headman a month ago. Realizing these words were now being used against him, he shouted, "Headman, my man, that act you carried out may be counted as rebellion against the State. If anything like this happens again between the villages of Çat and Yalıhüyük, I'll lock up both you and the headman of Yalıhüyük. Now go and get lost." As he dismissed the headman of Çat from his office, he added, "Oh, by the way, this rumor has come to my ears that the men of Çat are going to go to the Yalıhüyük Yayla and rape all the women. I hope there is no basis for this."

No one knew who could have started such a rumor or how it could have reached the village of Yalıhüyük. What was known was that, taking this rumor seriously, the men of Yalıhüyük had gone into action. On the second day of Bayram, barely a month after migrating to the yayla, they had transported with great haste and commotion their women, their children, and all their animals from their yayla back to the village.

The governor of Bozkır did not report to the higher authorities this unpleasant incident that had taken place between the villagers of Çat and Yalıhüyük. He realized that his friendship with the landlord of Yalıhüyük, known as Tahsin Beg, might make him appear prejudiced, and thus endanger his future. At the same time, he couldn't stomach having the words he himself had spoken in error a month before thrown back at him by the courageous headman of Çat. Considering his future possibilities for promotion, he kept saying to himself, I will soon request to be reassigned to a different town, and get as far as I can from this goddamn town of Bozkır, which is full of rebellious people.

Early the next morning, the governor sent two gendarmes to bring the Yalıhüyük headman to him. He admonished him in a serious manner. He told him he had heard that a young man from Çat had been beaten and wounded in the head. He said he had gotten the headman of Çat to promise him that the authorities would not be informed of this. He reminded the headman that in the eyes of the state, it was an unforgivable crime to block anyone's path or attempt grievous bodily harm. His agreement with the headman of Çat had been good for the people of Yalıhüyük, he declared, as it had saved them from the consequences of this great crime. The headman of Yalıhüyük, although the damage to his villagers, who earned their living from fishing and farming, was greater than that done to the villagers of Çat, promised never to harass them again.

The headman of Yalıhüyük managed to get the message through to his villagers about the warning given to him by the governor. From then on, neither the farmers nor the peddlers from Çat came under any kind of threat. This forced peace continued without a break. Under the leadership of Mehmet Mengene, headman of Çat, all the people of the village continued to enjoy the profit, however small, from their fertile land at Soğla Lake. In particular, those who earned a living by peddling in distant villages never forgot the debt of gratitude they owed their headman, Mehmet Mengene the smith.

Marriage by Abduction—
Emile and Durdul

It was the end of June, beginning of July, sometime in the 1950s. On one of the longest days of the year, the villagers of Çat were working feverishly to collect hay and firewood for the winter.

Mother and I were returning after a hot day collecting grass. We were a little late leaving our property, Çötü, and it was twilight when we got to the village. While we were unloading the grass, a commotion broke out in front of the house of our neighbors, Ibrahim and Leyla. We stopped to listen. A young woman was shrieking at the top of her lungs, "I spit in your mouths! I don't want your clothes! I don't want your silk. I will have Küpeli!"

After we had unloaded and spread the grass on the roof, we went toward the neighbor's house to eavesdrop. With sweet words, our neighbor Leyla was cajoling the girl who was screaming. "My love, my gentle girl, Emile, see here, this cloth, this silken scarf, this dress-length silk, they're all yours. If we only knew what else you want."

The young girl repeated her words, once again shrieking as loud as she could, "I spit in your mouths! Let the cloth be yours and the silk. I will have Küpeli."

The number of curious people standing in front of the nearby houses or on the roofs increased, each one telling the other what she knew. Mother had realized what was happening, and gave me a brief explanation. Leyla's older son, Memo, had abducted Emile. Earlier that day, while the poor girl was pulling wild weeds in her family's vineyard in the Met Stone area, Memo had snuck up and caught hold of Emile's arm, then dragged the girl away to a lonely place on the other side of the Ulu River. Who knew what flattery he had tried to seduce the girl, but by nightfall, he had not succeeded. Then, when darkness fell, reluctant to hurt Emile, he dragged her by force to his home.

This custom of abducting a girl was common among the poor families, but usually done by mutual agreement. The families of young men and girls old enough to be married might plan a marriage by agreement between themselves. "Our daughter is still too young, but if you wait two years, we'll give her to you," or "We can't give our daughter to anyone who hasn't done military service," or "Let your son get a suitable house and a stable, however small, before he marries, and we'll give our daughter to him." Many similar restrictions or conditions would be placed by the girl's parents. If one or both of the families were extremely poor, then there were fewer conditions. The girl's parents would say, "We've no money for a wedding feast. Tell us when you're ready and let your son come and carry off our daughter one day when she's by herself working in the garden or vineyard." A girl expecting to be carried off in this way would bathe herself that morning, comb her hair, and plait it neatly. Her clothes would be clean, if not exactly new. The young man would approach the promised girl while she was working in a garden outside the village, alone or with a friend, and pretend to threaten her. "Come, my girl, get in front of me, I'm going to carry you off."

The girl would reply coyly, "Go away, you son of an infidel. I won't be carried off."

Then the young man would say, "I'll teach you to cross me," and pull her by the arm and drag her away.

Crying, the girl would protest she didn't want to go. After pretending to drag her a little way, the young man, without the need for further struggle, would carry her off to a place where the trees and bushes were thick enough to shield them from distant eyes.

However loudly the girl shouted to make a show of resisting, she would not curse her future mother-in-law. The two young people would wait in their hiding place until dusk had fallen. They would share the food each had brought; the young man would take one or two candies from his pocket and the girl had hidden a few raisins or dried apricots in her waistband. This was the first time these two young people could come close to each other. It was a day they would both remember for the rest of their lives. After darkness fell, taking care that no one saw them, they would go quickly to the house of the young man's father. The son would open the door and the girl would enter. The son wouldn't go in, but go off to the coffeehouse.

The abducted girl knew what she should say to the people in her new home. To her mother-in-law and father-in-law, she had to say, "Mother, Father, your son came and carried me off. I have come to be your bride," and then sit down quietly.

They would reply pleasantly with words, such as, "Welcome, daughter, we're glad to see you. May God grant we get on well." It was more than likely that the parents already knew of the situation, and had already prepared a room for the young couple to spend the night in.

In my childhood, I witnessed one abduction similar to the one above. Young Durdul, our neighbor at the yayla, was the only living daughter of Şiraz, who, like many women in the village, was a widow. Şiraz was a poor member of the Apillar family. She had taken Durdul up to the yayla to make the year's supply of butter, cheese, and dried yogurt with the milk from their cow, while she busied herself in the village tending her small garden and gathering hay and wood.

Like most orphaned children, Durdul was a good-tempered girl, respectful to her elders, and hardworking. One day, she came to my mother and said, "Elder sister Karakaşli, I have to go to the village this evening. When the cows come down from the mountain, would you please milk mine, and keep the milk? We'll settle up when I get back from the village tomorrow evening."

My mother replied, "Of course I will, dear Durdul. Don't you worry. I'll milk your cow, use a stick to measure the milk, and keep it for you." Then she added, "Since you are going to the village later this afternoon, let my son Hasan walk with you and keep an eye on him along the way."

Durdul agreed, of course.

That summer, I was seven or eight years old. When afternoon came, Durdul arrived to say she was ready to go. My mother pressed a small jar of yogurt, tied firmly around the top, into my hands. "Tell your father I couldn't make any buttermilk, and he'll have to shake this up with water and make do for a day or two. In a few days' time, the cooperative milk will come to me. Then I'll send him plenty."

Durdul and I set off together with a few other neighbors. Something attracted my youthful attention: Durdul looked different than usual. She was cleanly dressed, her face seemed to sparkle, her hair under her headscarf was woven into neat plaits, and she looked beautiful.

The path down to the village was steep and rocky, and normally took three hours to walk. I, and another boy my age, went jumping from rock to rock while Durdul and a few other young women, older than us, gossiped among themselves as they went along.

The last part of the path from the yayla went along a small river, known as the Yayla River, which flowed through deep valleys. As evening approached, the sun seemed like a kind of halo over the top of the mountains. One of the older ones in our group remarked, "We've come most of the way and haven't far to go, so we'll be at the village before the call to prayer." At that point, we were walking near the place called Upper Bridge by a rocky ravine. Until then, our walk had been uneventful.

As we came to a narrow place known as "the rock on which the hooves of Blessed Ali's horse slipped," a young man jumped out of the undergrowth at the side of the path and stood in our way. He had a stick in his hand. We all stopped in astonishment. I realized that this young man was Abdul, the son of our neighbor, Blind Mehmet Ali, and my fear left me. Hastily waving his stick, Abdul dived in among us and, grabbing Durdul by the arm with one hand, he swung the stick as though to give Durdul a violent blow. Saying, "Walk, girl," he dragged her toward the bushes on the river side of the path. Durdul cried and moaned as they disappeared. A little while later, the sound of their voices was lost.

One of the women who knew what this was all about said, "May Allah see they get on well. It seems they arranged this. They'll wait on the hillside until it gets dark, and then they'll go to Abdul's home."

This was the first time the other child and I had witnessed such an event, and learned what an abduction was. That evening, those of us left behind hurried over the last short part of the way, and arrived at the village.

Let's go back to the story of Emile.

Mother and I had come to the village from Çötü that evening. The abduction of Emile reminded me of Abdul's abduction of Durdul that I had witnessed two years before. I thought to myself, So, there's a difference between being willingly abducted and being unwillingly abducted.

Even though, from time to time, the girl was abducted unwillingly and was not happy with the situation, she often resigned herself to staying in her new home. She might have parents who were unable to support her. Even if the girl was unwilling, she might accept her fate if her father forced her to agree, in order not to feel shame in later years, particularly if the families had agreed on the abduction. But that hot summer night, Emile never stopped shouting obstinately, "I will not stay here! I spit here in this house. I will have Küpeli!"

Emile was just fifteen years old, a beautiful girl with a faultless face and hands. The poor girl was fatherless, with only a mother and an elder brother in this world. Apart from her older brother, Yanık, she had no other male relative to rely on.

At this time, Yanık, one of the migrant workers from our village, would be hoeing cotton fields in who knew what landowner's field on the plains of Söke. Some of the villagers who went to hoe the cotton fields of Söke stayed on to irrigate the cotton fields. Yanık was one of the workers who would return home by the end of August. By that time, the deed would be over and done with. It was for that reason that Emile was shrieking her head off in order not to spend the night in the house to which she had been carried off. She went on screaming in the hope that perhaps one of the neighbors who understood how serious she was would tell the village headman, and he would rescue her from her lamentable situation.

Küpeli was a young man, motherless, and, one might say, fatherless as well. His widowed father, known by the nickname Berduş, meaning "useless," was a poor man who had become excitable and disoriented after his wife's death. He couldn't earn money, or, if he did, he couldn't keep it. Whatever he got, he spent without thinking. He was the kind of man who left his family burdened by oppressive need, and fully deserved his nickname.

Berduş had three sons, and a daughter, Fatma. He relied on his two eldest sons, Hacali and Küpeli, aged nineteen and seventeen respectively, to earn a living for the family. His fifteen-year-old daughter, Fatma, made bread and food for the family as well as she could, and struggled to raise her three-year-old brother, Ali.

Hacali and Küpeli hoed cotton in places like Söke. When they were at home in the village, the only thing they could do to earn a living was to cut young branches from the willow trees along the rivers and weave them into baskets. Both of them were polite young men. Their neighbors, who admired their industry, helped them as much as they could. Peddlers like Ismail, Hasanoca, and Rahim, would sometimes take Hacali, the elder of the two, with them and help him learn the art of bartering.

Both of these young men were calm and silent youths, but Küpeli was the better liked. His voice was so sweet that when he spoke, he seemed to sing. He also loved to dance at weddings, betrothals, or festivals, accompanying the local tunes by clicking wooden spoons. Everyone loved the way his hands, arms, legs, shoulders, his whole body, moved rhythmically in time with the dance tunes being played. At one time or another, who knew when, Emile must have seen him from a distance and fallen in love with him. Of course, Küpeli was not aware of this, and even if he had been, as a poor man, the possibility of marrying would never have entered his head. Even his elder brother, Hacali, was not married yet. Besides, who would give their daughter to a poor family?

Emile went on crying without listening to the constant words of entreaty. "Girl-bride, my dear lady-girl, my beautiful bride, stop crying. See what I'll give you, and what will I not give you! I'll hang gold on you. See, this house will be yours."

Emile kept repeating curse words and crying, so all the neighborhood people could hear: "I spit on your gold and everything here. I will have only Küpeli!"

That day was one in which Emile's mother, Ayşe, went as a day laborer to cut grass in a neighbor's field at Irmasan. When the poor woman came home in the evening, hungry and weary, her neighbors told her the news about her daughter. Ayşe immediately went and stood in front of Leyla's house. She spoke in a way likely to save the situation.

"Leyla, my sister, my neighbor, see, my daughter is still a child. Her age doesn't fit the government's rules. Now, I don't want to complain to the authorities. What's more, her elder brother, Yanık, isn't here at present. Let him come back from Söke. I hope to God he won't hear about this and leave off working to rush home. First, let's see my lamb, my dearest daughter, grow up. Wait and come in the proper way to ask for her if you still want her. If it's the will of Allah, we will give her to you. But, first, let Yanık come home. We'll talk the matter over. If he's willing, we'll wait until my daughter is of an age to get government permission to marry. Why not? Now, I'm taking my daughter home. Warn your son not to try to abduct her again. Come, daughter, Emile, we're going home."

Her mother's words calmed Emile a little, but she was still suspicious. "Wait, and if you still want her, we'll arrange the marriage according to our customs?" She was determined, whatever happened, that never in this world would she belong to Memo, Leyla's son. She quieted down, however, thinking, Maybe my mother was speaking cunningly in order to rescue me from here. Still sobbing after such a storm of tears, she clung tightly to her mother's arm.

While Leyla continued to speak entreatingly to Emile, mother and daughter got up and walked with determined steps toward their own home. The neighboring women went to comfort Leyla, the prospective mother-in-law, trying to improve the situation.

The pressure of summertime work made everybody, apart from the two families, soon forget about Emile's abduction.

In the middle of August, Küpeli, Yanık, and most of the cotton workers returned to the village. Afraid of falling into the difficult situation of another attempt at abduction, Emile's mother and her brother, Yanık, went to work with great secrecy. In order not to give anyone a chance to gossip, they arranged things quietly with Küpeli and his brother, Hacali.

In mid-September, the villagers were busy harvesting grapes and boiling cracked wheat. One day, after midnight, when bugs and birds were sleeping, two gunshots were heard, one after the other. These came from a double-barreled hunting rifle, which shot two bullets in succession. Following this, silence resumed. Those who heard the sound of the rifle did not worry too much. This sound was the customary way for a young man to announce to the world, "Tonight, I got married!"

It was that night that Emile became Küpeli's bride. Theirs was a marriage made in heaven. It was long and full of love, the kind of marriage seldom found in villages.

When a marriage began with an abduction, there was no celebration. For men, in particular, there was no form of entertainment. After the couple spent the night together, they first kissed the hands of the young man's mother and father. The father gave a plot or garden to his son, and the mother promised to give her new bride a heifer and a small cauldron or pan, or something similar. Then the newly married couple would go to their close relatives on each side of the family and kiss their hands. Generous relatives would press some bank notes into the bridegroom's hand, saying with feeling, "Here, children, take this. May it bring you good fortune and may you always sleep on the same pillow."

After visiting close relatives, the rest of the day belonged to the bride and those who came to congratulate her. The new bridegroom would not come home till evening. He either went to the coffeehouse to be with his friends, or would go with a few close friends to wander by the beautiful cold springs among the surrounding mountains and valleys.

That day, the new bride, together with the girls and young women who were neighbors or relatives, amused herself with an entertainment called the Bridal Ring. They would all congregate on the roof of the bridegroom's house to sing well-known, happy songs of that region, accompanied by those skillful or brave enough to play the tambourine. This music was very lively, and the girls and young women would dance for hours to the rhythm of spoons clicking like castanets in time with the tune. The older mothers and grandmothers encouraged the girls to dance happily together, and praised their daughters and those they saw as prospective brides. Such entertainments were a time for newly adult girls to show themselves.

A week after learning of Küpeli and Emile's marriage, our neighbor Leyla's son, Memo, abducted the more beautiful of two sisters of marriageable age from a poor family in the Ahmetli neighborhood. The bride, whose name was Mümine, moaned and wept a little the night she was abducted, but accepted her destiny when her future mother-in-law, Leyla, showed her a piece of double twist silk and two gold pieces.

The girls who came to a new neighborhood as newlywed brides were often as different as night from day. Some brought joy, virtue, and goodness to their new family and their neighbors, others were talebearers, and, as we say, loose tongued. They were experts at gossiping, and people were careful not to tell their personal or family secrets to such persons who could, as they say, "crack a millstone with their sharp gossip."

Mümine became one of the best-loved brides of our neighborhood. At hay time the following summer, each time I brought loaded donkeys to the village, she always helped me. Hoisting onto her back the bundles of hay I could not carry, she would carry them up to the roof.

In our village, there were many generous and kind people who spent as much effort as the parents in bringing up a child to be a good person.

Şenay, a Girl on the Yayla

1
Şenay

Tahsin Emmi was one of our most trustworthy neighbors. He did everything in the most compassionate way. No one ever heard him raise his voice to his wife or his children or to the pack animals that suffered the hardships of the family. Quite apart from never shouting at them, he never criticized them in even the slightest demeaning words. Tahsin was a person who didn't believe in the proverbial sayings "Those who don't beat their daughters will beat their knees" or "Crush a snake's head while it's young."

He kept fifteen wooden beehives, and when attending to their needs, he would never wear protective goggles. He moved so calmly that the bees flying around him never attacked him. If, very occasionally, a bee got entangled in his beard and stung him, he would merely say, "Why, bless you," and coolly continue finishing his work.

Tahsin Emmi's family went to the high-plateau pastures every year. The yayla they went to was not Sarot Yayla, where everyone else went. Tahsin Emmi, with his brother-in-law, Long Ahmet, and his wife's sister's husband, Hunchback Hüseyin, together with their families, would go to the yayla known as Bademli Yurt Yayla. This yayla was only fifteen minutes' walk away from our Oba, our little village of summer huts on the Sarot Yayla. Bademli Yurt Yayla had three springs and was surrounded on three of its sides by the Esenek Mountain and two hills, and backed by the heights of Çilehane. The center of this yayla was a very fertile plain where crops could be grown. The great-grandfather of Tahsin Emmi's wife, Fadime, had been granted the deed to this fertile area, in return for his notable services rendered during one of the Ottoman wars.

The local village headman would announce to the people of Çat the date when they might migrate up to the village yayla, Sarot. In contrast to this, Bademli Yurt, Çal Yurt, and Eski Yurt were private properties, so there were no restrictions on when the people who owned them could go to their yaylas. They would migrate there as soon as the snow melted, and only return to their villages in late November.

The weather at Bademli Yurt was cool. As a result, it was very convenient for planting potatoes. Their mountains and hills, where nothing could be planted, were grazed on by their animals. A boundary of stones had been made around this privately owned land, so that the grazing cows and herd of goats of the village would not stray onto it.

With its plentiful supplies of water and grass, Bademli Yurt Yayla was a very suitable place to keep the beehives in the summer. Tahsin Emmi kept about twenty beehives, and Long Ahmet thirty or forty. As Tahsin Emmi was a distant cousin of my grandfather, we were allowed to keep our four or five beehives on the same yayla.

Two of my best childhood friends, Zafer and Vehbi, spent their summers on Bademli Yurt Yayla. When my family first moved to our yayla, I would take every opportunity to go from our Oba to be with them on their yayla. One day, I was asked to look after my one-year-old brother, Mehmet, who was playing on the grass in the middle of Oba. I completely forgot about him and went off to the Bademli Yurt Yayla. My baby brother crawled into a muddy patch and his face and mouth got smeared with mud. Several women, noticing this, asked each other anxiously, "Whose child is this?" When my mother saw my baby brother, she rescued him, and when I came home that evening, I escaped with only a slight scolding from my mother, who seldom scolded anyone.

Like my father, Tahsin Emmi was a peddler. After moving to the yayla, when everything was settled, he would take his two donkeys and go to distant villages to sell pots. He had no field down at the village to look after. There were only a few fruit trees in his small garden. His wife, Fadime, was sometimes up on the yayla and sometimes down at the village, while her children who were not yet married would live on the yayla the whole summer. Tahsin Emmi would spend two days at the yayla, and, after attending to the bees and taking a look at how the crops were doing, would return to the village and continue his job of peddling.

Şenay was Tahsin Emmi's third daughter. After her older sisters, Fazilet and Huriye, got married, she became the daughter of the house and was the elder sister responsible for her younger brothers at the yayla. It was Şenay who looked after the children, milked the cows and sheep, and processed the milk. They kept only sheep, no goats, because in a confined area, sheep were easier to manage. It was the tradition to make unmarried young women responsible for serious duties, so they would learn what had to be done for the family and the household. Meanwhile, her younger brother Zafer took on the responsibility of monitoring the grazing of the family sheep and cows.

At the beginning of August, the village shepherd and all the families on our yayla would return to the village. The Oba was left empty. Those living on Bademli Yurt Yayla waited until November in order to harvest their crops.

2
The Abduction of Şenay

A man in our village known as Hamzaoğlu had five adult sons. As the family had no land to bring them any income, they earned their living by selling livestock and animal products. Hamzaoğlu was a Yörük who had sought refuge in our village. In fact, there were a number of families like his in the village: Komsoğlu, Hacıseller, Ankaralı, Yörük Hüseyin, Manav Eminasım, Yörük Kızı, Macar Kızı, Babaççılı, and Bekelelis had all taken refuge in our village, Çat, over the years. Hamzaoğlu and his sons would go to the Yörük tribes of Antalya and buy cattle from them to bring back and sell in Bozkır and the surrounding villages. They would not share their trading sources with even their closest neighbors or friends. People had only a vague idea of where the tribes or high-plateau settlements they went to were. One of the five sons of Hamzaoğlu, known as Seyit the Strange, was a very naive and harmless youth. The other sons were, in order of age, Mehmet, Kerim, Suleiman, and Fahri. They were all skilled and hardworking. Each had gotten married before

Fahri, the youngest. His father, mother, and brothers were slowly looking around to find a suitable young girl for him.

They learned that Şenay, who was of marriageable age, was living alone on Bademli Yurt. Alone, that was to say, because there was no older brother or father to watch over her all the time. Who would be afraid of the younger brothers the girl was looking after? Şenay had an older brother, but this young man was working far away as a day laborer. Her father was a docile man and mostly away peddling. It seemed to the Hamzaoğlu brothers that Şenay would be easy to abduct. Bademli Yurt Yayla was three hours away from the village at the top of a mountain. If she shouted or called out, who would hear?

One evening, they learned that Tahsin Emmi was at the village. Fahri and his older brother Kerim took two horses and set off for Bademli Yurt. They arrived after dark at Tahsin Emmi's house on the yayla. Şenay, who was about to go to bed, heard the sound of hooves, and, wondering if her father had come, went outside. Not recognizing the strangers, she addressed them, asking, "Hey there, have you lost your way? Do you need something?"

Coolly, Kerim replied, "Şenay, my girl, we've come to carry you off. Our intentions are serious and honest. We're taking you for our brother, Fahri. We've a long way to go now. The night will be very cold. Get yourself a covering or a shawl. We'll put you on horseback and go to one of the Yörük settlements."

"I don't know you," said Şenay. "Go and seek trouble on another mountain. My mind is set on a young man in the village I want to marry. You've come to the wrong place." Entering the house, she tried to bar the door, but the two strong young men forced it open.

Picking her up, the two tied Şenay on the back of one of the horses. Just then, her young siblings began to cry. Turning to the children, one of the abductors said, "Don't worry, children. We're taking your sister to a very good place. Tomorrow, we'll send word to your parents and they'll come and look after you." Mounting their horses, they set off at a good pace.

Tahsin Emmi's daughter, Şenay, was like her father. She certainly didn't know how to curse. As a child, she couldn't even manage to say to the mischievous children who pulled her hair or threw snowballs at her, "Go away, you beast! Go to hell, won't you?" Tied down on horseback by two unknown men, she could only say, "God will give you your just reward." In the dark of night, she had no idea where they were going.

The Hamzaoğlu sons knew very well what they were doing. It was simple: carry off the girl, keep her for at least a week on a Yörük yayla, treat her well, and if he could seduce her, do it. If he could keep the girl with him for a week, even if he couldn't seduce her, when she went back to the village, who would have her? In order to retrieve the family honor, her parents were bound to agree to a forced marriage. Of course, if the girl was feeling desperate and was forced into marriage, she'd take the first opportunity to throw herself into the raging waters of the Ulu River. It wasn't an unknown occurrence. Everyone knew of a bride who was treated like a slave, and had found her escape by plunging into the foaming waters of a river. No one could forget that the people responsible for this rotted away in prison for many long years.

Kerim and Fahri intended to journey all night till they came to Namaras, a settlement at the mouth of the Sesame Pass. There, no one would see them or guess where they were. But their calculations were wrong. Half an hour after they set off, it began to rain. It was possible that, in the act of carrying off the girl, they could catch pneumonia if they got soaked to the marrow in the freezing rain. A little while before the rain had started, they had stopped to drink from Meyre Spring, and knew they were near a tumbledown shelter called the Han in the deep valley of the White Mountain. The old trails in the high and mountainous regions used to have such shelters for voyagers in danger of freezing. The steep path up the mountain in front of them was like a series of steps to climb before reaching the Han. If they hurried, they could take refuge for the night in a corner of this Han before they got a thorough wetting.

These shelters were never without brushwood. They lit a fire and warmed themselves. Taking two blankets off the horses, they spread them out on the floor, telling Şenay to lie down on one by herself. From time to time, Şenay repeated, "You're tiring yourselves for nothing. I won't be of any use to you."

The older brother, Kerim, said calmly, "See here, lovely Şenay, you can now be counted as a bride. From now on, I'll call you Bridie and you will call me 'Elder Brother.'

Şenay retorted, "If I were you, I wouldn't roll up my trouser legs until I caught sight of the stream. I have my own intended bridegroom in the village."

Kerim answered, "We're going to keep you for a week, our Bridie, without anyone seeing. Who would take a girl who's been living with two men on the mountains for a week? See here, when we get back to the village, your mother and father will beg us to perform the nikah, the religious marriage ceremony, immediately."

They spent the night in the shelter. Kerim and Fahri had come prepared. They had brought food with them—bread, fried meat, cream-free yogurt, and onions.

Waking Şenay early the next morning, Kerim said, "Şenay, Bridie, we've a long way to go. Let's eat a mouthful of food before we set off."

In order to keep up her strength, Şenay ate a little.

After drinking from the small stream coming from the spring next to the Han, they climbed the narrow, rocky footpath, leading up like a staircase to the Namaras Yörük Yayla, which they reached after three hours or more.

That same morning, Şenay's younger brothers and sisters gave the news to their aunt Huriye, whose house was at the foot of the hill, telling her Şenay had been kidnapped during the night. Huriye hurried to the village and told Tahsin Emmi the situation.

The news that two men had come in the dark of night with two horses and abducted Şenay from Bademli Yurt Yayla exploded like a bombshell in the village. Those who heard of the event began to speculate as to which house the two young prowlers could have come from.

"I guarantee it's Hamzaoğlu's bachelor son and one of his elder brothers," was how the rumor went. A short time later, it was heard in every corner of the village that Hamzaoğlu's sons carried off Tahsin's Şenay from Bademli Yurt. Nobody knew where they had gone. When the village headman interrogated Hamzaoğlu and his wife, they denied any knowledge of the event, swearing that they didn't know where their sons had gone. Tahsin Emmi, Fadime, the relatives, and everyone else in the village was extremely angry. But no one had any news. No further news came on the second day, nor on the third. Tahsin Emmi's family grew more and more anxious. More and more neighbors and relatives began to say that when the kidnappers returned to the village, the matter would be looked on favorably. The Hamzaoğlu family were quite well-to-do, and the number of those saying, "Perhaps this is Şenay's kismet, her intended fortune," increased. Most of the people felt that, whatever happened, the matter was to be settled without informing the gendarmes, the local military police, or state authorities. Although they didn't say so openly, her family and close relatives began to approve of this idea.

Kerim and Fahri had taken precautions so that nobody caught sight of them on the road to Namaras Yayla. In any case, few people were on the road at that time of the year. The people who spent the summer at Namaras had gone back to their villages in Antalya by that time. Namaras Yayla was one of the furthest away from the boundaries of the village Çat. Since Kerim and Fahri had been sure they could use a high-plateau shack belonging to one of their relatives, a week before the event they had brought enough supplies of bread, cheese, and fried meat for ten days and stored them in the empty house.

They didn't leave Şenay without food or water, but instead, Kerim and Fahri tried to win her heart with their words, to get her to say what they were waiting for: "Very well, that's enough; I'll come to your house and be your bride." They promised Şenay many things in order to make her change her mind. But she dug her heels in, even when they promised, "When you're married, you and Fahri will live in a separate house. Your mother-in-law won't interfere in any way. We make a good profit by trading. We'll buy you the best clothes you could want. We'll buy you gold and a necklace worth five gold pieces."

She refused, saying, "No matter what, I will not be the bride in your family!"

In this way, nine days went by.

3
Şenay Runs Away to Mesut the Cutler

For nine days, the Hamzaoğlu sons, the kidnappers, used every honeyed word they could think of to convince Şenay. On the tenth day, Kerim, Fahri, and Şenay traveled back to the village Çat and arrived at the Hamzaoğlu house late in the night. But they didn't let Şenay go. She persisted in her refusal, saying, "I'm of no use to you. I won't be a bride in this house." In the hope that Tahsin Emmi and his wife, Fadime, would persuade their daughter to accept, a message was sent for them to come to the Hamzaoğlu house.

When her parents arrived, they found their daughter, Şenay, looking quite healthy. It was obvious that she had not taken ill or anything else on the high mountains. Her parents talked quietly with Şenay and asked her what she wanted. She had only one request: "I miss my home and my brothers and sisters a lot. First, take me home. Then I'll do whatever you want, Father."

Tahsin Emmi talked to the father of the Hamzaoğlu family. He agreed they could take their daughter home, but they had to promise that they wouldn't make a formal complaint to the authorities. Tahsin Emmi said, "Let my daughter come to our home to rest for a week. Then, as the traditions dictate, you will come like a proper father-in-law and ask for my daughter's hand in the customary way. At that time, we'll consider and decide what's the best thing to be done."

There was nothing to be said against such a reasonable proposal. Fahri and Hamzaoğlu were happy, knowing that the girl would not go against her father's decision. At least, that was how it had always happened in the villages.

Late that night, Şenay returned to her family home with her father and mother.

The village neighbors heard, of course, that Şenay had come back and was at home. Didn't Tahsin Emmi's children, in accordance with the saying "If you want news, ask the children," tell their friends that Şenay had come home, and was being kept hidden in the house? But all they had said was, "Our dear Şenay has come home."

After coming home, Şenay did not once leave the house. For five days, she stayed shut up inside. No news filtered through from the relatives and close friends who came and went. It was clear that her parents did not share their thoughts about their daughter's situation with either their neighbors or even their closest relatives. The neighbors grew more and more curious.

On the evening of the sixth day after her return, while the call to late-night prayer was being heard, a procession of five women filed down the steps of Tahsin Emmi's house. By chance, little Abidin, the son of a next-door neighbor, coming from his late-night visit to the outhouse, saw the silent procession of women. Not one of the women spoke. In the dark of night, it was impossible to tell who they might be. When Abidin got home, he told his mother, "Five or six women were walking in our alleyway, very quietly, going toward the upper part of the village."

His mother merely said, without paying much attention, "I hope it was for something blessed, my son."

The next day, the neighbors learned of the incredible decision that had been made during the five days Şenay had spent in her father's house. Şenay had rested and played with her siblings. Her married sisters had come to visit several times. Şenay had talked over her situation with her elder sisters for a long time and asked for their advice. In the end, her decision shocked the whole household.

"I will be Fahri Hamzaoğlu's bride on one condition," she said. "First, take me to the house of Mesut the Cutler, whom I love. If he and his parents accept me, I will stay there and be Mesut's wife. I don't care what anyone says. That's what I really want. If they say, 'We don't want someone who's probably been ruined up in the mountains,' and turn me away, then you can take me to the Hamzaoğlu house and leave me there. No engagement, no wedding. I will resign myself to my fate."

Her decision was incredible. It was beyond belief that anyone would take their daughter to a house where no one had asked for her hand in the proper way. No one would send a messenger to another family asking, "Will you please come ask for the hand of our daughter for your son?" Nor would anyone take his daughter to another house and say, "We have come. Here, take our daughter as your bride." This was a code of honor in the village. This was custom and tradition.

"Do you want to shame us in front of everyone? We can't do this," her parents declared.

Şenay, however, was adamant, and went on repeating her words.

Finally, on the sixth day, Şenay collected her belongings, tied them in a bundle, and made her final decision. "I'm tired of being shut up in this house. If you won't help me, in the evening when it's dark, I'll go all on my own to the house of Mesut the Cutler's family. I'll run away by myself to Mesut the Cutler. But if my mother, my sisters, and my aunt would come with me, I'd be very glad," she announced.

Seeing his daughter was so determined, Tahsin Emmi spoke. "Before this daughter of ours does something to hurt herself, let her go. She shouldn't go alone. You women, go along with her. May God bless this event."

That evening, Şenay arrived at the Cutler house, and, without any hesitation, said why she had come. The son of the house, Mesut, his father, and his mother were as delighted as if the bride had miraculously descended from the sky. With tears of joy in her eyes, Şenay kissed the hands of her new father and mother in her new home.

Only the two families and those close to them knew how Şenay from the yayla and the cutler Mesut got married. There was great respect and love in this marriage, which, together with modesty and simplicity, continued as though it would never end. The loving respect present in their relationship was reflected throughout the family.

After Şenay became a bride, her life was completely different from the way she had lived before. There was no need to milk cows or sheep to make butter, buttermilk, or cheese. In place of that, she rolled up her sleeves and worked in her husband's workshop, throwing fuel on the fire, using the bellows, and, if necessary, beating the red-hot iron in time with her husband.

Kerim and Fahri, who had prepared and acted out Şenay's abduction, thinking in their own minds that it was a good idea, certainly suffered great disappointment, especially Fahri. Since they had not done anything shameful to Şenay during the nine days of abduction, they were, however, quite proud of their own maturity. They were pleased that they had not gone to prison as, when they had brought Şenay back to the village, Tahsin Emmi had promised not to complain to the authorities.

In the village Çat, friction and arguments between the mothers of the children playing and fighting each other in the streets were common events; shameful incidents in the past would be brought up to rub the noses of their opponents in and blacken their names. Men did not do this. Still, to keep themselves from becoming the object of conversation in places like the coffeehouse or the market, these two young men, Kerim and Fahri, acted like shadows and became invisible for a time. These two brothers thought it safer to be out of sight, out of mind, and spent that winter trading in the Manavgat area. It was said later that Fahri got married and settled down there.

The Legend of Fiery Süheyla and Abdal Rüştü

1
The Cotton-Field Workers

The beginning of the 1950s brought many changes to the village Çat. First of all, the Democratic Party, also called the new party by the villagers, was elected to govern the country. Vowing to introduce all manner of freedoms, the new party completely overthrew the "old party," the Republican People's Party. Naturally, a person who promised to carry out the government's generous promises took over as village headman. This headman was Mehmet Mengene, the blacksmith, nicknamed "Forked Head," who was considered to be a just man, and was attentive to his neighbors' problems. The first thing he did was to change the attitude of the village watchmen. He prevented them from behaving in the accustomed unfeeling and tyrannical way toward the villagers.

Five years previously, several young men from the village—Akkoyun, Balcı, Karcı, Kumaş, Özüm, and Şahin—had been able to go to the İvriz Village Institute. In June of 1950, they came back to the village with their teaching diplomas and impressive new clothes. They had been appointed teachers to out-of-the-way villages of Konya, but before going to these schools, or to a village without a school, they spent three or four weeks talking in the village coffeehouse, encouraging fathers to educate their children.

In recent years, the paramedical teams sent to the villages had instituted the practice of inoculating the children against scarlet fever, measles, mumps, and whooping cough. In addition, infant deaths had decreased, and as a consequence, the population of the villages had quickly grown larger. Our fathers' generation had had two, three, or rarely, four or five siblings; now the families consisted of six, seven, or even ten or twelve living children. This increase began to give the parents difficulties they could not cope with. However, fortunately for the seasonal migrant workers and the newly adult young men, a rich source of income sprang up. A canal well supplied with water—or money—was opened on the plains of Söke in the Aegean region. As a result, the cotton-growing area there was rapidly extending, and this offered plenty of summer jobs. News came to the village that many laborers would be needed to work in the new cotton fields.

As the village Çat had the largest population in the district of Bozkır, for many years, most of the men had been going to earn a living for their family as laborers during the winter months. The men would work for at least six months in the fall or winter, laboring in the vegetable fields and orchards to earn money. My grandfather, known as Gunner Abdullah, who was a veteran of both the First World War and the War of Independence, had spent every winter, almost all his life, working in this way, either in Aydın or in Söke. When he came to visit his daughter—that was, my mother—in my childhood, he would tell us which villages he had worked for in either place, which garden he had worked in for which owner, and what kind of work he had done. Although I didn't know the names of most of the villages neighboring ours, I knew by heart the names of many villages of Aydın. Winter laborers like my grandfather spent the other five or six months of the year—the months when the heat in the Aegean region was unendurable—in our village. They spent the time planting and sowing the gardens and vineyards, and providing winter fodder for the animals, if there were any, and collecting wood for winter fuel. Elderly people, potters, blacksmiths, millers, and a few craftspeople would not go in the winter.

At the newly burgeoning cotton fields of Söke, the summer laborers found the work of hoeing and irrigating the cotton fields much more attractive than their previous work of winter labor in Aydın. The daily rate for a winter laborer was low and they could not save much. The saying "A day laborer has a pocket full of holes" showed that this kind of work for little pay did not allow much hope. News reached the village that hoeing and watering the cotton fields was a better way of earning money. "The harder you work, the more you get paid" was a maxim that gave great excitement, especially to the young.

Some experienced workers began to take on the responsibility of collecting the able, unemployed young sons of their neighbors and relatives and forming them into a team called "the Cotton-Hoers Gang." This foreman would find work for the fifteen to twenty youths he had collected by going to see the person responsible for the cotton field, the landowner or the overseer. He would bargain for his team's collective wages, which were not paid by the day but by the hectare, according to the amount of work done. The work the foreman bargained for was as follows: to keep the cotton fields free of the weeds that grew around the edges of the field where the cotton was as yet not fully grown, to hoe around the seedlings with a short-handled hoe, and to thin them out and heap up the soil around them. When the fields, bargained for by the foreman, had been hoed twice, the foreman would divide the total amount of money earned into equal shares for the foreman himself, the cook, and each one of the team of laborers. The team earned as much money as the number of hectares they had hoed; the more they hoed, the more they got. For that reason, everyone was expected to do his best.

Early every morning, when the cotton workers reached the edge of the cotton field, they would form a line. Every worker on that line was expected to move forward at the same pace. Naturally, those who were weak or couldn't manage to keep up became the butt of merciless jokes. Slow workers were not pitied by their team members. "My friend, hoe as quick as you can; your share will be the same as all the others in the end" would be the call for everyone on the same line to hoe at the same speed. Dried-up clay soil was not only more difficult to hoe than damp soil, but it also yielded less cotton. The owners of the field were extremely happy when they saw the laborers quickly hoeing all day long.

The life of the young cotton workers, who spent at least fourteen hours a day hoeing in the longest, hottest days of summer, was not one to bring joy to the heart. They sweated and swallowed dust from dawn to dusk, then were preyed on by mosquitoes at night as they slept out on the fields in their tightly closed tents. The plains of the Aegean region were stiflingly hot from May onward. The young men who hoed cotton fields there were often hungry and thirsty. They went on working, wearing the same clothes every day, which they became stiff with sweat and dust. Some of our villagers used to say, "At hoeing times, the cotton fields are absolute hell." However, at that time, when the daily wage of a builder's laborer was only one and a half to two liras, the "huge" amount paid to those who could find work in the cotton fields was very attractive.

2
Work Is Glory as Well as Gain

After a strenuous one and a half to two months' work in the cotton fields, each of the laborers there had in his hand a total sum of between four and five hundred liras, at least three times what a winter laborer would earn in six months. The young men, who had never before seen so much money at the same time, were able to taste the freedom of spending at least half of their earnings in any way they pleased before going back to the village. To the jacket and collared shirt worn by the teachers in the village and the officials in the town, they added a pair of breeches, a pair of flamboyant top boots with turnovers, a flat cap, a honey-colored string of prayer beads, and a cartridge belt, together with a nine-shot revolver. Before returning to the village, some of them grew a mustache for the first time.

For about a week after finishing work in the cotton fields and returning home, a young man paid little attention to the work and occupations of his family. He used this time to exercise his right to stroll around, to look and be looked at. In his new clothes and gleaming boots, his jacket slung over one shoulder and his cap set rakishly over his right ear, the young man would set off with measured steps toward the coffeehouses, taking care to show the revolver swinging in its holster at his side.

The coffeehouses of Musa and Sergeant Kemal in Çat drew these gloriously attired youths like a magnet. Coming from Karagaç, Ahmetli, Ömerli, and Cingiller on the opposite hills, these young men, backs stiff as ramrods, would swagger along the uphill streets leading to these coffeehouses.

3
Dressing the Lamb

Perched on the slopes of valleys, all the houses in Çat village had flat roofs. These roofs formed the dividing lines between the streets that, according to their location, were sometimes wide, sometimes narrow. The flat roofs of the houses, the most favored outdoor living areas, were the only level areas in the village. Looked at from a distance, the village neighborhoods looked like a series of steps, slowly rising above the rivers running along the bottom of the valleys.

All the women, old or young, waited for the return of the cotton-field workers with great excitement. The women or young girls who had business to do on the roofs that overlooked the roads leading up to the coffeehouses would look appraisingly at these adolescent youths with their flamboyant clothes and swaggering behavior as they came and went. They would talk quietly among themselves, with comments such as "Isn't that young man there so-and-so? He's become very handsome, God bless him." A gorgeous and handsome young bachelor would be well aware he was being observed from the roofs. Maybe it was the influence of these eyes, maybe from the confidence given by his fine clothes and the money in his pockets, who knew, but youths like him seemed to float along the streets as if their feet did not touch the ground. They appeared and disappeared like migrating butterflies blown by a gentle breeze.

The excitement of the young girls and their mothers increased each time they saw these youths walking along the streets. The mothers would begin to pester their husbands. At the first opportunity, they went to the town to have a dress made of an eye-catching new material. Made of artificial silk, this material was not only shiny, but had an overall pattern of colorful flowers and shapes. Upon seeing a girl wearing a dress of this material, with a waist-cinching belt, other girls would burst with envy. Mothers and daughters did not care whether there was money available or not. If there was a young girl in the family, this material had to be bought, debt or no debt. Strike while the iron's hot, as the saying goes. While there were magnificent young men strolling around the village, every family with a young girl, hoping she might be destined for a good future, simply had to buy at least a dress length of the new material known by them as tarla sattıran, or seller of fields. If there was not enough money for this, the father of a young girl was sometimes obliged to sell a piece of land.

Young girls wearing such dresses began to appear, and young bachelors, following them with glances from under their cap brims, started to dream all kinds of dreams. The first approach would come from the young man. A young man's closest friend in the world was his mother.

In a well-known story about a village lad doing his military service, his commanding officer asked him, "What is your homeland, son?" The youth answered, "My homeland is my mother, sir!"

In the villages, young men felt closer to their mothers than their fathers. They began to nag their mothers, pleading in the most winning way, "Mother, please go and ask for this or that girl." In the 1950s, custom forbade a young girl and a young man to speak to each other unless they were close relatives. This custom was strictly observed, especially since neglecting it might affect the honor of the girl or the family. The young men would be embarrassed to talk to their fathers about their feelings, but could easily share them with their mothers.

When a young man's mother felt her husband was in a good mood, she would begin by saying, "What about asking for the daughter of so-and-so for the boy? What do you think?"

The father would brush the question aside, saying, "Well, the asshole spent most of what he earned on clothing himself. Is it such an easy thing to go and ask for the hand of a girl? We'd have to buy presents, gold, most likely. Still, we'll think about it."

Without insisting too much, the mother would reply, "Oh, but the girl's thrifty as well as beautiful. There'll be lots of people asking for her. If we push ourselves a bit, we could get her married before others play their hand."

The young men returning from the cotton fields would fill the two coffeehouses, which became the scene of many interesting interactions. The ones who came first would order tea for the ones who came later. The first greetings made to the young man came from those already sitting on the wooden chairs in the coffeehouse. Each in turn would say, "Hello." Whether there was any feeling of competition, jealousy, or even the slightest ill will, to welcome each newcomer politely was the common coffeehouse rule. Conversation then started. Memories were shared of which gang worked on which landowner's field, how much money they shared at the end, where there were more or fewer mosquitoes, and things like that.

Even if a father was against his son wasting his time at the coffeehouse, he knew he must behave with moderation toward one who had just returned home after being absent for a time. A wise father would advise his son, "Son, since you're off to the coffeehouse, don't gossip and don't listen to gossip. Keep your cards close to your chest." The sons who listened to their fathers liked drinking their coffee or tea, playing the card game of Sixty-Six, and earning ten walnuts or one hundred grams of lokum, or Turkish delight.

Expert players of the game of Sixty-Six didn't like playing with beginners. A good Sixty-Six player could constantly remember the faces and the numbers of the cards he took, as well as those taken by his opponent and the scores. He was sure to know which cards were left on the table, and which were not yet in play. As his chance of winning increased, he began to crow louder. The beginners at this game in the coffeehouse watched carefully and saw how the experts competed with and jokingly insulted each other.

When a play between Mehmet, the blacksmith son of Eyüp, and Mad Abdullah began to heat up, all the regular coffeehouse goers would watch with extreme attention. They loved listening to the joking insults the two experts threw at each other. One time, the cards Mehmet had taken were good. He moved the deck to the side and said, "You're closed out, man," and played the ace of trumps.

Abdullah had to follow suit, so produced his only trump card, the ten of trumps.

Mehmet took his ace, turned it over, and banged it on top of the ten, implying a sexual act. Following this, he showed the queen and king, worth forty points, in his hand and said, "That's enough," meaning he had ended the game by making sixty-six points altogether.

"Take them, take them all. All the good cards came to you, and you puff yourself up and crow like your old rooster. I got half of your score, you know, by picking up nines and twos. You're only ahead by one game!" said Abdullah, turning over in his mind all the colorful insults he would throw at his rival if he had good trumps in his hand next time.

4
The Chatter of Guns

The neighborhoods of Çat, built on opposing sides of the valleys, rose in different directions. The gorgeous youths of the village took their strolls not only on the roads leading to the coffeehouses, but also on the roofs of the houses that were conveniently situated for this. After coming home in the evening, the young men began to wander over the roofs. In the Ahmetli neighborhood, the hand of one of them began to itch, and he took out his gun and fired a shot off into the air. Echoing back from the high, rocky mountains, the sound was heard by the whole village. Upon hearing the gunshot, another young man walking around on his roof in the Çat neighborhood immediately took out his gun and fired two answering shots. Another one on a roof in the Cingiller or Ömerli neighborhoods who heard the noise outdid the previous shooters by firing off three bullets. Not much later, the number of shots fired in each neighborhood increased, as did the number of spent cartridges. In the end, all the clips containing nine bullets had been discharged.

At the same time, other people, young and old alike, climbed onto the roofs to watch and listen to the racket. When I was in the village during one such summer, I was both quite young and a schoolboy, so I couldn't join in any competitions to show off my shooting ability. I just climbed onto the roof and watched the celebratory festivities in different neighborhoods. Once, when my Uncle Salih and I were on the same roof, he turned to me and said, "Nephew, the young lads are throwing money into the air for nothing, even though they don't earn money that easily . . . but that's youth!"

This competition to fire shots into the air seemed very much like partridges calling to each other at mating time. The partridges' calls would sound like a quarrel, stopping only when the birds became tired or darkness fell. The young men of our village stopped their rowdy firing into the air, when either the girl they had set their eye on had been asked for and given, or the cotton money in their pockets was finished.

5
Fire and Gunpowder: Explosion of Marriages

If you asked the fathers of daughters, they would say that this rowdiness was started by the cotton money; the fathers of sons would declare everything had begun with the invention of the shiny new material. What good would it do to argue until evening about "Which came first, the chicken or the egg?"

A merciless race to get married took place in the whole village of Çat. No one listened any longer to the precept "No girl can be promised to a young man who hasn't done his military service." One dress made from the new silky material was all it took for a family to head out with a gold lira or a necklace worth five gold pieces, to ask for a girl to marry their son. More and more families did this. When more than one "customer" was interested in asking for the hand of a particularly fine-looking girl, her parents were left in a difficult position. The fathers and mothers were well acquainted with the term "fire and gunpowder" when it came to young men and girls: if it was up to them, biology would dictate a whole lot of unplanned explosions! It was only natural for the parents to try to provide a secure future for their children. Girls who had completed their fourteenth year began to get engaged to be married at the end of the next cotton-field season. The government did not allow a girl under sixteen to get married, even if the parents of both families agreed. A solution to this was found, however: many families went to the town registrar with two witnesses to have their daughter's age changed to sixteen or seventeen. Those girls whose real age was eighteen were called "old maids," or said to be "left on the shelf" or "stale," which could be considered insulting. In short, the union of underage children increased.

During the time of the proposal and the engagement, the boy's mother would behave very sweetly to the girl's mother. Wherever they were according to the season, the produce of mountain, garden, or yayla would come to the girl's house as a present: a pitcher full of buttermilk from the yayla, a bowl of black mulberries from the garden, a basket of grapes, whatever was in season, would be sent to the girl's family. These presents, especially if brought by a future mother-in-law with a smile on her face, would be accepted with pleasure by the girl's mother. What mother would not be pleased to be giving her daughter to such a generous family? However, these smiles and goodwill during the time of the betrothal would end on the very day of the marriage, just like a soap bubble bursting.

The bridegroom's mother, who, for months, had brought presents and spoken sweetly with a smiling face, would give the young bride a job to do on the very first morning after she entered the house, even before the girl's wet hair had time to dry, and then find something to criticize. "Come, my angel, make some tea for us to drink. The day I became a bride, my mother-in-law made me cook tarhana soup. Tea is easy to make. Make it hot and brew it well. Cold tea can't be drunk." Her needling words would be expressed in a sweet and complimentary tone to the bride. But, in fact, these remarks were the first steps in a campaign to belittle and insult her.

Before evening on the same day, she would catch her son for a short minute, and whisper in a low voice only he could hear, "Oh, son, I say, may God bless you. They all praised her so much, saying she was so hardworking and so talented. But your bride, she hasn't even learned how to make a good cup of tea. Good luck to you. Even a plank can learn . . ." These words were spoken as naturally as eating a bit of bread or drinking a sip of water. On the happiest day of her son's life, she had to speak disparagingly of his young wife.

The young bride could still have been called a child. The young bridegroom was the same, and he was still his mother's little lamb. He listened to whatever his mother said. On the second night, as soon as they were alone together, this inexperienced and foolish boy would immediately blurt out the criticism his mother had made. Not knowing what had happened, this young bride, whoever she might be, having learned at home not to answer back, might stay silent. Or, the young bride, finding one or two loaded words to strike back with, might retort in a way quite unsuited to be heard by a husband who was his mother's little lamb.

This would be the start of a "cat and dog life" for this young couple. At the first opportunity, the young wife would relate to her own mother the barbed words she had been subjected to. Most of the time, the friction between the young husband and wife would not go beyond arguments. However, in some cases, the young husband would catch the "wife-beating sickness" of the village. This would precipitate the bride's escape home to her father's house. Some families would say, "Have patience, daughter." Others would say, "While there's no infant involved, leave and come home, daughter. Stay apart for a while. Maybe the boy will wise up. He's not going to listen to his mother forever, is he?" Sometimes, though rarely, the girl would be beaten by her own father and sent back to her husband's house. Very rarely, the story of a bride who had been beaten in both houses would be told in our village; her deliverance came by going to the bridge and jumping into the foaming waters of the river as if joyously greeting the spring.

In the 1950s, most of these child marriages ended in divorce. One of my brothers and one of my sisters experienced such child marriages.

Whether a young man or woman, a divorced person hardly ever married a person who had not been married before. But the second attempt to get married to another divorced person was not due to parental pressure. Somehow, the man or woman would find the courage to choose a partner from those who had also been married and divorced before. Within a short time, all divorced young men and young women in the village were able to get married again. Nobody was left out. The young people who married for a second time had more knowledge. Perhaps feeling that they would never get married again, or perhaps because this time they had made their own choice, the young couple managed to get on and take the good with the bad. If it could be said, "No one who married a second time ever got divorced," it would be a great thing, but this wouldn't be quite true.

6
Süheyla the Firebrand

Süheyla was known as the most beautiful young girl, not only in the Ahmetli neighborhood, but in the whole of the village. She was the youngest, the most lovable, and of course, the most spoiled of Redneck Ali's five children, all girls. Redneck Ali's four oldest daughters had gone as brides to neighborhoods far away from their own. In their old age, the mother and father very much wished that their youngest daughter, at least, could be married to someone they could call a next-door neighbor. With the hope of this, the mother became very good friends with the wife of their neighbor who had a young son, and the beauty and bearing of Süheyla supported the idea that no expense would be spared.

Two of Süheyla's older married sisters lived in our part of Çat, and she often came to visit them. Whenever she came, she always wore a dress of artificial silk, with a scarf of shiny silk on her head covering at least a part of her long hair, and tied loosely under her chin. The tendrils of hair escaping from under the scarf on her forehead, and the long, thin plaits that hung down across her breast, made her beautiful face even more attractive.

Süheyla's older sister Amme was married to a close relative of ours. Since my father was the eldest of the family, they came to us to celebrate every festival. Süheyla always came with her sister and her brother-in-law. I was then in the fourth grade in primary school. Without giving a thought to how young I was, I also had dreams of Süheyla, who caught everyone's eye.

In spite of there being many "customers" in other parts of the village, her mother and father gave her to Hüsnü, the son of their nearest neighbors. It was very important for them that their daughter's new house be near theirs, especially as they had no sons. It might happen that either mother or father would fall sick and need looking after. It was a great benefit for every family to have at least one daughter living near them. However much help a family might receive from a son in the village, it was from the daughter that most help would come, especially when the parents grew old. There was a saying in the village: "A daughter is the child to trust."

Süheyla left home as a bride, but not for long. It didn't last even a month. She didn't love her husband. He wasn't enough for her. With the excuse, "I have no intention of putting up with this boy," she returned to her father's house. With the connivance of the two fathers and mothers, who didn't want the event broadcast, few people heard that the two had separated. In any case, the formalities for an official wedding had not been completed. That divorce was just a quiet separation.

For some reason or other, the event did not become a subject for gossip, and another suitor arrived for Süheyla's hand. On the advice of her elder sister, married to someone in our part of the village, Süheyla married Nazmi, a young man who had recently completed his military service. Nazmi was a very hardworking and thrifty young man. He had no problem with having a wife who had been divorced. He was very happy. However, as the only way of earning a living was to become a migrant laborer, he was absent from the village for six or seven months of the year. Leaving Süheyla in the village, he continued struggling to earn money in far-off places such as Söke, Izmir, or Manisa. This second marriage did not bring happiness to Süheyla either. It lasted, with difficulty, for a year, then she went back, once again, to her parents' house. Many people in the village who married when still immature got divorced, and, after living as a single person for some years, became wiser. Süheyla's parents were not about to throw her out on the street. They did not object, even when their daughter was divorced again.

Six months or so passed by, then Süheyla married a third time. In Cingiller, there was a fatherless young man by the name of Alişan, who was known to be quiet and very honest. There were many who said, at first glance, that this third husband was a stroke of good fortune for Süheyla. Her father and mother, as well as her two married older sisters, were very happy, thinking that, at last, beautiful Süheyla, the baby of the house, their little rose, had found a good husband. Süheyla swore that, come what may, she would do her best to make this marriage work and not shame her parents anymore.

Alişan was also a migrant worker. He, too, spent six or seven months away from the village, earning a living in a distant place. Süheyla did not complain much about this, but spent her time waiting patiently for his return by tending Alişan's small garden in the village. Her mother and father were pleased, and even her brothers-in-law, who had felt shamed by Süheyla's previous behavior, were happy. This marriage went into its second year, and Süheyla began to feel that she had become a mature woman of the village. In the fall, after the grapes had been harvested and grape syrup made, Alişan provided his wife with what she would need during the winter, such as wood for fuel, kerosene, salt, matches, and oil to cook with that he bought from the market. After giving Süheyla what was left of the cash, leaving only enough money in his pocket for his journey, Alişan set off with five or six companions to work in Aydın again.

In Anatolia there is a widespread saying: if you leave a daughter to choose for herself, she will end up with either a drummer or a piper. The older generations certainly had experience with this. Otherwise, why would they have said it?

In winter months, the nights were long. Sometimes, neighbors or relatives came together, and while working at small handicrafts, would listen once again to enthralling tales of times past. When there were children in the house, famous tales of the legendary phoenix that lived in the seventh sphere underground would be told until they went to sleep.

7
Abdal Rüştü

Rüştü, a young man whose father was a potter in the Ömerli neighborhood, did not enjoy working with clay. He didn't want to learn from his father how to make pots. His father, Osman, was a very kind man and said to Rüştü, "Very well, son, go and be a migrant worker. But if you change your mind, I'll welcome you with open arms. Off you go, and God be with you."

For the first time in his life, Rüştü joined the migrant workers going to hoe the cotton fields in Söke. This young man who hadn't liked the physical labor of working in his father's cool pottery workshop, disliked working with cotton even more. He realized how oppressive it was to hoe during the long, hot days on the dusty earth and to battle for sleep with mosquitoes at night. Already dark complexioned, Rüştü became even darker, working all day under the hot sun. Upon seeing him turn such a color, the other workers began to call him "Abdal Rüştü." He didn't mind this at all. He remembered the saying "Mouths aren't sacks to be sewn up by hand." He went on working patiently until he had completed his three-month task of hoeing and watering the cotton fields.

Unlike the other cotton-field workers, Rüştü did not spend the money he earned on clothes and a pistol. He remembered how, for years, he had admiringly listened from a distance to the tunes Ali the Fiddler played. He decided to spend a third of the money in his pocket on a good instrument. After finishing work in the cotton fields, he didn't return with his companions to the village, but instead, went to Izmir, the nearest big city. There he found a store that sold musical instruments. He listened to experts playing, and after consulting them, bought a very nice banjo. He stayed in Izmir for a while, learning how to string and tune his instrument, how to hold the plectrum and strike the strings, and how to play a few tunes by going to the musicians in the music stores.

After buying presents for his father, mother, and siblings, and a modest set of clothes for himself, Rüştü returned to his village, banjo in hand. Telling himself he must learn to play songs and folk melodies, he worked from morning to night on his banjo, sometimes in tune, sometimes not, but never anywhere near his own house. He knew his father would be irritated by the constant sound of the instrument, tuned or untuned. He had to find a place where he wouldn't upset his father or annoy his neighbors.

One of Rüştü's friends from childhood was Jackal Osman, a fatherless young man who earned a living for himself, his mother, and her sister as a master cutler. His house, with his workshop underneath, was not close to those of his neighbors. The level space in front of it, big enough for a chair or two, suited Rüştü's needs. Osman worked all day in his workshop by himself. It was lonely work pumping the bellows, using worn-out shovels as steel for making knife-blades, heating and cutting goat horn for the handles all by himself. The idea of having Rüştü there in front of the workshop appealed to him. As long as he had a companion to say a few words to now and then, he saw no problem in listening to the "noises" Rüştü made on his banjo. About a week after returning to the village, Rüştü started to practice playing the banjo in front of his friend's workshop. Even when it was rainy or snowing, he continued playing in a corner of Osman's workshop.

It was then I learned that Rüştü was a distant cousin of mine, two or three times removed. Osman's workshop was fifty or sixty meters from our house. From our balcony, we could see and hear Rüştü playing. Once, while eating on the small roof that served as a balcony, my mother turned to my father and said, "I'm fed up with this constant noise grating on my ears."

My father said gently, "Rüştü's father is a relation of mine. It's obvious the boy's enthusiastic and is trying to learn a skill. We should be pleased. We don't sit on the balcony from morning till night. It doesn't bother us too much."

From the first, those who sat on the balconies of houses near Osman's workshop or passed by it on the street didn't care for the sounds that pierced their ears. Rüştü took no notice of their harsh words, such as

"Enough, man, you've given us a headache." He would simply answer politely, "Auntie, Uncle, this is a very difficult skill. I'm sorry I can't become an expert without practice," and went on playing.

After taking up his banjo in the morning and tuning it as well as he could, he would try to pick out the notes of a folk tune running through his head. He repeated the same notes many times. Toward evening, those who heard him began to recognize the tune. The ones who occasionally said, encouragingly, "Well done, Rüştü," began to increase.

Rüştü would play, over and over again, each of the folk songs sung at weddings, and in particular, the ones loved most by the people of the Bozkır area. Untiring, he continued to play all through the year. As he became better, he began to sing the words to the tunes he played. Although at first his voice was a little hoarse, people began to like it more as time went by. In the end, people sitting on their balconies or roofs would peer over and ask each other, "Who's that singing folk songs so beautifully?"

Without taking any notice of whether the days were long or short, and after practicing all through the winter and summer months, when fall came, Rüştü began to feel he played the banjo well. After he felt more confident, he would sit, late in the evening, on his father's roof in the Ömerli neighborhood and begin to softly play and sing a few of the pieces he was familiar with. Then Rüştü began to join the musicians who got together on Friday evenings to play in front of Long Musa's coffeehouse in Çat. After playing the banjo without a break for one and a half years, he showed the longtime musicians of the village that he had become a very good player. He impressed, in particular, the expert fiddler, Ali, and began to find work with him at weddings in the neighboring villages and towns.

8
Drums Sound Pleasant from a Distance

Cingiller, where Süheyla lived in her third husband's home, and Ömerli, where Rüştü lived, were the smallest neighborhoods of the village and close to each other. In the evenings, the sound of Rüştü's playing could be heard at Süheyla's house. The area between the two neighborhoods consisted of one small garden after another, crossed by a narrow path only just wide enough to walk on. To the right and left of this path, wild apple and barberry trees, wild roses, and brambles grew so thickly that no one from the Çat neighborhood on the other side of the valley could see anyone walking along the path without looking very intently.

Süheyla had been without the loving care of her husband for many months. Some evenings, she walked sedately along the path to Ömerli and passed near Rüştü's father's house. Once, she was daring enough to knock on the door and ask Rüştü's mother to lend her some salt. Rüştü was sitting on the balcony playing his banjo and she complimented him, saying, "Mr. Rüştü, health to your hands, how sweetly you play."

Rüştü was taken by her musical voice. He replied, "Thank you, Mrs. Süheyla. I'm just practicing."

Without delay, Süheyla quickly returned home.

There were people with eyes and ears everywhere in the village. Such people tried to come up with a rumor about everyone they saw whether human or animal, making up something about every scene, incident, or sound. They were experts at choosing their words carefully. Whether man or woman, they tried to appear as if they were innocently minding their own business. They never made a song and dance about anything. Two or three soft-spoken words would drop gently from their lips, but their tongues were forked. Slippery, poisonous comments would puff softly from their mouths like a mild breeze. There's a saying to describe such a person: able to grow worms in a bowl of salt. Such persons used hypocritical or devilish ways of speech. In fact, the rumors they started soon reached everyone's ears; like the mud in a swamp, they flowed and increased. These stories spread like a contagious disease.

It was Süheyla's misfortune that, one evening, someone whom we might call a devil saw her walking calmly toward the Ömerli neighborhood. This person, whose nickname was Roly-Poly, was going to the coffeehouse to listen to the news on the radio. He whispered his suspicions in one corner of the coffeehouse: "As I was leaving the mosque after the evening prayer, please God forgive my sins, but I could not help seeing a young woman walking in the bushes toward Ömerli."

Süheyla's eldest brother-in-law, who was known as Mad Kerim, happened to be in the coffeehouse then. As her elder sister's husband, he felt that any gossip suggesting light behavior on the part of Süheyla would reflect badly on his wife and himself. He warned Süheyla, somewhat threateningly, against going on her own to other neighborhoods in the evening.

A man isn't called mad for nothing, and there certainly was an alarming reason for this. When he was angry, Mad Kerim would swear at his wife, his children, and even at his neighbors, and everyone knew he would beat anyone who was weaker than himself or unprotected. Such people, in reality cowards, were to be found in every village. Of course, Süheyla was frightened, and contented herself with listening to Rüştü's music from a distance, rather than going to Ömerli.

Her brother-in-law, in order to show he was serious, couldn't stop himself from spying on her from time to time. On some evenings, he would walk to the coffeehouse by way of Cingiller and Ömerli, even if this made the road longer. Süheyla could now no longer go to Rüştü's house. In time, Mad Kerim's suspicions lessened and he began to swear heartily at the malicious people who had unjustly accused his sister-in-law, calling them vicious gossips and baseless liars, as though he himself had a pure soul.

Some evenings, Süheyla would go to her sisters, Amme or Canan, who lived in Çat and whose husbands were also away in Aydın. She listened to the old stories they told, but couldn't fully concentrate on what was being said. After noon each day, her attention was fixed on the sweet sound of a banjo coming from Ömerli, accompanied at times by a soulful tenor voice.

9
Who Won the Lottery?

One New Year's Eve, what Süheyla's brother-in-law had feared would happen came about. That evening, he was at Long Musa's coffeehouse until late, listening to the radio and playing cards. The coffeehouse was full to bursting. As it was New Year's Eve, the winning ticket for the big prize in the state lottery was to be drawn. Even those who hadn't bought a ticket were waiting with great curiosity to see which number would win the million-lira prize, even in which city the winning ticket had been sold. Even those who seldom went to the coffeehouse were there that evening to enjoy the excitement of hearing on the radio the number that was drawn.

Hüseyin the Basketmaker, a devil with prayer beads, came to the coffeehouse after saying his late-evening prayers at the mosque. As soon as he saw Mad Kerim, he said, as if murmuring to himself, "Why, man, at the mosque this evening, I couldn't remember my prayers and mixed up the ones I know as well as I know my own name."

Without any suspicion, but thinking he had some news to tell, two-faced Abdul said, "What could have happened, my friend, to muddle your mind like that? Do tell us."

Basketmaker Hüseyin replied, "I was late for prayers, so I came straight down from Cingiller. I saw a shadow like a woman going toward Ömerli. I didn't see her face. God knows, I don't want to point the finger at anyone."

Upon hearing this, Mad Kerim's ears pricked up. "Why, I swear to God, I'll kill that no-good infidel," he said, getting up and leaving the coffeehouse angrily.

Knowing how angry and bad-tempered Mad Kerim could be, eight or ten young men immediately ran out of the coffeehouse after him, racing into the darkness. Trying to calm him down, his friends followed him, repeatedly begging, "Hey, my friend, wait a bit. You may harm someone. It's better to keep your wrath until morning. Cool down."

One of these was Gambler Kamil. "Hey, in no time at all, the state lottery will be drawn. We were going to have fun listening to it on the radio. Where did all this spring come from?" he said, trying to make them smile.

Rüştü's house was on the other side of the valley, on a hillside above the road leading from Çat to Ömerli. The house was less than two hundred meters from the road as the crow flew. But the Yayla River ran along the bottom of the valley, and it was impossible to cross directly; there were high banks along the riverside and terraced gardens. In order to go from Çat to Ömerli, it was necessary to go via Helim Gully and cross the wooden bridge there.

Rüştü was sitting on his balcony, smoking a cigarette, when he heard the noise coming from across the valley, and said to Süheyla, sitting happily beside him, "Get up, girl, I'm afraid we're in for it, it seems. Go quickly and hide in the hay barn. I'll walk out as if nothing has happened, as if I was calmly going to the coffeehouse. If anyone asks where I'm going, I'll say I'm going to hear about the lottery. No one will suspect anything."

In the hay barn, he quickly covered Süheyla with hay. Then, with his cigarette in his mouth, he began to walk with steady steps toward Çat. At the bridge, Rüştü came across the people coming from the coffeehouse, but the Mad Kerim gang either did not recognize Rüştü in the dark or they were so intent on finding Süheyla, they hurried on.

When they arrived at Rüştü's house, Mad Kerim and his companions searched through the rooms, the stable, and the hay barn by the light of a torch. Just as he was about to say, "Enough, friends, there's no one here, girl or bride," Mad Kerim caught sight of a small piece of cotton cloth among the hay, and began to curse. He recognized it as part of Süheyla's red dress. He attacked his poor sister-in-law, hidden as she was, with blows and kicks. The others he had come with prevented him from doing further damage, and together, they all took Süheyla straight to the house of the village headman, who was at that time Hese the Potter. They wanted the headman to start legal proceedings so that this woman, who could destroy the village's morals, would be sent to Konya and delivered to the brothel there.

Little time passed before everyone at the coffeehouse, waiting for the state lottery to be drawn, heard the news. A heated discussion followed. One of the young men frequented the coffeehouse, a sensible young man who thought sending Süheyla to Konya was wrong, began to speak in a persuasive voice, saying, "Look, friends, young people from neighboring villages, as well as ours, go to the brothel in Konya. Süheyla's presence there would lay our villagers open to slander from other villagers. Our young men wouldn't stand for that. This would give rise to dangerous quarrels between the youths of two villages. Terrible injuries might happen. Our young men are never without a knife or gun at their waist or in their pocket. Come, let's not broadcast this event; let's keep it under wraps. Let's tell her father, Redneck Ali, to keep her at home and not let her out for a whole year. In any case, he will say, 'My honor is shit now,' and punish his daughter accordingly." The villagers liked this solution and, without more ado, the village headman closed the case.

The next day, Rüştü, knowing that he would be subject to shaming words by the villagers, never left his father's house. That evening, tucking his banjo under his arm, he left the village without a word to anyone. Wherever he went, Rüştü felt his conscience prick him. Even when playing his favorite songs and tunes, he was imagining what Süheyla's situation must be like.

Rumor had it that Redneck Ali had chained his daughter up in the stable alongside his donkey. He had put enough food in front of her for her to survive, but did not show his face to his beloved daughter for many weeks. This was whispered around the village, and created a shadow of fear among all the young girls and brides of the village, and even among the young men.

The rumor of her being chained up next to the donkey had reached Rüştü. He said to himself, "You useless scoundrel, Abdal Rüştü, you who call yourself a musician. A man without honor, what good will your craft do you? Go back to your village and clean up your filthy mess."

He soon set off along the road home. That evening, he pleaded with his father, his uncle, and Headman Hese, and sent them to see Redneck Ali. The next morning, both the parents, Rüştü, Süheyla, and two neighbors as witnesses, went to the registry office in Bozkır. The two were then officially married according to state law. From Bozkır, they went straight back to Rüştü's house. Both of them were happy. Without any wedding celebrations, festivities, or entertainments of any kind, they began their married life.

In time, Rüştü and Süheyla brought four sons into the world. Each of these infants, born with the sound of their father's music in their ears, grew up to become a successful musician. Each son became a master of a different instrument—the banjo, the violin, the lute, and the drum. Each of them took up another way of earning money apart from their music, but they continued to treat themselves and those around them to musical feasts, and so kept alive the legacy of Abdal Rüştü.

Bozkır: Friday Farmers' Market

In the 1950s, Fridays were market days—hot summer days full of dust, hucksters, and noisy crowds. With a string bag, a basket, or a shopping bag in hand, customers rubbed shoulders with each other among the stalls. Villagers from Yolören were the first there, spreading their cucumbers, zucchinis, eggplants, tomatoes, onions, and garlic on cloths on the ground, ready to be sold. The same area was shared with those selling butter, honey, raisins, and grape syrup.

My father and I liked to get to the market early. The night before, we were on the road from evening until morning. That week, our peddling journey had been to the Uluören Yayla of Çalmanda. We had finished our trading there by noon on Thursday, and walked all night to arrive at the Friday market in good time. We arrived in Bozkır just as the sun was about to rise. We unloaded our animals in a corner to the north of the market, in front of a street lined with shops. With great dexterity, we emptied our saddlebags and sacks and spread out our goods where people usually sold butter and honey. I laid one of the empty sacks on an untaken space on the dusty ground. Father took the saddlebag, heavy with pots of salted butter, off his shoulder and placed it on the sack.

On one side of us, a neighbor of ours, whom my father respected and called Uncle Ismail, was busy arranging two pails, both full of honey. When necessary, one of these two neighbors could leave their goods in the care of the other, whom they trusted, and go around the market to get what they needed. In fact, Uncle Ismail and my father were fairly close relatives. On the other side of our display of goods were the bags of Abdullah from Asarlık village, who was selling grape syrup and last year's raisins. Abdullah, Ismail Emmi, and my father often saw each other at the market. Father frequently bought the leftover raisins and grape syrup from Abdullah at wholesale prices and took them home, ready to sell on his next trading excursion.

One of the regular market women, Kirez from Çat, appeared, saying, "Good trading to you, brother Ismail, Rahim. I'm late to the market this morning. I couldn't find an empty space to set out my goods. I'll just squeeze in between you, and squat down here." She put down her small, patched saddlebag on a space as big as a shoe, near our display of goods. Father wasn't about to turn away his mother-in-law, my granny. He immediately pulled our butter pots a little further back and she spread out the goods from her bundle. Uncle Ismail and Abdullah from Asarlık made no objection, but they couldn't hide their sour looks. When they saw she had only a few green onions picked in the early morning from her garden at Mantaki, two or three kilos of early potatoes, and a basket of mulberries picked the day before to sell, they greeted her happily, saying, tongue in cheek, "Kirez cousin, is that all you've brought today?" Competitive sellers in the market all knew the proverb: A white dog does damage to the cotton seller.

The marketplace consisted of small, separate areas where three or four salesmen would spread their goods back-to-back. In the narrow spaces between these areas, the customers would stroll, net bags or bundles in hand, or saddlebags on shoulder, looking at the hucksters incessantly crying their goods, asking the price, and bargaining to obtain what they needed.

The market's first customers were usually office workers who started work at nine o'clock. They wouldn't bargain for long, but take what they bought, hand over the money, and walk away quickly. Avoiding the hot and crowded afternoon, the middle-aged and older women of Bozkır would come to the market before lunchtime to look around and fill their capacious net bags with necessities.

At that day's market, one of our neighbors was a Yörük, two were vegetable sellers from Yolören and Kozağaç, and behind us were grape molasses sellers from Aladağ. My father liked the Yörük market goers. In fact, in summer, they were the most persistent and quick-acting salesmen and customers for their needs. From May to September, our sturdy fellow countrymen from the villages of Antalya, who lived and grazed their animals in their yaylas in the high valleys and on the slopes of the Taurus Mountains, would load their camels with their products of butter, cheese, soft cheese, wool, and sacks, and bring them to the Bozkır market. As both coming and going involved a long eight- to ten-hour trek, they were in a hurry to sell their produce quickly, buy what they needed, and return home. When the market was slow, Father would buy the remaining goods from the Yörüks for a bargain price and sell them in the neighboring villages.

At the market that day, normal butter found customers at three and a half liras a kilo. The butter the Yörüks sold was very fresh. Churned two days before, at the most, it had the smell of fresh buttermilk. That day, their unsalted butter, smelling of saffron from the uplands, went for three liras seventy-five kuruş. A Yörük called Esat, whom Father was friends with, wanting to sell his goods as soon as possible in order to go to the grain market and buy wheat and barley, sold what was left of the butter and soft cheese to my father at a discount of thirty-five kuruş. By adding salt, we could keep the butter for longer and sell it at a later market. One of our villagers had previously ordered some soft cheese for winter from Father, so the cheese was sold to him for a small profit.

The Yörüks, handsome people with sunburnt cheeks and hands, who lived on the high uplands and were our neighbors on the summer pastures, would come to the Bozkır market with small camel caravans. Every Thursday and Friday in the summer months, these small caravans, each consisting of three to five loaded camels led by a donkey, would fill the roads and trails leading to their summer pastures. The camel caravans would move very slowly along the narrow, uphill tracks. Even though the villagers from Çat, Dere, Sorkun, Karacahisar, and Kuruçay, who shared the same paths, complained about crowding the roads and trails, they were happy that the Yörüks bought generously of the area's products.

The grain the Yörüks bought at the market was taken to the water mills established along the Ulu River at Çat, Dere, and Sorkun villages. There, it would be ground during Friday night and Saturday morning, then the Yörüks would load the sacks of flour onto their camels and return home. Fruit and vegetables were the most valuable presents they could take back to their families, who, during their long stay on the high uplands, lacked such things as summer apples, plums, fresh grapes, cucumbers, green beans, and other fruits and vegetables.

Uncle Ismail sold pure honey, mostly from his own traditional hives. He could easily sell a big pail of honey to officials he knew, complete his sales before noon, and return home. If a customer who hadn't bought honey from him before asked, "Is this honey really pure?" he would reply, "Sir, my product is renowned," which the buyers in the market knew was the same as saying, "If you don't like it, bring it back."

We had two big earthen containers of butter to sell at the bazaar that had been acquired by barter from many families in the Uluören Yayla of the village Çalmanda. We bartered various pottery vessels such as water pitchers, storage jars, and yogurt churns in exchange for butter, the amount of which had previously been bargained for piece by piece. Every family in Çalmanda could produce plenty of butter, because they were mainly goat, sheep, and milk cow owners. That Thursday afternoon, my father had picked up the few unsold pots and knocked on doors on the outskirts of the Uluören Yayla, bartering them for butter quite cheaply. In order to keep the butter from melting, we walked the fifty-five kilometers to Bozkır in the coolness of the night, and reached there early Friday morning. On one such trip, the night was very warm. When we got to Bozkır, the butter had become quite soft. The first thing we did when we arrived was buy a bag of snow from the snow sellers, and cool the butter by immersing the vessels in the bag. The wooden spoonful of butter we showed to the buyer would look more attractive and more appetizing if it seemed firm.

The snow sellers used to place their goat-hair sacks full of snow between the sites of the drapers and the pottery sellers. Apart from the snow sold wholesale to the ice cream vendors, the rest would be sold off retail, in amounts costing twenty-five kuruş, fifty kuruş, or one lira, without using any scales; larger pieces would be sold for as much as could be bought. In the heat of summer, the thirsty buyers and sellers in the market would buy a beaker or a jugful of what was known as snow water. Buyers who wished to drink this didn't complain either about drinking from the same vessel as the other customers, or about the goat hairs found in the water in the cup.

In our village Çat, five or six hardworking families were engaged in the snow business. On the hottest days in summer, Cenderme's son Kerim, Manav Emine's son Ali, Niyazi the sesame seed seller, basketmaker Köle, and Hüsnü Karacalar would go up to the highest crevices on the slopes of the Taurus Mountains where snow had collected throughout the winter, cut up the half-frozen snow and put it into sacks, load it onto donkeys, and walk all night down the mountain to reach Bozkır early on Friday morning.

Whenever we needed snow, we got it from our neighbor, Niyazi, who gave it to us at a reasonable price. Niyazi would finish selling his wares by noon, go to the bakery, and come back with a piece of hot, fresh bread. He would beg my father for twenty-five kuruş' worth of butter to spread on his bread, and my father, without saying, "I can't even weigh twenty-five kuruş' worth," would give him half a spoonful.

The bakery was one of the shops surrounding the market. The villagers would congregate in front of it, crowding on top of each other in order to take home a present of the market bread, pide. The women and children, who were afraid of being squashed and trampled on, would wait like strangers at the edge of the crowd. They would wait until a male acquaintance or relative came to help them. Those who were lucky enough to get a pide or two, fresh from the wood-fired oven, would take it, burning their hands, and wrap it in a cloth as they went away.

Like Uncle Niyazi, we, too, had gone hungry from the evening before and ate a hot pide from the market, spread with a spoonful of butter, as both breakfast and lunch. The salted butter melted as soon as it was spread onto the hot bread, some of the larger grains of salt looking like tiny snow crystals frosting the bread. We put a piece of hot bread, maybe a little undercooked, into our mouths, and, steam from the buttery morsel burning our palates, let it slip down into our stomachs without chewing. The salt crystals would be crunched like roasted garbanzo peas. I can still feel the taste of it in my mouth. If Uncle Ismail had not left after finishing his sales, we would mix the scrapings of honey from his pail together with the scrapings of butter from the bottom of our storage jars and gobble the mixture down. When I remember this, I become a child again.

The pottery market, consisting mainly of people from Çat and one or two from Sofran village, was next to the junior high school. In general, vessels used daily, such as ewers, cooking pots, pitchers, and jugs, were sold there. Pitchers sold by the Sofran villagers were preferred for drinking water, as they were made of thicker clay than those of Çat, so they kept the water cooler in the heat of summer. The Çat master potters made sound, durable water vessels and large and small storage pots, using special kinds of clay from their own mountains. Large storage pots were difficult to carry for an inexperienced person, so they were not sold in the market. That kind of pot was tied by ropes to the harnesses of donkeys and mules, and taken to be sold in faraway villages by the itinerant packmen from Çat. These villagers did not use money for buying and selling. The peddlers used a system of bartering, exchanging their goods for the produce of the villages they visited.

The cutlers displayed their goods right next to the potters' stands in the market. There were more than twenty smiths in Çat who provided all the cutting tools, such as the spades, bill hooks, and pruning shears needed for tending and pruning the gardens and vineyards in Bozkır and all the villages. They would make the tools needed to shape the grindstones for the mill keepers, and repair and sharpen their blunted spades and axes. For their raw material, they used steel from tools that were completely worn out and unusable. The heat for the smiths' forges came from the charcoal made and brought by the villagers of Sorkun and Kucca. The handles of the cutting tools were made of the plentiful goat horn available. Knives and saws were made in all shapes and sizes, big and small. Younger smiths would make daggers, not for cutting with, but ordered by some people for self-defense, but these were never sold at the Friday market. Trading these defensive weapons was kept secret by both buyers and sellers.

The shoemakers displayed their goods at the wooden bridge near the pottery sellers. Expert shoemakers from Hocaköy village would supply all the footwear needed in Bozkır and the surrounding villages. Their handiwork included overshoes, moccasins, pumps, half boots, and long boots made from the hide of local animals.

The shoemakers got the leather they needed from the neighboring village of Pabuççu. The men from Pabuççu would periodically travel to all the villages over a wide area to buy and collect salted and dried raw hides, and bring them back home for the elaborate tanning processes resulted in leather suitable for making shoes. When a Pabuççu villager went around to the other villages to buy their dried leather, he bargained in a very aggressive way. If he liked a piece of leather, the Pabuççu buyer would say, "Why, what a worthless piece of leather," and beat it on the ground. The widespread saying, a Pabuççu beats the leather he likes on the ground, came from this. The local saying, a Pabuççu strikes the ground with the leather he likes, is also used when a man criticizes his loved one in front of other people.

According to the peddlers and other travelers to Pabuççu village, all the houses there smelled heavily of yeast and newly tanned leather. One of the well-known stories about Pabuççu in the Bozkır area was this:

A bride who was new to her husband's house, after living there a month, said to her mother-in-law, "Mother, when I first came to this house as a bride, it smelled very badly of leather. Since I came, I have washed and wiped everywhere and kept it very clean, so now it doesn't smell of leather anymore."

With a twinkling smile, her experienced mother-in-law said, "Yes, my dear, when I was a bride, at first, I did the same."

A small rock hill rose up sharply in the center of Bozkır. Stones cut from the left side of this monolithic rock that rose up sharply in the middle of the marketplace were shaped for use in construction work. The area cleared then helped to extend the market area. Every year, this area, used for the grain market, grew a little bigger. The villagers who earned a living selling their dried grains would bargain fiercely when selling the wheat, barley, garbanzo peas, lentils, flax seed, and black peas from their rows of sacks. On Fridays in the autumn months, in addition to grain, sellers would produce broken wheat, for use in a pudding called aşure, or keşkeklik or tarhana, other forms of cracked wheat.

Each side of the market was bounded by small shops selling all types of things: drapers, grocers, two bakers, a halva sandwich vendor, two butchers, a doctor's office and a pharmacy, three tailors, two coppersmiths, one tinsmith, an expert saddler, four farriers, and a watchmaker who also sold newspapers and magazines. The store of Şakir the watchmaker had a special attraction for me; every Friday during the summer holidays, I could find there an out-of-date newspaper or magazine to satisfy the longing I felt for something new to read on the comings and goings to the distant villages.

In one corner of the market, turning their backs on this rock hill in the center, were the governor's office and the jail attached to it. On Fridays, the villagers who had walked perhaps five, six, or even seven hours with their laden pack animals not only did their shopping, but also tried to take care of any official business they had to do. The thick wooden jailhouse door had a small hole or opening in the middle through which a head could be poked. Perhaps this was why the jail was referred to as the hole by the Bozkır villagers.

All day long, elderly fathers, mothers, and especially wives who had husbands in the hole would sit and wait in the shade of the governor's office. When their turn came, each of them would come face-to-face with the prisoner at this narrow opening and share news of family troubles and disputes. They provided these close relatives with gifts, clothing, and the other necessities they had bought at the market. I was too afraid of the gendarme standing, gun on shoulder, in front of the prison to dare go up to the hole and look through it, much as I would have liked to.

Women coming to the Friday Farmers' Market in Bozkır visiting their relatives in prison in the 1950s

The cattle market was on the wide plain on the Kozağaç side of the Ulu River, which cut through the middle of Bozkır. All animals were bought and sold there. Some villagers would sell one or two sheep or goats, or a cow with a calf, for something they needed badly. Donkeys were the easiest to sell, and the most convenient to use of all the pack animals sold at the market. Most of these belonged to a skillful salesman from the village of Aslantaş, whom we called the Trickster. Those who earned a living by trading animals were usually called this. They were such persuasive talkers and good animal handlers, and so skillful at cheating, that people were always wary of trading with them. In fact, a trickster was expert at passing off a lazy donkey as one that was quick and full of life. Jumping onto a bareback donkey with an encouraging click of the tongue, the trickster would prick it with a three-nailed goad so dexterously that, without heeding the weight on its back, the animal would rush off at speed among the other animals and convince the naive buyer that it would be a lively pack animal. A salesman like this, who had all the tricks up his sleeve, could sell the laziest donkey he had to a customer desperate for a pack animal.

A person who had once been burned by the trickster's tricks would get a friend or relative to go with him when he wanted to buy a donkey. Thinking that it would not be so easy for the trickster to pull the wool over their eyes if they were together, they would try not to be cheated. It was an odd thing that being an expert salesman seemed to be part of one's genes. In America, one is advised never to go alone to buy an automobile from a dealership. In fact, even if you know what model it is you want to buy, those tricky salesmen can induce you to admire and buy a model you'd never even thought of, which had been left in his hands.

Although mules and horses, valued as pack animals or for riding, were sold at the cattle market, it was seldom that animals such as a bull for breeding or a pair of oxen were sold there. Those who needed one of these would go to villages to find a person wishing to sell or who had been recommended to them, or order one specially from a trickster.

There were animals at the market that were not for sale. In general, a villager who came to market with his loaded donkey or horse would tie the animal up in a safe place in the garden or stable of a Bozkır dweller for a charge of ten kuruş. Some market vendors, however, either because the animal was valuable, or because they did not want to spend the ten kuruş, would bring a child with them. The boy, or sometimes girl, would take the halter of the animal, freed of its load, and lead it to the cattle market, where the child would wait until the father came, often late in the afternoon. Even if hungry and thirsty or in need of a toilet, that child never let go of the halter of the animal entrusted to him or her. The child would sit in a dry spot among the animal dung, and wait. Some of the buyers might ask, "Child, is that donkey for sale?" to which the child would reply, "Uncle, my father will be here soon. Ask him when he comes." In the summer months, the Friday market would be very hot. In order to subdue their hunger and thirst and conquer the feeling of being forgotten, these children would drift off into the world of dreams.

Decay and Dissolution

1
A Delayed Time Bomb

One disastrous effect of the First World War, followed closely by the War of Independence, was a significant decrease in the number of men in the villages of Anatolia. When I was at primary school, for example, the grandmothers of most of my friends were widowed. They were the older women whose husbands had become war victims on one battlefront or another.

The members of the new civil service set up under the newly proclaimed Republic came from among those officers who had managed to survive the war. These war veterans, now the new administrative officials, knew that the independence of the nation depended on an increase in the population. Naturally, they banned any form of education regarding birth control or family planning, and the sale or practice of any tool or method for carrying this out. In fact, in order to increase the population quickly, they encouraged the birth of children, and found ways to promote this among young couples in an attractive way. One of these was to give a slight increase in a civil servant's salary for each newborn child. But the most effective way was to allow conscripted young soldiers to go home to see their families on compassionate leave. Many of the eighteen-to-twenty-year-old village youths who got married before they entered the army were very happy to get leave during their training period, and also made use of this to increase the population. It was quite usual for a married soldier who had spent his month's leave in the village to find he had a new child when he returned home after being discharged.

To combat the great number of child deaths caused by infectious diseases, the government instituted a program of immunization against such diseases, the success of which also caused a population rise. The two-to-three-children families known by our grandfathers turned into seven or more in our fathers' time. Families with nine or even ten children could be seen. The number of primary-school-age children in our village of Çat in the 1950s was between two and three hundred. Previously, in our grandmothers' time, before the use of inoculation or vaccination against infectious diseases had begun, even though eight to ten children might be born, only two or three of those would survive childhood. Our mothers, however, might have eight or ten living children, and it became hard to look after them all. Our grandmothers, wishing their children to survive, had given them names such as Dursun, Durali, Durmuş, Durdu, Duriye, Allah Verdi, and Yaşar, meaning, "survived," "stay with us," "gift of God," and "live long." Our mothers, however, being tired of giving birth and taking care of children, began to give their sixth or seventh children names such as Fazıl, Fazlı, Yeter, or Söngül, meaning "enough," "extra," "no more," and "last rose." It was quite common for many of the fathers, who had to suffer the burden of providing for their big household, to curse and swear, "F——those who are fertile, and those who plant the seeds."

2
Firearms: Fortune's Foe

My junior and senior high school years were spent away from the village in a far-off boarding school. When I returned to the village for the summer holidays, I would spend three months working as my father's helper. We used to go peddling, loading our pack animals with the different kinds of pots produced in our village, and taking these to barter for the most plentiful produce of the distant villages we went to. We would spend Friday and Saturday in the village, as well as one or two days during the week if we were not off on a peddling trip. On such days, in order to listen to the news on the radio, I would go in the evenings to the coffeehouse. Considering me an adult and a young man of the village who had gained knowledge and understanding, the villagers there would pay me compliments, such as "Come now, Hoca ("teacher"), tell us something we know nothing of so our brains don't rust away."

The young men who went to hoe cotton would return to the village with a great number of handguns, which they enjoyed showing off to each other by firing them into the air at night on the roofs of their houses. It was also the custom in later years for the bridegroom and the younger relatives to fire a number of shots into the air at village weddings. I had always worried about the shots they fired, wondering, Do the bullets fired straight up in the air go on rising forever, or do they sooner or later melt and disappear?

When the villagers at the coffeehouse asked me to give them some information, these shots fired into the air immediately came to mind. By chance, that year in our physics class, we had studied the way an object is thrown into the air at a certain speed: Under the influence of gravity, the speed of the object shot into the sky soon drops to zero, and it falls to the ground. What is interesting is that the speed with which it falls to the ground is the same as that with which it was thrown into the air from the ground. In the same way, a bullet fired into the air fell to earth again after reaching a certain height, and the speed at which it fell to the ground was the same as that at which it was fired from the gun.

I explained this with great enthusiasm to the villagers, who then objected, saying, "How is this possible, Hoca? In this village, thousands of bullets have been fired into the air and no one has seen a single one of them return. Who knows how many heads would have been rained on by these bullets by this time."

"It's only by great good fortune that an accident like this hasn't happened," I added. "A bullet, fired directly into the air as straight as a poplar tree stands tall, will fall just a little away from where it is fired."

They again objected. "Hoca, that's not right. If it were, by now, a bullet fired in this village would have fallen on at least one person's or one animal's head."

While I was wondering how I could explain it so they would believe that what I said was true, Gunner Abdullah, a veteran of the War for Independence, helped me out. "Neighbors, our young Hoca Hasan's words remind me of something that happened during the War for Independence. One morning, during the Battle of Sakarya, we were preparing to join the battle on the front line. Our officers told us that the enemy front was just behind the mountain ahead of us. We were ordered to capture the top of the mountain and drive the enemy from their position. We moved forward, climbing the hill at great speed. Suddenly, bullets started to rain down on our backs and heads. It was as if they were being fired from behind us. Right and left of me, my comrades were being hit in the back. It turned out that the enemy commander was a cunning brute. With the help of field glasses, he had seen our soldiers climbing to the top of the mountain early that morning. He had ordered the enemy soldiers not to fire straight up in the air, but at an angle. The shots so fired came over the top, turned in the air, and were raining down on us. Our officers realized what was happening but, while we were trying to find shelter for ourselves, a great number of the soldiers were killed. One hundred and seventy of us went into battle that morning. The number counted at roll call that night was only seventeen."

Neither the explanation I gave based on a scientific knowledge of physics, nor Gunner Abdullah's reminiscences changed the villagers' custom of firing shots into the air.

The population of the village Çat in the 1950s was around three thousand, and this custom of celebratory gunshots into the air lasted until about a decade later. By extraordinary good luck, no one suffered from this way of celebration, which had started with the coming of the cotton-hoeing era. The words spoken by scholar Hasan in the coffeehouse had long been forgotten. But finally, what was to happen, happened: a bullet fired into the air at a wedding celebration fell and hit a man called Kara Mustafa, and became lodged in his head. The man didn't die. He was blinded in one eye, but he survived. No inquiry was held to find out whose gun the shot had come from. It was many years later that our people learned by seeing detective films on television that marks inside the barrel of each gun would identify every bullet fired from it, in the same way a fingerprint identifies their owner.

3
A Son Fires at His Father

No one gave a thought to the fact that the number of guns in Çat village meant that sooner or later, a family catastrophe would occur, or that an unexpected murder would inevitably happen from someone's lack of care. To own a gun was thought by the younger men, in particular, to signify manhood and bravery. Although guns were kept away from the women and children, it wasn't in the young men's interest to listen to the saying "A weapon does the most damage to its owner."

One of the villagers, known as Scrubby Hüseyin, was a veteran who had survived the First World War and the War for Independence. He loved to reminisce about his memories in front of an audience at the coffeehouse. He spoke of war as a fearful and very stressful occurrence, and his eyes would fill with tears when he remembered his comrades who had died in battle. "It's a great sin to declare war and destroy the youth of a country, unless the fatherland is being invaded," he declared. The listeners would hear him in silence and try to imagine the scene in their minds.

Before Turkey had been proclaimed a republic, Veteran Hüseyin had married two different women, but, like several others, was not affected by the new laws. These marriages had been given special immunity from any charge under the new laws, and the men were recognized as having two wives. Before the new laws were announced, if a man was married to a woman who could not have children, it was considered normal for him to take a second wife, and this, being in accordance with Sharia rules, was quite a common occurrence in the villages.

Like most of the men in the village, Veteran Hüseyin was quite short-tempered, and at home, took out the stress and strain of the day by beating his wives and children. Hüseyin, who had no children by his first wife, had one son from his second, a youth of eighteen called Dursun. Dursun was one of the youths who spent their earnings from working in the cotton fields on clothes to show off.

Returning home from the coffeehouse one evening, he saw his father beating his mother with a stick. When Dursun tried to intervene and separate the two, the father started beating his son. Dursun, in his rage, did not remember the saying "A son should never lift his hand against his father." He immediately pulled out the gun at his waist and shot his father five times in the stomach. Then, when the man fainted, he took him in his arms, tied him onto the donkey in the stable, and went directly to Bozkır. There, he hired a jeep and drove to the hospital in Konya. An emergency operation to patch up his intestines by removing suitable parts from seventeen different places saved his father's life.

At the trial, Veteran Hüseyin pleaded, "Judge, sir, it was all my fault. I forced my son to do it. Judge, sir, I'm an old veteran soldier. My son is very dear to me. Forgive him and give him back to me. If I fall down tomorrow, I will need his support."

The judge put an end to the trial by saying, "I sentence this young man to six months imprisonment. Let him cool his heels there for a while and come to his senses."

After serving this very short prison sentence, Dursun went back to live with his father again.

4
Blood Feud

This story is about a blood feud that had no beginning and no end, but brought death to three young men.

Two of the people concerned in this event were cousins who grew up in the same neighborhood of the village. They were born at the same time to a brother and a sister who hated each other. They lived to grow up, but their stars never shone on them. Feelings of rivalry and jealousy, most probably stirred up by their families, turned to an animosity that benefited no one. This animosity, according to the young men of the village, did not come to a successful end, despite the intelligence and education of the two young men.

One of these cousins, Medali, had graduated from the village institute in Ereğli and became a teacher in a village in the province of Çumra. When the schools went on holiday, Medali, like the other teachers, spent part of it back home in our village with his father and mother.

The other cousin, Birahmet, didn't have the opportunity to continue his education after primary school, as he was fatherless. He became a successful soldier during his time of national service, and came back to his village with the rank of sergeant. After passing an exam, he became a watch guard responsible for the safety of the canal carrying water from Beyşehir Lake to the Plain of Konya. Birahmet's uniform for his new job was, of course, as showy as that of any police or army officer. He was also given a splendid horse to ride around on his frequent visits to check the flow of water in the canal and open or close the sluices accordingly. A necessity of his job was the Mauser rifle he proudly carried on his shoulder. As the stretch of the canal under his supervision was between Bozkır and Seydişehir, from time to time, he would come to our village to visit his mother and sister. His entry was eye-catching as he rode into the village on his horse, with his rifle on his shoulder and looking quite as smart as any officer in his official uniform. There is no doubt that the youths who saw this state official, who grew up in our village, were filled with envious admiration.

But real animosity could be seen in the eyes of his uncle's son, Medali, his enemy from childhood. A young man in the flower of youth, now a village schoolteacher, Medali dressed neatly and soberly. His five years of education at a village institute had taught him modesty. Whether this modesty was real or whether this young teacher was like a coiled snake twined among the roots of a bramble bush, no one knew.

During the previous few years, the paths of Medali and his childhood enemy, Birahmet, had not crossed. One had been busy getting an education, and the other was doing his military service. The two had then been separated by their new duties, so there had been no opportunity for either to show his enmity toward the other.

Medali's father and mother were both alive. Moreover, they were among the well-off families of the village. Certainly, Medali drew great courage from his father, Hamzaoğlu, who could freeze the air around him, and his three paternal uncles, who were always ready to bite.

Birahmet's mother was alive, but otherwise, he had only one sister. His mother was known to be the village's best maker of pekmez, grape syrup. They were a fatherless family without the power to say "Hsst" to a dog.

One day, by chance, these two cousins met on the road coming from the town. They passed without greeting, and, seemingly, without seeing each other, though each took a sideways glance at the other as he went by. With his splendid uniform, Birahmet looked by far the superior.

Medali could not stomach the way his cousin rode into the village in his eye-catching uniform, or his pompous attitude toward the villagers.

One evening, after treating his resentment with a "medicinal dose" of rakı, a strong, vodka-like spirit made of grapes and aniseed, Medali arrived in front of Birahmet's mother's house at midnight. He let fly a volley of bullets at the door and windows, and gave voice to a loud war cry, "Come out! You fucking lily-livered coward. You won't escape from me by hiding under your quilt like a woman!"

Aroused by the shots and the shouting, the neighbors, too frightened to come out, began to observe what was going on from behind a crack in the curtain or the door. Birahmet was also awakened. He loaded his rifle with bullets in case he needed them. Creeping slowly to the window, when his eyes had become accustomed to the darkness and he could see Medali like a dark shadow, he took aim, pulled the trigger, and hit his enemy right in the middle of his forehead. Before Medali could say, "Oh Mommy, I'm dying," he fell, sprawled out across the street.

At the first trial in court, the judge set Birahmet free, quoting the precedents of forced entry and self-defense. Birahmet returned to his salaried job as though nothing had happened.

As it was not established from the evidence produced at this trial whether Medali had been killed by a bullet that entered his head from the front or by one fired from behind, the high court quashed the first trial and ordered a new one. Medali's head had to be exhumed and sent to Ankara for a qualified doctor's diagnosis. As the body had been deep in the ground for at least three months, it was beginning to rot. The smell was overpowering. As the two gendarmes detailed to cut off the head and take it to Ankara could not stand the smell, the head was put in a bag and tied on top of the jeep. Even then, the smell was noticeable. During the night journey between Bozkır and Konya, the gendarme driving noticed that the smell had gone.

Apprehensively, the driver stopped the jeep, took a look at the roof, and realized that the bag was not there. Knowing that to lose a vital piece of evidence in a murder case was cause enough for a prison sentence, the unhappy gendarmes, a master sergeant and sergeant, retraced their steps. The driver shone the powerful headlights of the jeep on the road as he proceeded slowly along, while the other used the light of his flashlight as he searched frantically for the parcel. As it was a round parcel and the road sloped downward, it might have bounced and rolled away, unseen, into the grass. However, it was the object itself that was of the greatest help in their search. The terrible smell that filled the air and turned their stomachs came to their aid. After searching for an hour, they found the bag and carried it the rest of the way, safe inside the jeep.

The doctors verified the first verdict by looking at it and making a thorough examination. Birahmet was once more acquitted, and returned to his job.

The Hamzaoğlu family burned for revenge, and were so full of rage that they were willing to sacrifice Murtaza, the youngest son, still a boy, to achieve this. Although Birahmet had not suffered in prison for Medali's death, he did not feel his life was happy or without care. He could not forget the saying "Water may sleep but an enemy never does. He was vigilant at all times, his infrequent comings and goings to the village to see his mother all taking place under cover of darkness.

Three years passed, and Murtaza grew and his body filled out. Gun in hand, he began to lie in ambush at night on the road to the village under a big rock at a place called Karakuz. He had often heard his elders say, "One of these days, Birahmet will surely come to visit his mother." After a long wait, one night, his brother's murderer was about to approach the village.

People had seen and recognized Birahmet shopping at Bozkır's Friday market, not in uniform, but wearing civilian clothes. One of them set off to tell the Hamzaoğlu family, almost running to the village to give them this news. Without delay, an ambush was set up before dark and they said, "Tonight is the night for hunting."

Birahmet waited until it was totally dark to approach the village. The road through the valley was in complete silence, apart from the sound of the waterfalls, big and small, that cascaded into the Ulu River. When he got to the Karagaç Bridge, he dismounted and walked, leading his horse. He crossed the bridge and began to climb up the hill toward the neighborhood where his mother's house was. Although the horse was walking slowly, the sound of horseshoes aroused Murtaza, who was nodding off.

It took only a second for him to decide who was coming. Not stopping to wonder who else might be coming to Karagaç at this time of night, he raised his rifle as if to aim, and waited for his target to come nearer. He could hear the sound of hooves and, despite the darkness, he could make out a tall man walking in front of the horse. This was the minute he had waited many days and nights for. Adjusting his aim once more, he pulled the trigger.

Breaking the silence of the night, the terrible noise could be heard in every corner of the village as it echoed in the mountains around the valleys. Some lads, still sitting in the front of a coffeehouse, made a joke about the noise, like, "Someone probably has shot his brother-in-law," but it could not dispel the uncomfortable feeling there. The sound of gunfire meant one of the two things: either it was a young man announcing his marriage to the world, or it was another life lost, another hearth extinguished.

Before morning came, the dreadful news had reached the farthest corner of the village.

The next day, without waiting for the gendarmes to come and arrest him, young Murtaza went to Bozkır to give himself up to the Karakol, the gendarmerie post. He believed he had protected the honor of his family. Both his father and mother had told him repeatedly, "Son, don't be afraid. You have protected our family's honor. We'll sell whatever we have, all our possessions, to pay for a lawyer to defend you."

Murtaza arrived at the gendarmerie Post. When the officer there asked him what he wanted, Murtaza said, "I shot my enemy and protected the honor of my family."

This saying was familiar to the first lieutenant who was in charge of keeping public order in the area. "Is that so, young man? I've heard these words a lot from the bums out in the east, and I've dealt with them as necessary. I never expected to see one of them in front of me here." The officer then called his assistant and said, "Book this dog and lock him up. I'll inform the district attorney."

Murtaza rotted away in prison for many long years.

5
Decay and Dissolution

Not many years had passed before Father and I began to see rapid changes in the life of the distant villages that we had gone to for many years as peddlers. In the 1960s, the changes in these villages seemed like a cauldron of milk placed on top of a raging fire. The milk simmered, bubbled, and boiled over, then simmered, bubbled, and boiled over again.

Farmers who had had difficulty making ends meet from the proceeds of small gardens, fields, or vineyards died. Their children, who ranged from five to ten in number, began to split the family land up into small strips so each would get a share. The shares were not sufficient enough to make a living for any of the siblings. Where a living was earned from keeping livestock, the family's herd of fifty to sixty goats and sheep, and maybe two or three milk cows, were divided among the children, which was insufficient for any one of them to make a living.

The literacy campaign that had started in the 1950s sped up and reached a peak in the 1960s. Among the generous promises made by politicians seeking votes was a promise that there would be a junior high school, a senior high school, and a religious senior high school in every township. The dreams of every father and mother who endured the trials and difficulties of making ends meet was to educate at least one of their sons to become a civil servant, to have a more comfortable life than they had themselves. Fathers and mothers whose lives had been full of struggles, always trying to come up with ingenious solutions to make ends meet, however small, were hoping one of their children might be harnessed for life to a salaried job with a regular income. Naturally, being educated or in the process of getting an education was the cause for the young men to be jealous or bear ill will toward each other. The upcoming generation of each village began to form three basic groups: those who made a living involved with religion, having been educated in Koran courses and the religious Imam Hatip high schools; those who were graduates of art schools or teacher-training colleges or had a salaried government job such as under-officers in the military or the police; and finally, those who were seasonal migrant laborers in places like Istanbul, Izmir, Aydın, and Konya.

The military administration, which came in with a coup in 1960, relaxed the ban on free speech, publications, and the press in general. With this unlimited "freedom," at the time of the new elections, the old or newly formed political parties took up a stance based on three main platforms. These were: a platform based on religion, religious beliefs, the mosques, and similar concepts; a platform based on social justice, workers' rights, and land reform; and a platform based on ultranationalism and repeated retellings of famous historical incidents under slogans like "Fatherland," "Flag," and "Sakarya."

Before long, especially during preelection days, politicians worked on their separatist aims by using insulting and demeaning epithets for those who were not of their party. These were: ultraconservative or fanatic, leftist or communist, and racist or fascist.

In every village, the politicians spread butter on the bread of those whose leanings were in sympathy with theirs. In order to attract votes, the promises of every political party gave their supporters the hope of obtaining concessions. In their speeches and declarations, the politicians fanned the ambitions of a large number of young people who dreamed of a door opening on a salaried job in the government or in a state-owned factory or business, without the need to sweat or put in any effort. The young people who listened to the politicians became estranged from each other, even if they came from the same family. As a result, the former custom of inviting all the villagers to a wedding was no longer observed. Political differences began to influence the young when marrying and establishing a family.

The supporters of these politicians, in particular the young, began to use three separate words they had created to bad-mouth and demean each other: fanatic for the religious-minded, fascist for the extremely nationalistic, and communist for those who were left-wing socialists. Each of the groups behaved like enemies toward the others, and this situation was reflected in the village coffeehouses and meeting places. The division among the young reached such a height that the unity of many families began to fracture as their members joined different groups. The politicians encouraged this division in such a cunning way that disagreements among individuals or groups of people quickly turned into bitter enmity. Being neighbors, old friends, relatives, or even siblings was not enough for people to live together harmoniously.

In the Demiray family, for example, three brothers were badmouthing each other with these insulting words: fanatic, communist, and fascist. Their father and mother were devastated by this unhappy situation. The older brother, Halim, who had worked all his life as an agricultural worker on the plains of Söke, was a supporter of land reform; he was regarded as a socialist and was considered a member of the communist group. His brother, Ahmet, who had completed his religious education by taking a Koran course, then becoming an imam and believing that religion and moral teaching could solve every problem, was of the fanatic group. Another brother, Kenan, who admired the former army officers who had taken up politics and went on repeating slogans like "Fatherland," "Flag," and "Sakarya," had become a member of the fascist group. These brothers did not speak to each other. They would visit their father's house at different times. This situation made their father, Ibram, and their mother, Raziye, as well as their younger sisters, very unhappy. How could they agree with any of these beloved but incompatible young men, while trying to survive, without becoming involved in the damnable politics? The unlucky parents knew the well-known expression for this sort of situation: if I spit downward, there's a beard; if I spit upward, a mustache. The only solution seemed to be to let them live their own lives.

When another brother, Abdullah, who had lived for long years away from home, came to visit during Bayram with his wife and children, he could not believe what he heard and saw. The coffeehouses, the places where people gathered together, were now run as if they served three different types of people. At the entrance to the village, the wall of the historical bridge over the Ulu River was covered with ugly expressions containing the words "communist," "fascist," and "fanatic."

Visiting his village and his family after many years away, Abdullah was astonished at what he saw. He had had no idea of the division caused there by the bitterness between the villagers. It was difficult to understand how the three brothers could have turned into such enemies. Abdullah loved all three of them, but he realized that he could not meet with them all together in a friendly way.

On the first day of Bayram, relatives who were not much interested in politics came to visit Abdullah and his wife and children. "Communist" Halim's wife, Amine, along with her two children, came to visit too. However, before entering the house, Kenan's wife, Sadiye, told her that the atmosphere in the house was very intense, and asked Amine to come and visit the next day. So Amine and her kids turned away, unhappy. Late that night, when Halim came back from the coffeehouse, his wife, Amine, complained to him: "I took the children and went to your father's house to pay our Bayram respects, but I didn't go in. That is to say, I was kind of driven away. The wife of his fascist brother Kenan said, 'Everyone's in a bad mood. If you come in there'll be a fight,' so we turned away from the door and came home."

Halim swore and cursed everyone for their religion and beliefs, including his parents, sitting and drinking a bottle of rakı, which gave him courage. At about two o'clock in the morning, Halim took his gun and started toward his father's house. Waking up, his anxious wife tried to hold him back, but was unsuccessful. She tried to wake up one or two of the neighbors, shouting, "There'll be murder! Come and help me!" But Halim had already reached his father's house and was on the balcony, shouting at those inside.

This is how Abdullah told the next part of this story: I was fast asleep when a loud voice woke me up. I couldn't decide whether I was still dreaming when I heard someone shouting repeatedly: "Come out, all you fucking fascists and fanatics! Open this door!"

Then I heard my mother's voice: "Your father isn't here, Halim. He's in the house above."

I was in a nearby room, with my wife and children sleeping side by side on the floor next to me. I didn't make a sound. The threats and curses uttered by the voice coming from the outside door continued.

Then I heard my sister, Esma, sleeping in the same room with my mother, pleading: "Would you force your way into the house at night, big brother Halim? Don't do it, please! Don't shame us in front of everyone. Go home and we'll talk about it tomorrow."

Halim answered, "This trouble all began with you, you unbelieving I don't know what!" and fired a shot from his gun.

My mother and Esma kept quiet. If the small children and their mother in the next room were awake, they didn't utter a sound. Afraid, we all took refuge in silence.

Before long, my father came out of the house above where he had been sleeping. He persuaded Halim to go back home with his wife. When morning came, we saw that the bullet Halim had fired had gone straight through the door and lodged itself into the wall opposite. Halim had escaped lightly, without causing a disastrous family tragedy on the day of Bayram. We decided to keep the incident a secret within the family and tell no one. I cut our Bayram holiday short and took my family back to Konya by the first available vehicle.

Seven years passed before Abdullah and his family visited the village again. What didn't happen in those seven years?

Agricultural machinery increased. The young men were no longer needed in the cotton fields of the Aegean area, so, having lost their source of income as laborers, they left in great numbers to go to the big cities, especially Istanbul. They lived in ramshackle neighborhoods near the industrial areas of the cities they went to, five or six of them living in the same room, to save money. These exiles desperately missed their mothers, their fathers, their villages, and their children, if they had any. They returned once or twice a year to their village, if only for a few days. Living far away from the animosity they had experienced in the village, they began to make a new life away from home. Gradually, they grew accustomed to living where they were, and cut their connections with the village.

In their own words, they had "cold feet" for the work in the village, such as cutting hay or tending to the fields or gardens, which brought little or no income. As their financial situation in the city improved, little by little, they began to bring their wives and children to live with them. First, the newcomers from the villages would make do with a rented tenement for a few years, and all the members of the family took up jobs, without caring whether they were good or bad, in order to save enough money to prosper as a family. Later, they began to buy boxlike apartments to live in.

For the children who started school in a big city, especially those born there, the village was not a place to live in permanently. Living in the city, they enjoyed the time spent in the village during school holidays, or the few days they stayed there at Bayram time, visiting the relatives left behind there.

6
Tended, a Garden—Neglected, a Stony Wilderness

Every man who grew up accustomed to life in a village, whether living all year round there or spending six months of the year away from it working to support a family, certainly wished to spend his last years there. Previously, similar to the story about a nightingale bird that lived in a golden cage wishing to fly off to the thorny bushes, those who held jobs away from home would finally return to the homes left to them by their forefathers, and enjoy spending their old age with the young people and children of the family. All of this changed. Increasing numbers of grandchildren and great-grandchildren began to leave the village for distant places and different cities. The young no longer felt any warmth for their home villages. Instead of living in the villages with their enemies, those who did not wish to be involved in political differences that quickly turned to quarrels chose to go and settle in Istanbul or other big cities. They lived and worked there under very poor conditions at first, but gradually, their lives improved, and they settled and put down roots.

In this situation, their parents were left in the village to grow old without hope of support. Many of them, who had neither son nor daughter in the village to look after them in their old age, were unable to look after their gardens properly. They couldn't prune or dig the earth around the vines. Whereas before, no one would tolerate the overstepping of their boundaries by as little as a centimeter, those still living in the village no longer cared for the land they had formerly cultivated, and it became neglected and worthless. Even the four or five families still living in the village began to buy what was needed, rather than produce anything to sell or use themselves. After a short period of neglect, those same gardens, fields, and vineyards, possessions that had earlier been fought over among the siblings, became like a wilderness or wild woodland. The waterside gardens and fields were soon covered with quick-growing wild thorny bushes, becoming fit only for wild boars to give birth and multiply. The land of Anatolia, which had been cultivated for thousands of years, fell into disuse.

The flat roofs of the houses needed constant attention. When it rained in the fall, they had to be rolled over, and when the winter snow fell, they had to be cleared and made waterproof. Neglected, the flat roofs covered with earth, and the walls, made of stones and adobe, began to fall into ruin.

When the young abandoned their villages, no one was left to carry on the traditional crafts of making clay pots, forging iron, or milling grain, and as a consequence, there were no products to take to barter in distant places and no one left to peddle these. Motor vehicles increased.

Travel became easier. People sold pack animals that had been used for peddling. Those who didn't sell them set them loose in the mountains, saying, "Let them at least be food for the wolves and the birds." The use of plastic for water jugs and storage vessels increased. For Çat village potterymakers, the market for clay pots decreased to almost nothing. Many potters gave up. The smiths also had to give up their work, as it was cheaper to buy imported knives and cutting tools. As the products of the village craftsmen decreased, the number of peddlers soon dwindled away to nothing.

There were no longer any pack animals. It soon became impossible for the old people left in the village to keep domestic animals like hens, cows, sheep, and goats for eggs and milk. Words connected with the care and nurture of animals and poultry fell into disuse. A multitude of the special words connected with the tools used in field, garden, or vineyard that had been used for thousands of years disappeared from the Turkish language. For the children born in cities, their grandparents' lives seemed like a legendary tale which they only half comprehended.

Today, the animals that produce meat and milk and the poultry that lay eggs are kept shut up in closed buildings and fed on prepared branded products that contain antibiotics and hormones to stimulate growth. Such processed products are sold to the public as nutritious food.

People do still live in the villages, even if only a few. Many of the children who migrated to the big cities and produced families of their own returned to the flat-roofed houses, covered now by corrugated sheets of metal, to visit their relatives still living there, and spend one or two weeks in the village during the summer months.

The lives of those who migrated to the big towns cannot be called ideal. The young girls in particular, who, in the villages would have been involved in every kind of activity, live enclosed lives in a restricted space, first in ramshackle shacks, and then later in a concrete building divided into a number of small apartments. Quite apart from the lack of fresh air and greenery, sometimes they do not even see the sun. These apartments, jostling side by side or joining one to the other, are like a concrete jungle. My youngest sister, who lives in Istanbul, once said mournfully, "Another spring came and went, and I never heard a bird sing or saw a flower open." At an early age, she already looked like an old woman. This woman had spent her childhood in the village of Çat among the mountains and valleys where the fruit trees blossomed with a thousand colors, and, together with wild almonds, roses, and buckthorn, provided fruit and seeds for the birds to feed on; corncockles, cornel cherries, may, and barberry, together with native trees growing wild, adorned the surrounding area.

As for me, Hasan Ali Çelik, I left the village at the age of twelve for the purpose of education. Starting with the then-valued İvriz Village Institution, I was able to get higher levels of education, which enabled me to work as a professor of mathematics, and live in America. Over the years, I experienced many sad moments, every time I visited and observed the desolation of the village of my birth.

Finally, in 2015, the administration then in power removed the word *köy* (village) from the Turkish language. Every village from then on was to be recognized as a district belonging to the nearest city, and by which it was administered. Many sayings and many phrases, in which the word *villager* appeared, often used with epithets, such as brave, noble, modest, hardworking, simple, traditional, or salt of the earth, are now meaningless.

Elegy for a Lost Culture

Was there one time a village
far away in the distance?
That isn't our village.
Whether we go there or not,
it can't be our village.
No children play joyfully
in the streets or on roofs;
no brides or young girls
wearing bright, shining dresses
dance and play on the roofs.
No hens cluck around,
poking beaks in the trash;
no cows, sheep, or goats come
home from their grazing,
with mooing and baaing
in search of their young ones
before evening falls.
No street dogs there, searching
for something to eat.
The gypsies, the Abdals,
no longer come begging,
crying out at each house,
"I'll tell you your fortune,
my master, my sister, my rose."
The donkeys so burdened

*are not to be seen there,
nor the men of the plains
lining up at the mill.
Puttees to the knees
in the midst of the winter,
the Yörüks and Dongruls,
their camels all loaded
with rolling pins, firewood,
great crocks and small basins,
come peddling no more.
The mountains still breathe out
sweet fragrance of thyme,
but the cheep of the partridge
is silent, unheard.
On its thorn bush, the magpie
no longer brings news
from loved ones afar.
No one now is collecting
the harvest or produce.
Houses emptied of foodstuff,
of sacks filled with hay,
have no use for the baskets
of grapes to make syrup,
or the clay jars to fill with
flour, cracked wheat, and grain . . .
Rich red clay from Yuvalca
feels no smoothing hands.
Nor are branches collected
from woodlands for kindling,
to light up the kiln
where the potters fire pots.
No longer are jugs, jars,
bowls, basins, and crockpots
produced in the villages.
Gone are their crafts.
No more to be seen.
Faithful pack animals,*

horse, donkey, or mule,
which trotted to market
with saddlebags full,
and brides even rode
on the way to their wedding.
The grandmas have no one,
no homecoming laborer,
to greet with sweet words,
"Welcome, my dear child."
Grandfathers no longer
tell stories of battle,
who fought at Çannakale,
Yemen, Sakarya, and Gallipoli,
no tales of "At Afyon,
we beat up the enemy."
There once was a village,
a long way away now,
but no longer a village.
A municipal district
we no longer belong to,
far off in the distance,
is what it's become.
And we are in exile,
here, there, or wherever . . .

ACKNOWLEDGMENTS

I count myself fortunate in that, as a child, I was able to observe with great curiosity the changes that began to appear in the village way of life, which had continued unbroken for hundreds of years. While the people were able to continue the traditions and customs handed down to us from our forefathers, I belong to the generation that witnessed innovations being implemented little by little, and tried to adapt to them.

I never saw the responsibilities placed on children like me at an early age by our families as a crushing burden. On the contrary, the arduous duties that we were given, greater than our years allowed, were the steps we had to take toward maturity. Our fathers, mothers, and relatives devoted themselves to helping us grow and develop, protecting us while, at the same time, guiding us toward tasks we could only just manage. When I was six years old, I carried my brother's clothes around the house of the one who had wished ill upon him. At eight years old, when my mother injured her knee, I undertook the task of providing food and warmth for her and my three younger siblings. At nine years old, I was entrusted with the duty of taking the donkey loaded with flour to the high-plateau settlement called the yayla, four hours' walk away, all by myself. I consider the efforts we children made to carry out these hard tasks of great benefit in helping us grow up.

As one who came from a village and had the opportunity to see many different ways of life, I cannot remain silent about the destruction of the culture in which I was raised, which had been the way of life for hundreds of years but which is now completely forgotten.

I am grateful to my parents for giving me courage to leave the village and to get an education, which allowed me to have a life that they could not have dreamt of themselves.

I am deeply thankful to my dear friend, Caner Arabacı, for editing the Turkish version of the book. With indefatigable energy, he read the book and generously shared his thoughts.

I am grateful to Angela Rome, who patiently translated the Turkish text to English. My violin partner, Jim Forrest, patiently read the English translation and helped me to change key words from UK spelling to American spelling. I am grateful to him.

I am grateful to Jessica McKelden of Reedsy, who patiently edited the English text.

I am grateful to Mark Fretz and Evan Phail at Radius Book Group for their production work.

Unbounded love and support of my family members Neriman, Aysan, Aytek and Tantek, who have helped me to continue on this project. I am indebted to my daughters, Aytek and Aysan, for their tireless reading and editing of the English manuscript.

Hasan Ali Çelik

Kirez and Abdullah

Fatma and Rahim

ABOUT THE AUTHOR

Hasan Ali Çelik was born in the village of Çat (now Çağlayan) [in the Taurus Mountains] near Konya, Turkey. A graduate of the Middle East Technical University and the University of California at Santa Barbara, he is Professor Emeritus of Mathematics at California State Polytechnic University. Dr. Çelik lives and gardens with his wife in Claremont, California.

CPSIA information can be obtained
at www.ICGtesting.com
Printed in the USA
LVHW091049170323
741758LV00005B/220